JUSTICE AND SELF-INTEREST

This volume argues that the commitment to justice is a fundamental motive and that, although it is typically portrayed as serving self-interest, it sometimes takes priority over self-interest. To make this case, the authors discuss the way justice emerges as a personal contract in children's development; review a wide range of research studying the influences of the justice motive on evaluative, emotional, and behavioral responses; and detail common experiences that illustrate the impact of the justice motive. Through an extensive critique of the research on which some alternative models of justice are based, the authors present a model that describes the ways in which motives of justice and self-interest are integrated in people's lives. They close with a discussion of some positive and negative consequences of the commitment to justice.

Melvin J. Lerner is Distinguished Professor Emeritus in the Department of Psychology of the University of Waterloo, where he founded the Division of Social Psychology. The majority of his research efforts focus on the theme of justice in people's lives. Much of that research has been summarized in several volumes, beginning with *Belief in a Just World: A Fundamental Delusion* (1980), which was awarded the Quinquenual Prize from the Society for the Scientific Study of Religion, and continuing in several coedited volumes: with S. Lerner, *The Justice Motive in Social Behavior: Adapting to Times of Scarcity and Change* (1981); with Gerold Mikula, *Entitlement and the Affectional Bond* (1994); and with Leo Montada, *Responses to Victimizations and Belief in a Just World* (1998) and *Current Societal Concerns about Justice* (1996). In addition, Lerner is the founding editor of the journal *Social Justice Research* and was the corecipient of a Max-Planck-Forschungspreis and a Lifetime Achievement Award from the International Society for Justice Research.

Susan Clayton is Whitmore-Williams Professor of Psychology and Chair of Environmental Studies at the College of Wooster. She has published extensively on topics related to justice as well as the natural environment. With Faye Crosby, she wrote *Justice, Gender, and Affirmative Action* (1992), which received an award from the Gustavus Myers Center for the Study of Human Rights in the United States, and with Susan Opotow, she coedited a volume of the *Journal of Social Issues* on "Green Justice" as well as *Identity and the Natural Environment* (2003). She is also the coauthor (with Gene Myers) of *Conservation Psychology: Understanding and Promoting Human Care for Nature* (2009). Clayton is a Fellow of the American Psychological Association and has served as president of the Society for Population and Environmental Psychology.

Justice and Self-Interest

TWO FUNDAMENTAL MOTIVES

Melvin J. Lerner

University of Waterloo, Ontario

Susan Clayton

The College of Wooster

CAMBRIDGE
UNIVERSITY PRESS

CAMBRIDGE UNIVERSITY PRESS
Cambridge, New York, Melbourne, Madrid, Cape Town,
Singapore, São Paulo, Delhi, Tokyo, Mexico City

Cambridge University Press
32 Avenue of the Americas, New York, NY 10013-2473, USA

www.cambridge.org
Information on this title: www.cambridge.org/9781107002333

First published 2011

Printed in the United States of America

A catalog record for this publication is available from the British Library.

Library of Congress Cataloging in Publication Data
Lerner, Melvin J., 1929–
Justice and self-interest : two fundamental motives / Melvin J. Lerner, Susan Clayton.
p. cm.
Includes bibliographical references and index.
ISBN 978-1-107-00233-3
1. Social justice. 2. Justice. 3. Self-interest. I. Clayton,
Susan D., 1960– II. Title.
HM671.L37 2011
303.3′72–dc22   2010034220

ISBN 978-1-107-00233-3 Hardback

CONTENTS

LIST OF FIGURES AND TABLES

FIGURES

TABLES

PREFACE

The 1980 monograph *Belief in a Just World: A Fundamental Delusion* concluded with a "last thought." It contained the following recommendations concerning what should happen next:

> Much remains to be done. As scientists and people who care about one another we need to understand more about the social psychological processes which generate this commitment to deserving and justice. Why do people care about justice? This concern is ultimately tied to the need to solve the riddle of what decides the particular form that justice takes in a given situation. At times, people feel that justice is served when people's needs are most effectively met; at other times, people's deserving is seen as relative to their effort, their contributions to a task, their station in life, [or] what they can win in a fair competition (Lerner, 1975). And both of these sets of problems are inextricably bound up with the way people decide who is in their "world," and what place they have in that world. (Lerner, 1980, p. 194)

The present monograph reviews the contributions of many investigators over the past thirty years in order to provide answers to those centrally important questions. Consistent with the style adopted in the earlier volume, we generated a narrative that provides the reader with our thoughts as we examined a wide range of theories and data. Much of this narrative consists of critical analyses and arguments for rejecting and reinterpreting entire lines of research as well as the theories that generated them.

In order to integrate the relevant material needed to provide answers to the central questions of the origins of people's commitment to justice and the forms that it takes, it was necessary to detail the way in which much of what had been published in the most prestigious journals and monographs was irrelevant or just plain wrong. In our review of the research, some of the most visible and active areas of contemporary research were found wanting, at best. That includes much of what has been published under the rubric of economic psychology, procedural justice data and theories, evolutionary theories, and infrahuman data, and an array of experiments employing simulations and vignettes that generate misleading conclusions.

Fortunately, and happily, several among the most recent generations of investigators produced sufficient, ingeniously generated experimental findings to enable us to piece together an outline not only of the origins of the justice motive but also of how justice and self-interest interact in people's lives: an initial stage of automatic preconscious processes including justice and self-conceited scripts, and the personal contract, is followed by a second stage in which norm-based motives tend to dominate, and then by a third stage in which people often react in terms of "prepared solutions" to the often-conflicting demands of justice and self-interest.

It has been a long time, and an often bumpy journey, but we feel this volume integrates an extensive array of studies to represent a worthwhile advance in our understanding. We may not have presented the last word about the origins and forms of justice and how they interact with other, self-interested motives, but as some of our discussion of important real-world problems reveals, we know a great deal more about how the justice motive appears in people's lives than we did in 1980. There is even more reason to believe now that justice is a central and pervasive motive. Recognizing the importance of the justice motive, and the various circumstances and forms in which it influences people's lives, offers the opportunity to avoid many tragic events and promises constructive solutions to important problems.

1

Contesting the Primacy of Self-Interest

For more than fifty years, prominent social psychologists have portrayed the pursuit of self-interest as the primary motivating force in people's lives. This perspective is common among the general public, in which it is often taken for granted that people will only do what they are paid or otherwise rewarded for doing. It also reigns among other academic disciplines, such as economics and evolutionary psychology. Although the former focuses on maximizing financial gain, and the latter on maximizing reproductive success, they both take individual self-interest as the fundamental driver of behavior. The primacy of self-interest is an implicit assumption that underlies much public discussion and policy.

Self-interest, however, falls short in explaining some common human behavior and emotional experiences – cases in which people appear to act against their own interest or to feel guilty when their acts promote their interests. Because we will spend the bulk of the book describing and explaining these cases, we start with some illustrative examples. We examine the postdecision consequences experienced by two remarkably different decision makers: corporate managers (Levinson, 1994; Smith, 1994) and caregivers of elderly parents (Brody, 1985; Brody, Dempsey and Pruchno, 1990). In both cases, decisions that negatively affect others, but that have adhered to all the requirements of rational self-interest, have been seen to result in serious emotional consequences for the decision makers. This regret, reluctance, and guilt, we argue, demonstrate the power of the justice motive.

ILLUSTRATING THE IMPORTANCE OF JUSTICE

Corporate Managers

The institutional structures and mechanisms that support thoughtful, "rational" decision making are ubiquitous and are readily apparent in virtually all corporate enterprises. It is a given, and a moral mandate, that all decisions are the products of more or less careful considerations of the costs and benefits of alternative courses of action. Because of this virtually sacred institutionalized practice, corporate executives have been surprised and greatly concerned when the most thorough and extensive use of their thoughtful deliberations did not prevent the postdecision appearance of costly and entirely unanticipated tragic consequences. These consequences include the experience of debilitating, demoralizing levels of shame subsequent to downsizing decisions by many of the managers who were involved. Typically, that demoralization as well as signs of resentment and disaffection also appear among a significant number of the remaining employees (Armstrong-Stassen and Latack, 1992; Brockner, 1990; Kozlowski et al., 1993).

The embarrassing, undeniable fact is that the cost-benefit analyses that preceded the important corporate decision did not include the substantial costs of the "irrational" assessments of harm doing and blame. Their predecision procedures insured that by all the relevant societal standards and rules, no one could be blamed, so no one should feel guilty, ashamed, or resentful. Given the circumstances they were faced with, the publicly affirmed consensus was that they had done what was best for all the relevant stakeholders. They could not have acted otherwise while fulfilling their obligations. So why the postdecision guilt, shame, and/or demoralizing anger?

A closer examination reveals that the essential elements of the critical event include the market-induced or at least market-instigated efforts to reduce costs of production. To accomplish that, the decision was reached to downsize by discharging a significant number of otherwise qualified employees. These employees were to be let go with relatively little advance notice and compensating benefits.

To be sure, in each instance the decisions regarding whether or not to reduce costs by downsizing the labor force and how to accomplish this were not arrived at lightly. They occurred only after extensive, elaborate efforts to arrive at the wisest course of action for the corporation and the stakeholders, including the remaining employees. The decisions as to whether and how to downsize were the end product of all reasonable efforts to acquire any relevant information and the subsequent consideration of all available alternatives.

Typically, as a consequence of the extensive deliberations it was openly recognized by all concerned that each employee was let go because the economic realities left the management with no choice. Or at least it was left with no better, wiser, more economically and, thus, morally appropriate course of action. Given that remedial action was required in order to save the organization, it was considered to be the most "fair" or least unfair alternative for all concerned. That was the consensus view of the downsizing affirmed by all levels of management, at least until it actually took place. Once having arrived at the decision to downsize, highly qualified social psychologists were often involved in assisting management in their attempts to devise procedures that conveyed the appearance of being fair to those affected as well as the remaining employees (Greenberg, 1990). Nevertheless, when management informed the designated employees that they were to be discharged and their income shortly would end, many of them, management as well as the employees, experienced a new emotional reality: the compelling effects of the justice imperatives not considered during the decision process.

Apparently, the managers were not prepared for the painful experiences they encountered. The possibility of that happening had not appeared in the deliberations. Why would it have? Management was convinced that what they were doing was in the best interests of all the stakeholders, including the remaining employees. Presumably, by the time the employees were informed of their job loss all of the relevant issues had been thoroughly examined, discussed, and factored into shaping the final decisions. Management was convinced that to arrive at any other decision would have been foolish, irresponsible, and even immoral.

But then, as described by a manager involved in a downsizing, "nothing – not over-work, not confusion, not lost perks, not apprehension – is as deadening to managers' morale as firing subordinates" (Smith, 1994, p. 46). The feelings of guilt for having harmed innocent victims may be recognized: "What makes the flood of dismissals in recent years especially distressing for managers is that so often workers have been fired not for cause but because their skills were no longer needed" (Smith, 1994, p. 2). Did the managers not know that?

All of management knew well in advance that the employees were to be discharged not because of any lack or failure on their parts, but because their skills and efforts were no longer needed in terms of promoting the welfare of the corporate stakeholders, which constituted the "big picture." A psychologist who has been repeatedly consulted in order to deal with this postimplementation problem described an important factor that had not been considered by management. In his award-winning address to the American Psychological Association he pointed out that:

> The conscious guilt any manager of conscience has about terminating someone else without cause is compounded by the unconscious guilt that arises from the sense that he or she is destroying the other.   (Levinson, 1994, p. 429)

Apparently, in his extensive consultation with companies that had downsized, Levinson discovered that the managers' conscious experiences of guilt emanated from cognitive-affective processes of which they were unaware. Because of the preconscious sources of their guilt, those who were demoralized with guilt could not have anticipated or easily coped with the painful emotions they were experiencing. Management had gone through considerable prior efforts to insure that the acts that caused others to suffer were entirely rational and appropriate responses to the market conditions with which the managers were faced. Above all, prior to taking the required actions, managers were convinced that, according to the societal norms for assigning blame and culpability, they were not harm doers: they were doing nothing ethically "wrong"; they were merely meeting their obligations.

Why would they have anticipated being overwhelmed with guilt feelings? They had no way of knowing that, after implementing their decisions and being confronted with the suffering of their "victims," those justifying thoughts could not dispel what they were experiencing. The awareness of an innocent person's suffering because of something they had done automatically elicited the emotions of someone who had committed a terrible injustice. All that rational norm-based thoughts could do was to make them feel as if they were being "irrational."

Over time, and for some sooner rather than later, other less painful ways of expressing the compelling justice imperatives might appear in the form of blaming or derogating their victims, or generating illusions that their victims were not victims after all. Those laid off would eventually be fully compensated, even "better off," in the future (Maes, 1998). But for a considerable period of time the managers joined the employees, their friends, families, and co-workers in suffering for the employees who had been victimized by the corporate decision, the managers' rational decision that took away the jobs.

Caregivers for Elderly Parents

The second set of tragedies, similar in dynamics to what has just been described, has appeared among children, typically daughters, of elderly parents. (We explore this situation further in Chapter 9.) In the typical scenario studied by Brody (1985), daughters had provided considerable and increasing amounts of daily care for their elderly parents for an extended period of time. Eventually they felt compelled to move their deteriorating parent into a nursing home so that he or she would receive the daily care and supervision required. Similar to the managers involved in downsizing, before deciding to institution-alize their parents the daughters engaged in extensive problem-solving efforts focused on finding the best solution for the parent's well-being. The experts they consulted, physicians, gerontologists, or social workers, explicitly included the consequences of various alter-natives for the other "stakeholders" who would be affected by this decision: the caregivers and their immediate families.

To understand the interpersonal and psychological dynamics of this tragic outcome, it is important to recognize the events and circumstances leading up to and following the recommended decision to institution-alize their parents. It begins with an increasingly common event. Elderly parents typically turn to their children, or their children's spouses, for help when they can no longer take care of themselves. In this society, typically, when this occurs a daughter takes on the role of primary care provider or actual caregiver. Eventually, however, the daughters experi-ence considerable and increasing amounts of emotional stress as well as "role" exhaustion. The costly physical and emotional demands of caring for one's elderly parents' daily needs are compounded with the conflicts they create in meeting obligations to one's spouse and children, as well as in continually denying their own needs and desires. These emotional and physical stresses include the anguish of witnessing the unrelieved deterioration and suffering of an especially loved one and, in spite of all the best efforts, his or her increasingly imminent death.

Eventually, with sufficient undeniable evidence of irreversible deterioration, expert professional consultants, as well as family and friends, unanimously recommend that the care providers must place their parents in a nursing home. Typically, the professionals assure care providers that along with providing their parents with the care they require, this move will mean that their own stresses will be greatly relieved. The increasingly demanding, often overwhelming burden will have been lifted.

Unfortunately, as Brody (1985; Brody et al., 1990) and others have reported, these previously overstressed and overburdened daughters often do not experience the promised emotional relief when their parents are moved to a nursing facility. Apparently, in response to their parents' continuing deterioration and suffering, the daughters often experience feelings of guilt that were entirely unanticipated. In spite of the enormous sacrifices experienced over the long periods prior to the placement, many of these daughters report feeling more depressed and stressed than they did prior to placing their parents in a caregiving facility. They feel that somehow, in spite of what everyone says, they let their parents down. They failed to protect their parents the way that their parents had nurtured and protected them. Is that irrational?

Any objective observer would be able to offer rational, sensible arguments for why they have no reason to feel guilty. Not only did they not harm nor fail their parents in any way, they continually sought to make the best decision for all concerned, including and especially their elderly parents. Unfortunately, those thoughts and that reasoning reflect only the application of societal norms for determining blameworthiness and culpability and have no direct influence on those preconscious processes that are actually generating the guilt feelings. The preconscious "reality" is that regardless of what occurred up to that point, as the result of "my decision to institutionalize my mother she is now living among strangers and is suffering and very unhappy," and thus "I caused her to suffer." The emotional effects of the preconscious script that "bad outcomes are caused by bad people" may be consciously expressed in various forms: "She is suffering because I am an ungrateful, selfish daughter."

The distressing consequences of the justice imperatives elicited by the daughters' awareness of their parents' continuing suffering may lead to various additional reactions. Considerable evidence suggests that "harm doers" may find ways to derogate the victims, attempt to compensate for their harm by gaining moral credits through doing good deeds, or go into denial and try to blot the experience out of their conscious awareness by avoiding the victim (Lerner, 1980). For very understandable reasons, efforts to persuade the guilt-ridden daughters to be rational and come to their senses will accomplish very little in preventing or ameliorating the appearance of any of these reactions.

These examples, along with a vast body of research that we will discuss, lead us to conclude that the desire to be fair is a powerful force that is not suppressed by logical reasoning and that has consequences that are inconsistent with self-interest. It is ironic that so much justice theory has been devoted to explaining why the justice motive arises from self-interest.

A BRIEF REVIEW OF JUSTICE THEORY

Although language conventions offer several related terms for the form of justice that appears in various contexts – *fairness, deserving-ness, entitlement* – the common element is an "ought" imperative that is experienced preconsciously or cognitively represented as courses of action linking people with their outcomes and the appropriate treatment of one another. Early justice theorists recognized that there could be more than one way of defining justice. For example, justice could prescribe that all individuals receive equal outcomes, outcomes in proportion to their input, or outcomes in proportion to their need. How is the operative rule determined? Walster, Walster, and Berscheid (1978, p. 6), integrating the perspectives of earlier influential theorists (see, e.g., Adams, 1963; Homans, 1958), asserted "Individuals will try to maximize their outcomes" as the first proposition in their General Theory of Social Interaction. The assumed dominance of self-interest shaped their view of how the desire for justice appeared in people's lives. They, for example, derived the predictions that individuals, in their omnipresent efforts to maximize their outcomes, will naturally select and promote the rule of fairness that offers them the greatest benefits, or, if they believe it is more profitable they will simply ignore any considerations of fairness.

Similarly, Deutsch (1975) in a highly cited essay, "Equity, Equality, and Need: What Determines Which Value Will Be Used as the Basis of Distributive Justice," observed that people, in each encounter, naturally adopt the rule of justice that they believe will promote their values or goals. This instrumentally self-serving theme also appears in the proposal by Messick and his colleagues (see, e.g., Messick and Sentis, 1983), that in every encounter people initially decide what outcomes they prefer and then elect a rule of deservingness that offers the best promise of justifying their most preferred outcomes.

Later, several investigators (e.g., Lind and Tyler, 1988) in their efforts to present a theory of procedural justice as distinct from distributive justice, tried to demonstrate that a desire for fair treatment is not only different from but also can supplement and override a desire for fair outcomes. However, they also located people's desire to be treated fairly in self-interested motives (Brockner and Wiesenfeld, 1996). Their explanation for why people become upset when they are treated unfairly, especially by those in authority, pointed to the implied lack of respect, leading to a loss in public esteem. They then tied the fear of lowered public esteem to the potential loss of access to those desired material resources that are mediated by their status as a bona fide member of their group (see, e.g., Tyler, 1994; Tyler and Blader, 2003). Supposedly, people become upset by unfair treatment because of the implied threat to their ability to get what they want, that is, to maximize their outcomes.

More recent theorists reinforced this consensus by identifying automatic and preconscious processes to explain how self-interest acquires its dominating and controlling influence. According to Moore and Loewenstein (2004):

> Self-interest is automatic, viscerally compelling and often uncon-
> scious ... the automatic nature of self-interest gives it a primal
> power to influence judgment, and make it difficult for people to
> understand its influence on their judgment, let alone eradicate its
> influence. (p. 189)

Similarly, echoing the automatic and primary themes, Epley and
Caruso (2004) argue that

> First, people are automatically inclined to interpret their percep-
> tions egocentrically. Second, people are automatically inclined to
> evaluate those egocentric interpretations as good or bad, positive
> or negative, threatening or supporting. Finally, moral judgments
> about fairness and unfairness are based upon these automatic
> evaluative responses. (pp. 181–2)

Skitka et al. (2009) have offered an updated version of Deutsch's (1975)
and Walster et al.'s (1978) assumption that people's goals and values
determine how they employ considerations of justice. Skitka proposes
to integrate the research literatures on distributive and procedural
justice along with her work on moral mandates within the same
theoretical framework. In this model, people's justice judgments reflect
perspectives that are elicited by their "goals activated in current memory." According to Skitka, those goals can involve material needs and
the social exchange of material resources, which lead people to adopt a
perspective to promote rational self-interest; social concerns based on
the need to belong to a group and concerns about social status, which
cause the person to be concerned with fairness of procedures; and,
completing the triumvirate of motives and perspectives, fundamental
beliefs about right or wrong, or moral mandates, which require people
to evaluate fairness in accordance with those beliefs.

Skitka's theory encompasses multiple motives. Although it affirms
that people care about morality for reasons independent of self-
interested needs, it still portrays most justice motives as arising from
self-interest and specifically defines justice decisions in many cases as
based on people's economic and/or social wants and needs. We will say

more about Skitka's approach in future chapters. For the present, it serves as an eloquent confirmation of the essentially unchallenged persistence of social psychologists portraying people's concerns with justice, that is, how justice appears in people's lives, as primarily an instrument of other, more directly self-serving motives and goals.

That leads to the obvious question: given that persistent consensus, why would anyone doubt that people care about justice in the ways and to the extent that it serves other more central personally valuable goals?

CHALLENGING THE SELF-INTEREST DOGMA

In retrospect, the essentially unchallenged persistence of this consensus is truly remarkable. From the outset, there were good reasons to question the portrayal of self-interest as the primary source of motivation in people's lives. To be sure, the drive to maximize their own outcomes seems to characterize how some people typically behave and even what appears to motivate many people in very competitive encounters. Over the years, an abundance of empirical studies have documented their participants distorting or ignoring considerations of justice presumably as they attempt to profit themselves (see, e.g., Montada and Lerner, 1996; Vermunt and Steensma, 1991). But at the same time, a wealth of evidence typically not discussed by these investigators provided substantial reasons to question those findings and reexamine that literature. Sufficient evidence was provided to require a reformulation of how self-interest and the themes of deservingness and justice influence how people behave and treat one another.

Easily accessible casual observation and introspection readily contradict the view that people are solely or primarily driven by the desire to maximize their outcomes by doing what is most pleasurable and avoiding that which is noxious, painful, or unpleasant. They are often motivated by what may be descriptively identified as *ought imperatives*. As the term suggests, these experienced imperatives explicitly instruct and impel people to do those things that they should and avoid those they should not do. People clearly recognize that these ought imperatives often conflict with a self-interested cost-benefit analysis. It is a commonly experienced fact of life that these two sources of motivation compete with one another on those frequent occasions when people believe they have to choose whether to do the "right thing" or that which is more profitable or pleasurable. The theorists described in the preceding text may concede that other sources of motivation often appear but then insist that they are inevitably overcome or shaped to serve the person's self-interest. Is that supported by the available evidence?

Moving beyond introspection and self-reports, the common cultural heritage provides more objectively verifiable evidence for at least two distinct, often-competing motives and the frequent successful influence of justice imperatives. One can point to folktales like the story of the grasshopper and the ant as well as to more formal literary, philosophical, and religious texts that describe and recommend ways to resolve the classic human conflicts between "ought" and "want." Certainly it is not always the case that "wants" invariably prevail over or shape the ought imperatives. Many members of society devote themselves wholeheartedly to causes that advance justice for groups to which they do not belong: animal-rights advocates epitomize this phenomenon. Possibly the most visible testimony to the omnipresence of the power of justice over self-interest can be found in society's enormous investment in institutions designed to detect and punish the relatively few members of society who violate the rules of justice and harm others in order to gratify their desires. The belief that freeloaders and harm doers should be "brought to justice" is sufficient to motivate great sacrifices of time, money, and personal comfort. Interestingly, recent research suggests that even many nonhuman animals have some sense of justice to which, in some cases, they subordinate their own self-interest (Bekoff and Pierce, 2009; Brosnan and de Waal, 2003).

Social analysts and philosophers have recognized the pervasive influence of the justice form of ought imperatives in people's lives. Typically, however, they attribute these imperatives to a form of self-interest: in order to promote their own welfare, aggregates of people have come together, at some earlier time in human history, to construct a "social contract" (Rawls, 1971), as well as to establish the supporting institutions that train each generation to recognize and internalize the contracts' rules of conduct. These philosophers, similarly to some social psychologists (see, e.g., Walster et al., 1978), often locate the motivating force for creating and adhering to the social contract in people's desires to maximize their collective outcomes. The common view is that individuals have been taught to follow ought imperatives and do the "right things" because of the promise of greater profit and/or to avoid internally or externally administered punishment costs. This represents an enlightened form of self-interest. Although typical and generally accepted, that explanation ignores or has great difficulty explaining easily documented contradictions.

A rationally enlightened form of self-interest may often motivate people's compliance with societal norms (Miller, 1999). However, considerable evidence does not easily fit within any discernible short- or long-term self-interested goals. This is particularly evident when people's emotionally charged reactions to a serious injustice, either to themselves or others, impel them to pursue a costly course of action that predictably includes their own suffering, deprivation, or even death. It is a matter of common observation that people, when sufficiently aroused and driven by their injustice-elicited emotions, often act reflexively without considering what would be most beneficial for them either immediately or in the long run. These often-irresistible justice-restoring attempts to punish harm doers or come to the aid of victims are often too costly and occur too rapidly to be the product of a self-interested decision to gain later benefits or avoid even greater suffering for oneself.

When confronted with this kind of evidence, biologically oriented theorists have attempted to rescue the image of an all-dominating self-interest by locating the benefactor of the individual's costly self-sacrificing acts in the "gene pool" that included the actor's genetic makeup. Ostensibly, an all-dominating "selfish gene" impels everyone to engage in costly actions in order to promote the welfare, and the long-term survival, of those who manifest kinship-based cues, that is, who appear to carry the same genes. Although there is evidence that people often have a preference for those who are similar or genetically related to them there is no direct evidence for the existence, much less all-powerful influence, of such a "selfish gene."

Ultimately, in the absence of credible evidence demonstrating a dominating self-interested motivation it is possible to simply insist, as some theorists have (e.g., McClintock, 1978), that a person's costly attempts to restore justice are no less a form of self-interested act than their pursuit of any of their other desired goals. Their assumption is that people who voluntarily risk their lives or sacrifice their resources in the pursuit of justice are simply doing what they want, expressing their preferences on that occasion and thus engaging in an act attributable to self-interest.

WHY MOTIVATIONAL MODELS MUST INCLUDE THE JUSTICE MOTIVE

That approach may seem to offer an irrefutable theoretical parsimony. In actuality, however, there is nothing parsimonious in ignoring or obfuscating the crucial issues.

For example, assuming that costly efforts to maintain justice are invariably motivated by a self-interested preference requires serious investigators to rephrase the important questions while offering no guidelines for where to find the answers. Obviously, if one assumes that all behavior is motivated by self-interest, then in order to understand and predict people's behavior one must know when and how the preference for justice appears as the dominant "self-interested" motive, effectively trumping virtually all other desires. Similarly, it is necessary to know what antecedent events, including developmental processes and interpersonal dynamics, are unique to a dominantly compelling self-interested desire for justice, rather than the desire to maximize any or all of one's other desired outcomes including the biologically basic desires to avoid pain and death.

The search for meaningful answers to those fundamental questions has typically turned to the ways children are shaped by their social milieu. Apparently, in the normal course of development children learn what resources are desirable and the rules for acquiring them. They also learn specific rules of entitlement concerning who is entitled to what from whom and the sanctions that follow from meeting or violating those rules, that is, the terms of the "social contract" (institutionalized status-roles). In addition, they learn the various kinds and categories of people who inhabit their world and their relative social value: who is good or bad, better or worse. Finally, along with appearing in their thoughtful decisions, much of what is learned becomes overlearned and is manifested as automatic habitual reactions to specific cues. The motivation underlying all of this – what is learned and when it is manifested – is typically attributed to various forms of self-interest: rewards and punishments are instrumental in the learning process, which includes the habitual modes of responding, and both the anticipation of benefits and the attempt to increase benefits to oneself often dominate the process of deciding how to behave.

What children adopt and learn from their environment, however, provides the beginning of an explanation but only the introduction: people may often do the "right thing" either because it has become a reinforced habitual response to certain cues of entitlement or for various clearly self-interested reasons. Having described the most familiar arguments for the various ways self-interest influences people's behavior, it is now possible to get to the most critical evidence.

Neither the anticipation of something desirable for compliance or undesirable for failure to comply, nor the expression of a habitual response, can adequately explain the uniquely central and pervasive role the theme of justice plays in people's individual lives as well as their interpersonal relations. Any plausible social psychological theory regarding how justice appears in people's lives must incorporate the following observations:

- In Western societies the pursuit of justice is not simply one of the cultural values and personal goals. It is the only goal/value that can sanction, and at times require, the deliberate sacrifice of all the other desired outcomes: people's property, freedom, and even their lives. Arguably, there is no other secular value with such power in human transactions. In Western societies even the most egregious violations of religious values do not legitimize or justify the taking of human lives. That is not the case in those societies or extremist subgroups in which the distinction between sin and injustice has been erased.

- At the more mundane, but no less significant, level of human affairs, rules of deservingness and justice in the form of entitlements – obligations and privileges – pervade and are the central motivating components of all the various status-roles individuals occupy in their daily lives. These ought imperatives provide the glue and fabric of human relations. By defining in each situation who is entitled to what from whom within particular relationships, such as student and professor, parent and child, drivers on the highway, and so forth, these rules of entitlement (deservingness) exert an unparalleled automatic influence on how people treat one another in virtually every context.

- On most occasions, simply as a matter of course people meet those well-understood obligations to others and expect to enjoy the privileges to which they are entitled. Without being consciously aware of what is guiding their behavior, most people, most of the time, naturally follow the rules that define who deserves what from whom. Instructors in introductory sociology and psychology classes often demonstrate the powerful omnipresence of these implicit obligations/ought imperatives by acting in ways that violate them: inappropriate dress, forms of address, and so forth.

- Similarly, if one observes how most people actually behave in their daily lives, it is apparent and essential for a civilized society that, rather than directly pursuing self-interest, most people, most of the time, willingly follow the rules of deservingness to earn what they want and need, and they become upset at times to the point of costly corrective efforts if they become aware that others, as well as themselves, are unjustly harmed or receive less than they deserve.

- Finally, when describing fundamental psychological processes, along with the truisms that people prefer pleasure to pain and a greater rather than lesser share of commonly desired resources, considerable additional evidence reveals an astounding overriding principle: no amount of those desired resources can actually satisfy people if they believe they deserve more or they are being treated unjustly. At the other extreme, people will often accept, or at least tolerate, the most miserable deprivation if they believe that is what they deserve: it is their just fate (see, e.g., Crosby, 1976).

To Summarize

Contrary to the assertion that self-interest appears automatically and assumes the role of the primary motive in people's lives (see Epley and Caruso, 2004; Messick and Sentis, 1983; Moore and Loewenstein, 2004), easily available evidence clearly suggests the influence of a pervasive justice motivation that is independent of and often in conflict with self-interest. The central importance of the justice motive is evident in its unique power to sanctify the sacrifice of lives, liberty, property, and virtually all other values, as well as its dominantly pervasive influence on how people treat one another and go about their daily lives. Finally, the sense of deservingness or justice sets the limits and minimal conditions for when people are either satisfied or disturbed by what their labors and the fates have given them.

LOOKING AHEAD

The discussion that follows will argue that the self-interest–based theories only apply to a specifiable, rather limited set of circumstances and must distort or ignore much of what happens in people's lives: what they care about and how they treat one another. We provide an alternative theoretical framework that portrays people as primarily and automatically committed to following rules of deservingness and justice as they go about their daily lives and are confronted with critical events.

In the remainder of this volume, we develop the argument for the importance of justice as a motivator of behavior. We start Chapter 2 by discussing why justice would be relevant and explaining why the acquisition of a sense of justice is part of the normal developmental process. Chapter 3 explores the impact of a concern with justice on the processing of information about other people, and on reactions to events involving oneself – including actions like those of the managers and daughters described earlier in this chapter. In order to understand and counter the way current theories of justice overemphasize self-interest, Chapter 4 will critically review some of the research on which these theories are based. Chapter 5 will investigate the definition of *justice* further, examining the relationship between procedural and distributive justice and their relevance to morality. In Chapter 6, we discuss the way in which deservingness and justice are assessed, and we present a model in Chapter 7 that assesses the relative influence of justice and self-interest, integrating them into a more comprehensive theory of behavior. Chapter 8 will situate the initial evaluation of justice within a context that is socially and temporally extended. In Chapter 9, we develop the specific example of institutionalizing elderly relations in order to illustrate the way that justice is experienced and integrated with self-interested motives in people's lives. We close in Chapter 10 by examining some of the negative consequences of the drive for justice in understanding the ways in which people behave and respond in public situations and the ways in which these consequences can be alleviated.

2

Why Does Justice Matter? The Development of a Personal Contract

The recognition of a pervasive and central concern with deserving-ness and justice in people's lives raises a challenging question: how can one explain why justice imperatives, the commitment to deser-vingness and justice, have a uniquely central place in peoples' lives? Some have attempted to answer this question by speculating about prehistoric evolutionary events or by extrapolating from the behavior of infrahuman organisms, but a considerably more accessible place to begin the search for the origins of the justice motive in humans is with the normal course of human development as it unfolds in a relatively stable environment. Examining the cognitive capabilities and learn-ing challenges that characterize children as they grow and mature suggests how acquiring a sense of justice can be a standard and important part of development.

DEVELOPING A SENSE OF DESERVINGNESS

As children develop and learn more successful ways of gaining what they want, they typically pursue a more enlightened or rational form of self-interest instead of attempting to directly gratify their desires. This represents a natural transition from being dominated by what Freud (1953) termed the "pleasure principle" to following the "reality principle." The innate tendency to focus on the immediate gratifica-tion of urges is replaced by the use of more indirect and socially sanctioned methods, based on a longer time span, that integrate individual desires with societal expectations and standards. Of particular interest is that, while following a more enlightened form of self-interest, children's behavior increasingly complies with rules of deservingness and justice (Damon, 1975; Piaget, 1932). Conceivably, an understanding of the processes that account for how that transition occurs can offer some insight into the origins of the commitment to deservingness and justice.

The theory offered here begins with the maturation of children's cognitive abilities. As infants develop in a relatively stable social and physical environment, and their cognitive capabilities expand, they are increasingly able both to remember previous experiences and to imagine alternative courses of action and their various consequences. The ability to recall and comparatively evaluate several alternatives eventually empowers the child to choose a course of action that promises to provide the greatest pleasure in the long run. Self-interest remains the guiding concern, but rather than being dominated by the desire for immediate gratification, the more mature child recognizes that appropriate efforts can lead to the acquisition of greater and more secure outcomes and has the ability to remember the desired sequence of events leading to their acquisition. In effect, the maturing cognitive resources enable the child to replace attempts at direct gratification with the more profitable reality principle: pursuing self-interest in this more enlightened way promises greater gains at a later point.

A second component appears when children have the repeated experience in which ultimately acquiring the more valuable outcomes typically depends upon the deprivation of immediate gratification and engaging in extended efforts. Repeated experiences of manipulating their environment to gain desired resources, together with adequate memory and comparative evaluations, are the only teachers a child needs to recognize that as a rule it takes more time and concerted effort to build bigger, get more, and go further. Their own observations provide ample and compelling evidence that

greater, more valuable outcomes typically require greater investments of self-deprivation and focused effort. The results of these
repeated experiences establish the building blocks, or elements, for
the emerging commitment to deservingness: justice.

Something more is required, however, for that commitment to
occur. The third element is the development of the self-control
required for the child to make the transition from directly gratifying
present desires to the more "rational," less pleasant, and more costly
investments of effort and postponed gratification. A large and growing body of research emphasizes the importance of self-control and
the significance of the ability to delay gratification in predicting future
success (Baumeister and Vohs, 2004; Mischel, 1961: Mischel, Shoda,
and Peake, 1988). That transition from present to future focus requires
that the child engage in what can be portrayed as an inner dialogue.

To control the urge for direct gratification, the child's intelligent
"voice" must enter into a "personal contract" with him- or herself. To
achieve the necessary control, children promise the impulsive part of
themselves that the relatively painful denial of that which is immediately available, delaying gratification, and engaging in costly efforts
will be appropriately rewarded by the eventual acquisition of greater
and more desirable outcomes. Greater benefits require greater investments of self-denial and effort over a longer period of time.

The rationally self-interested voice can prevail over the omnipresent
impulsive urges and guide the child's behavior as long as the promise is
fulfilled. However, any failure to acquire the promised outcomes generates the prototypical experience underlying the justice imperative: the
disappointed gratification voice claims, "I was promised. I gave up
doing what I wanted and did what was required, so I am entitled to,
I deserve, X." When that occurs, the viability of the personal contract to
give up immediate gratification and engage in the required acts of self-
denial and effort is in jeopardy. The rational self, recognizing the
ultimate advantages of maintaining the personal contract, is impelled
to produce additional promises and support to maintain control. In

essence, the justice imperative is the psychological manifestation of the imperative to act in order to preserve the child's commitment to deservingness rather than indulging in immediate gratification.

Any reappearance of either the experienced desire for direct gratification or failure to obtain the anticipated self-promised outcome can reawaken the impulsive internal voice that questions the value of the personal contract. In effect, giving up the pleasure principle and accepting the self-denial and efforts of the reality principle requires an ongoing act of faith and self-control: the child must believe in the inevitability of the anticipated later, greater benefits that they deserve. In order to control their urges for direct gratification so that they can engage in the more profitable concerted goal-seeking efforts, children must persuade themselves that the world in which they live and function is constructed so that they can and will eventually get what they have tried to earn and deserve. Given the inevitable experiences of failure and disappointments, at these critical points they must reassure themselves that their future self-deprivation and extended efforts will be appropriately rewarded.

Finally, the crucial transforming events occur when, with increasing age, children must deal with increasingly greater demands and opportunities that invariably require costlier investments for longer terms. This final component of the commitment to deservingness appears as the child adapts to the inevitable uncertainties and greater risks of failure that follow from having only limited control over the required longer-term investments. In order to maintain the required increases in self-denial and self-control, they must transform the conditional personal contract into a firm, virtually noncontingent, binding commitment. Once the child has made that commitment, failures and uncompensated losses may have inevitable emotional consequences initially, but they are no longer able to jeopardize the commitment and may, in some circumstances, intensify the personal resolve to follow rules of deservingness (see, e.g., Goldberg, Lerner, and Tetlock, 1999; Hafer, 2000a, b).

In this manner, the emerging adult's commitment to deservingness, though initially rooted in self-interest, under normal circumstances eventually becomes a functionally autonomous motivation that guides goal acquisition and relations to others. Various motives and goals may ultimately influence their behavior, but in each encounter, as a result of having made this commitment, people will initially seek out and follow rules of deservingness. To do that, rather than focusing on the opportunities for self-gratification in each encounter, they must automatically attend to and habitually assess who is entitled to what from whom. As a consequence, in each encounter the automatic and primal response becomes the assessment of entitlements rather than self-interest.

TRANSFER OF DESERVINGNESS TO OTHERS

How the personal commitment to deservingness is related to the experienced imperative to see that others get what they deserve is less clear and probably somewhat more complicated. Some investigators have suggested that empathically experiencing the fates of others (Hoffman, 1970; Messick and Sentis, 1983) elicits the imperative to maintain their deservingness. Certainly it is possible that an emotional connection to another allows people to experience the outcomes experienced by those others as if they were personally relevant. Dan Batson (e.g., Batson, Early, and Salvarini, 1997) is well-known for his experiments demonstrating that people who are induced to feel the stressful emotions that may be experienced by the victim of misfortune are more willing to help and less likely to abandon that person to his or her fate. It has also been proposed that people naturally recognize that their ability to deserve their desired outcomes is vulnerable to the same events that affect other people, implying that if others are mistreated they are in jeopardy of suffering the same fate.

One implication of this is that the justice imperative is derived from, and dependent upon, the person's commitment to deservingness.

This implies that people's commitments to their own deservingness may take priority over the derived imperative of justice for others. Consistent with this possibility, Miller (1975, 1977) found that people avoided the opportunity to provide financial aid to innocent victims when that would entail their receiving less pay than they deserved for themselves. Whereas, if they believed their own deservingness would not be threatened, they were more motivated to reduce the victim's undeserved suffering than increase their own financial outcomes.

There is ample anecdotal and experimental evidence, however, that witnessing injustices inflicted upon others, even in contemplation, often elicits strong emotions and justice-restoring behaviors (Darley and Pittman, 2003; Goldberg et al., 1999; Keltner, Ellsworth, and Edwards, 1993; J. Lerner, Goldberg, and Tetlock, 1998). Some experimental evidence demonstrates that witnessing some injustices inflicted on others may create a greater imperative to punish the perpetrator than does directly experiencing the same undeserved fate (Meindl and Lerner, 1983). Consistent with common observation, it is reasonable to expect that the intensity of people's reactions to injustices inflicted upon others would be influenced by the observer's relation to the victim. It is not unusual for people to attempt to restore justice, regardless of the associated costs, when the people for whom they feel responsible have been victimized, but remain relatively indifferent when a potential competitor or outgroup member suffers the same unjust fate (Correia, Vala, and Aguiar, 2007; Meindl and Lerner, 1983).

To Summarize

Under normal circumstances the initial drive to get what one wants becomes psychologically transformed into a personal contract that develops into the functionally autonomous commitment to deserve what one wants and get what one deserves. Ironically, as a result of this commitment to deservingness, any reappearing impulses to directly gratify their desires and evidence that someone has received more or less than she or he deserves may be experienced as threats to their commitment. Eventually, as a result of their commitment to their personal contract, the person automatically avoids or neutralizes threatening information by denying and reinterpreting threatening events or by generating additional evidence confirming the justness of their world.

BELIEVING IN A JUST WORLD

The "belief in a just world (BJW)," which is supported by a large body of research (Hafer and Begue, 2005; Lerner, 1980; Montada and Lerner, 1998), refers to an implicit but pervasive belief that the good and bad outcomes a person obtains are commensurate with what is deserved. As such, it is meant to portray people's fundamental assumption concerning their own ability to get what they ultimately deserve, but it also implies that people recognize the existence of various social and physical circumstances, "worlds," that are more or less dangerous or filled with uncontrollable forces. Claudia Dalbert and her colleagues (Lipkus, Dalbert, and Siegler, 1996) generated evidence supporting the theory that people's belief in the justness of their own "world," or being able to get what they deserve, can be reliably distinguished from their beliefs concerning the justness of the worlds others occupy. Their evidence also suggests that the former is, typically, more critical in determining people's behavior. A recognition that injustice sometimes occurs does not necessarily infringe on a person's belief that their own world is just, but it may threaten that belief and thus elicit defensive responses.

According to the theory presented here, the viability of children's personal contracts depends upon a requisite degree of confidence that they live in a world in which their investments and incurred costs will ultimately produce their desired outcomes. It would be appropriate to infer the extent of children's commitments to deservingness and justice from the strength of their self-reported BJW, or from their general willingness to delay gratification for greater outcomes (Braband and Lerner, 1975; Long and Lerner, 1974). But once the individual has reached the stage in which the conditional personal contract has been replaced by a functionally autonomous commitment to the justice motive, theoretically because the individual's BJW has lost its functional role, the strength of individual's BJW may have no necessary relation to the commitment to justice. Compelling examples of the distinction between someone's BJW and commitment to justice can be generated in casual conversations. It is very easy to find people who recognize and are willing to state that the world they live in is not "just." Many innocent people are victimized and very often people do not get what they deserve. At the same time, however, they are strongly committed to justice principles and experience strong emotion-driven imperatives when confronted with an injustice. These people admit they would like to believe that justice inevitably prevails, but they clearly recognize that is not true of the here and now.

If for most adults there is no necessary functional relation to the individual's commitment to justice, what are the psychological origins or functions of these measures of BJW, and/or what psychological processes do they reveal? One place to begin is with the manifest content of the measures: what would lead people to report their agreement or disagreement with the beliefs that people get what they deserve or deserve what they get? Possibly, people who have lived in a protected and benign environment or, conversely, one filled with chaos and danger might simply be reporting their experiences. Or, for these people, believing in the justness of their world is relatively comforting, and they are the kind of people who hold similar comforting beliefs, like being optimistic about the future. That optimism and desire for comfort and security may also be caused by, or at least associated with, a more general system of beliefs, such as an organized religion or political ideology (Rubin and Peplau, 1975). Conceivably, underlying experience-based fears or a future-oriented sense of threat may provide the motivating force for the adoption of those comforting beliefs (e.g., Kay and Jost, 2003).

There are additional possible correlates of BJW beliefs, but the important point is that those correlates would neither depend upon nor indicate the extent or nature of people's commitments to justice and deservingness. Those commitments would be revealed in the strength of their reactions to being confronted with an emotionally arousing injustice. There are some reasons to think that those people who strongly believe they live in a just world would be less likely, because of those beliefs, to perceive or recognize some injustices, or to reflect those beliefs as a form of "prepared response" (see Chapter 8) to signs of an injustice, for example, by finding fault with the victim. But those belief-consistent reactions would not necessarily reveal the strength of their commitment nor be motivated by attempts to restore justice. It is conceivable that some people may maintain their previously functional beliefs in the justness of their world long after they have lost their functional significance. But nevertheless they would, in adulthood and probably late adolescence, simply function as more or less strongly held beliefs.

Some evidence suggests that immediately prior confrontation with an injustice enhances people's attention to justice-related events and their justice-restoring reactions to the current injustice, but the evidence provides no indication of how individual differences in self-reported BJW mediates or influences these reactions. In one experiment (Hafer, 2000a) those measures appeared as a correlate of the extent of the participants' heightened attention to justice issues; however, there was no evidence of causal relations. Even absent compelling answers to the important questions concerning how people's commitments to their justice motive relate to their reported BJW, it may be instructive to consider the evidence describing the functional correlates of BJW.

In one very early experiment, Miron Zuckerman (1975) reasoned that people who more strongly believe they live in a world in which people get what they deserve will be especially likely to reflect this belief in their reactions to immanent critical encounters, that is, encounters in which the person has only partial control and something bad might happen. To examine this, he initially obtained measures of undergraduate students' beliefs in the justness of their world. Then, at a later point in time, separated from and with no obvious link to the initial assessments, someone telephoned the students and asked them to volunteer to be a participant in an experiment, a rather altruistic act. The key element in this experiment consisted of simply varying when the students were called. Zuckerman employed two different time periods for these calls, one during the middle of the semester and the other just prior to exams.

His reasoning was confirmed: relatively few of those whose help was solicited during the middle of the term were willing to help the caller and agree to participate in the experiment. Just prior to exams, however, those students who had previously indicated a relatively strong belief in the justness of their world volunteered to benefit the caller at a remarkably higher rate. Those with low BJW scores did not. The findings are consistent with the prediction that someone who believes they live in a just world, one in which good things happen to good people, when confronted with a critical event would be inclined to improve their odds for attaining a good outcome by being especially good themselves. Because good things happen to good people, if I do something good, or a good deed, that will help my grades on the exams.

Much later, Tomaka and Blascovich (1994) confirmed a related hypothesis: the belief in the justness of one's world, combined possibly with a note of self-conceit, may provide a functional amount of reassurance when confronted with a challenging potentially stressful task. If I am confident that I will get what I deserve and I am a good person, then with this implicit promise of success, I am more likely to perceive a potential stressor as a challenge that can be successfully overcome rather than as an anxiety-inducing threat. To examine this process, the researchers had their participants complete a measure of their BJW (Rubin and Peplau, 1973). Subsequently, they employed a series of measures to assess participants' stress and coping-related physiological responses, self-reported levels of arousal and threat, and their performance when confronted with two simple, but challenging tasks: for example, beginning with the number 2,549, mentally do (and report) serial subtractions of 7 as rapidly as possible.

Their comparisons of the reactions of the top and bottom half of their respondents, as categorized on the basis of their BJW score, revealed meaningful results. When reacting to both essentially similar tasks, those higher in BJW, in anticipation and during the task, showed greater signs of physiological coping and fewer signs of physiological stress reactions. These differences were consistent with their participants' verbal reports and, as anticipated, their performances on the critical tasks were remarkably better than those with lower BJW scores. Although the design of this experiment could not rule out the possible influence of other individual differences that may have been conflated with the BJW measure (e.g., optimism), the pattern of findings was consistent with the expected influence of a strong belief in the justness of one's world on people's level of confidence and their subsequent ability to successfully cope with potentially stressful encounters.

The pattern of physiological arousal assessed in this experiment suggests a potentially interesting approach to understanding how the construct measured by the BJW scales differs from the motivation involved in the commitment to justice. Of particular interest were the relations between the participants' changes in skin conductance (a measure of stress-based arousal) and their BJW. The high BJW participants in the Tomaka and Blascovich (1994) experiment exhibited fewer changes in the skin conductance, that is, less threat-based arousal, than their low BJW participants. An earlier experiment by Markovsky (1988), however, employing essentially the same measure of physiological arousal (changes in skin conductance), reported increased stress-based arousal among the participants who had just experienced an injustice: they had been either over- or underpaid for their work. Apparently, considering the findings of these two experiments, it makes sense to infer that although the experience of an injustice is stressfully arousing, the strong professed belief in the justness of one's world can enable people to minimize that level of arousal by, according to Tomaka and Blascovich, construing the arousing event as a challenge with which one can cope.

What is the relationship between people's commitment to justice and the strength of their belief in the justness of their world (BJW)? Evidence we will review in Chapter 3 indicates that for a period after being confronted with an injustice, people are more vigilant, even preconsciously, to cues of deservingness and justice (Aguiar et al., 2008; Correia et al., 2007; Hafer, 2000a) and more motivated to construe subsequent events to be consistent with justice scripts: "good things happen to good people" and "bad things happen to and are caused by bad people" (Callan et al., 2006). They also engage in efforts to promote justice by punishing harm doers (Goldberg et al., 1999; J. Lerner et al., 1998) and compensating victims (Simmons and Lerner, 1968). It appears that people's attempts to reestablish justice can elicit reactions that would be consistent with the motivation to believe they live in a just world, for example, victim derogation (Aguiar et al., 2008; Lerner, 1971b), but that does not indicate that their BJW had a causal relation to their reactions or even influenced how they expressed their imperative to restore justice, for example, by compensating a victim or punishing a harm doer. Rather, the extent or severity of their justice imperative, for example, as revealed by the extent of their injustice-elicited "anger," determines the strength of the person's justice-restoring reactions: the greater their anger the stronger their reaction (Goldberg et al., 1999; J. Lerner et al., 1998).

THE PERSONAL CONTRACT
THEORY: EXPERIMENTAL EVIDENCE

These rudimentary theoretical conjectures concerning the development of the personal contract, its role in the individual's commitment to deservingness and justice, and the central importance of this commitment in human motivation, suggest hypotheses that are amenable to empirical examination. Several experiments have generated a considerable body of evidence that sheds light on these hypotheses. One central hypothesis is that people who have developed a stronger commitment to their personal contract, a process that is affected but not completely determined by the developmental stage, are also more likely to follow rules of deservingness and justice rather than attempt to maximize their outcomes.

One of the earlier experiments examined the proposition that children's commitment to deservingness begins with and emerges out of their willingness to control their urges for immediate gratification in order to gain more profitable later outcomes. In this research, Gary Long (Long and Lerner, 1974) gave children the opportunity to donate some of the money they had earned for testing a toy to other children who were fortuitously denied that opportunity. In constructing the experiment he reasoned that young children, in this case nine to ten year olds, would vary in the extent to which they had become committed to their personal contracts, and the degree of their commitment could be reliably inferred from their willingness to forego immediately gratifying their desires for later, larger rewards.

If the theory is correct, then those children who were more willing to delay immediate gratifications would be more influenced by considerations of deservingness in deciding how much of their pay to keep or donate to the unfortunately deprived other child. Furthermore, it was reasoned that if they have a personal contract with themselves, this responsiveness would reflect their own private commitments to deservingness. Whether they donated more or less of their pay would be essentially a private act not designed to gain the approval or avoid the condemnation of others, whereas the donations of those less willing to delay gratification, that is, still lacking a sufficiently viable personal contract, would be most influenced by the possible sanctions of an audience.

To test these hypotheses, children from grades three and four participated in two separate testing sessions with differing experimenters, so that the children would be led to believe that these were two separate experiments. In the first session, the experimenter presented the children with a series of choices between a relatively small desirable object, which they would be immediately awarded, and a considerably more desirable one, which required their waiting a week. Although they were asked to make several such choices, they were assured of receiving one of the objects. By counting the number of small and immediate, as opposed to later and larger choices, the experimenter identified those children who were more or less willing to delay immediate gratification for the later larger rewards (see Mischel, 1961). For purposes of the research those above the median were designated "High DG [delay of gratification]," and those below, "Low DG."

The children's commitments to deservingness were then assessed in a later separate session conducted in a trailer by a different experimenter. In the second session they were paid for playing and evaluating a game that was to be commercially marketed. After receiving their pay the children were given the opportunity to donate some of it to other children who, they were told, because of time limitations, would not be able to participate and earn the rewards.

To distinguish between children's commitment to deservingness, rather than generosity or altruism, the experimenter led half of them to believe they did not deserve all the pay they had received. These children were told the amount of pay they received was actually appropriate for older and more experienced children, but because it was already prepackaged in envelopes they were given this undeserved overpayment. Similar procedures had been shown in previous studies to lead adult employees to experience the feelings of having received more pay than they deserved (Adams, 1963). The other half of the children was led to believe that the pay they received, actually the same amount in all cases, was the appropriate compensation for children their age.

The comparisons of the children's donating behavior confirmed the main predictions. The High DG children who believed they had been fortuitously overpaid donated considerably more of their pay to the relatively deprived children than did similar High DG children who believed they deserved all of their pay. Furthermore, this responsiveness to their own deservingness was not affected by the presence or absence of an audience when the High DG children made their donation. The High DG children donated similar amounts when the experimenter was in the room and when they believed their donations would remain anonymous because the experimenter had left the room.

By contrast the Low DG children's donations were uninfluenced by whether they had been overpaid or appropriately paid, that is, their own deservingness. In either case, they donated relatively little to the other children. They did appear to recognize, however, the social value of donating their pay to the deprived children. They donated almost as much as the High DG children when they believed the experimenter was observing their behavior. As expected, they knew that donating some of their pay was the socially desirable thing to do (the "social contract"), and so to gain favor or avoid negative sanction the Low DG children gave considerably more when the experimenter was present then when they believed no one would know the amount they gave.

These findings were encouraging because it was possible to predict that those children who were typically willing to postpone gratifying their desires to gain later more desirable outcomes were particularly responsive to issues of their own deservingness and appeared unconcerned about the social desirability of their behavior. They were willing to donate the "undeserved" pay to those less fortunate and just as willing to keep the pay that they deserved for themselves. This occurred regardless of whether or not they believed others would know what they had done. Those children less willing to delay gratifications were unresponsive to issues of deservingness while being sensitive to the normative expectations of those in authority.

A subsequent experiment (Braband and Lerner, 1975) found that high DG children, from grades five and six, as determined by the same prior assessment procedure, were predictably influenced by information concerning the source of another child's dependency in determining whether or not to come to his or her aid. The other child's need for help was described as resulting from either an externally caused accident or the victims' careless behavior. As expected, the High DG children volunteered considerably more help to the more deserving innocent victim of the accident than when they believed the victim had been carelessly negligent. The Low DG children offered relatively little help regardless of the victim's innocence.

These experiments provided remarkable support for two critical elements in the personal contract theory of deservingness. One is the predicted relationship between children's willingness to delay gratification and their commitment to the principle that people should get and have what they deserve. Those children who were more committed to their personal contract, as measured by their willingness to delay gratification, only gave help when the other child was a truly innocent victim who deserved their help, and similar others gave considerably more of their pay to the unfortunately deprived child, but only if they had been paid more than they deserved. The second confirmation involved the hypothesis that the children's commitment to deservingness was internally driven. As expected, the donating behavior of those children more willing to delay gratification, though highly responsive to their own and the other's deservingness, was uninfluenced by the anticipation of possible social sanctions: either praise or condemnation from an adult observer.

Carolyn Hafer (2000b) examined another central element in the personal contract theory of the commitment to deservingness: the impact of the common experience wherein a person deprives him- or herself in order to invest in future outcomes. Hafer recognized that most university students in pursuing their education must make considerable and ongoing investments of personal sacrifices in effort and economic resources. If the personal contract theory is correct, then making students vividly aware of their great investments in the future would also make them more vigilant and protective of the belief that they live in a just world in which people get what they deserve. As a consequence they would be more easily threatened by the awareness that an injustice, or undeserved suffering, has been inflicted on an innocent victim. To counter this threat and maintain their trust in the justness of their world they would be motivated to deny that an injustice had actually occurred. That denial required persuading themselves that the "innocent" victim actually deserved her fate by virtue of her inferior character or misbehavior. In this manner they could persuade themselves that an injustice had not occurred. Bad things did not happen to an innocent, good person.

To test these hypotheses, Hafer presented university students with a vivid portrayal of a victim: a student suffering from the effects of a sexually transmitted disease (STD). She varied the extent to which the victim deserved her fate by informing participants that the STD had been acquired either accidentally (innocent victim) or through negligence (culpable victim). Subsequently, they were asked to evaluate the extent to which the victim was blameworthy, personally similar to them, and of good character.

The findings revealed that the students who had previously described what they imagined their lives to be like after graduation and beyond resisted the possibility that such terrible suffering might be accidentally inflicted upon an innocent, desirable person similar to them. As expected, these students portrayed the explicitly "innocent" victim whose STD had been accidentally contracted as equally blame-worthy and undesirable as the same victim who had brought about her STD by her irresponsible negligence. The other students, whose equally great investments in their future were not made salient, that is, they had previously described their daily activities, were much more willing to recognize the innocence of the accidentally infected victim. They portrayed that same innocent victim's character in a much more positive light and described her as essentially blameless for her suffer-ing while condemning the negligent victim. Apparently, making their investments in the future salient impelled many students to deny the apparent suffering of an innocent victim. She was viewed as neither an innocent nor a desirable person.

Callan, Shead, and Olson (2009) found an additional equally ingenious way to examine these processes. They reasoned that if the personal contract theory is correct, then witnessing a clear instance of someone's undeserved suffering should threaten the viability of the personal contract and at least temporarily reduce the observers' own willingness to put off immediate gratifications in order to achieve future benefits. To test this they presented their participants with the same vivid portrayal of the young woman suffering from an STD that Hafer had used in her research (Hafer, 2000b). Some of the partici-pants were led to believe the victim's recklessness had led to her contract the disease, while others were informed that her STD was the result of medical personnel having provided her with infected blood following an automobile accident. In other words, she was an innocent victim. Immediately following that experience, the parti-cipants were given a series of choices between various rewards that differed in magnitude and delay.

The results nicely confirmed the main hypothesis. Those who believed they had witnessed the terrible suffering of an innocent victim (evidence of an unjust world) were less willing to delay grat-ification than those who believed the victim was negligently responsible for bringing about her own suffering. The time between the witnessing of the victim's suffering and the measure of willingness to delay gratification had to be rather brief, given the demonstrated willingness of observers to find ways to persuade themselves that no injustice had occurred. Nevertheless, the remarkable, theoretically significant findings of these experiments provide compelling evidence of the causal link between people's belief in the justness of their world and their willingness to defer their own gratification in order to earn larger, later, rewards, that is, invest in their futures.

In Summary

The search for the origins of the central and pervasive influence of justice in people's lives led to an examination of the normal process of human development. A child's growing cognitive abilities include enhanced executive control over his or her instinctive impulses and the ability to understand the causal connection between actions now and consequences later. These abilities combine with attempts to generate greater and more secure desired outcomes to generate a personal contract based upon delaying the immediate gratification of their impulses in order to earn and deserve later, greater outcomes. To maintain the personal contract in a complex and changing environment eventually requires most people to make a commitment to deservingness and justice for themselves and others in their world. This commitment leads people initially in each encounter to automatically and preconsciously determine who deserves what from whom.

A fundamental issue remains concerning the relative importance of the individual's commitment to deservingness and justice: how important is its influence in relation to other motives? According to the theorists cited earlier, one of the reasons self-interest dominates people's behavior is because it shapes their automatic, preconscious initial reactions to significant events (see, e.g., Moore and

Loewenstein, 2004). The personal contract theory offered here, however, predicts that individuals' initial and primary reactions to these events are driven by the person's commitment to deservingness and justice. Fortunately, the findings of recent experiments speak directly to these alternative and apparently contradictory hypotheses.

3

Commitment to Justice: The Initial Primary Automatic Reaction

The personal contract–based theory of the commitment to deservingness and justice stands in stark contrast to contemporary self-interest theories on at least two key issues. One of these, the most obvious, concerns what people care about, or what motivates their decisions and actions: do people invariably and primarily attempt to promote their own welfare and gratify their desires, or are their initial reactions guided by their commitments to deservingness and justice? The related second issue involves the underlying psychological processes in people's reactions to an occurrence of consequence: does their initial, automatic, and often unconscious egocentric and egoistic reaction give self-interest "primal power" to influence their judgments (Epley and Caruso, 2004; Moore and Loewenstein, 2004)? Or, because of their commitment to justice, do people initially focus their attention on the question of who deserves what? According to the personal contract theory, peoples' central commitments to deservingness and justice would naturally lead them to automatically attend and respond to cues of what has happened to whom. Their initial automatic reactions would include preconscious evaluations of someone's outcomes together with evaluations of the person's entitlements as a function of who they are and what they have done. Discrepancies between those two evaluations – outcome and entitlements – elicit justice imperatives composed of affective responses and efforts to eliminate the discrepancy. Although this occurs automatically as the initial preconscious reaction in response to the salient cues in an encounter, subsequent and more thoughtful controlled processing often modifies and alters these reactions in specifiable ways.

Recently generated evidence speaks directly to these theory-driven and critical issues: the automatic and preconscious processes that initially occur when people witness an apparent injustice.

Considerable previous research has examined hypotheses derived from the proposition that people's reactions to victims are influenced by the extent to which they do not deserve their suffering or deprivation. This was assessed by confronting participants with victims of greater or less undeserved suffering. The victim was inflicted with extended versus brief duration of suffering (Lerner and Simmons, 1966; Simons and Piliavin, 1972); the suffering was mild versus severe (Stokols and Schopler, 1973); and the victim was portrayed as innocent or negligently responsible (Simmons and Lerner, 1968). In each case, greater or less deserved suffering led to measurably greater efforts to restore justice, either by derogating the victims' character to match their fates or by attempting to help and compensate the victim.

Although those findings confirmed important hypotheses, they relied on plausible inferences based upon comparing participants' reactions in various experimental conditions. Recently, however, several investigators have taken on the task of generating more explicit and direct evidence of the processes underlying those reactions. They have focused on describing the automatic appearance and influence of justice imperatives in people's reactions to witnessing an injustice.

Carolyn Hafer published the first of these highly illuminating experiments (Hafer, 2000a). In her study, she presented all of the participants with the same vividly compelling report of an injustice: another student had been robbed and severely beaten. She then employed an ingenious procedure to test the hypotheses that witnessing the victimization of the student would lead the participants to become concerned with the violation of justice that had occurred, and that this concern would impel them to find ways to reestablish justice. Although the participants would be unaware of the processes that were driving their reactions, the experimenter would be able to observe and measure them. According to the theory, all of this would occur automatically and preconsciously.

To assess these reactions, Hafer had her participants engage in a "second experiment" immediately after witnessing the injustice. That experiment consisted of a signal detection task in which the participants were to respond as rapidly as possible when they detected the color of a stimulus word. There is considerable prior evidence that in this task the delay in detecting the color of the target word reliably indicates the extent to which the perceiver has been attending to and processing the content of the word rather than simply identifying the color as instructed. This procedure is particularly well suited to assess the influence of preconscious processes because the content-based interference typically occurs at exposures below the threshold where perceivers are able to consciously visualize and report the actual content of the stimulus word (Williams, Mathews, and MacLeod, 1996). In this experiment, the theoretically critical stimulus-words denoted issues of justice, fairness, deservingness, and so forth. The control words, of equal length and familiarity, included those denoting harm, story content, and neutral events. To test the main hypotheses, the extent of the injustice was varied by informing some of the participants just prior to engaging in the signal-detection task that the perpetrators had been apprehended and punished, so that justice had been at least partially restored, while others were told that the perpetrators had gotten off scot-free.

The main hypotheses were nicely confirmed. Those participants who believed the perpetrators had not been punished revealed significantly greater interference-delay times in identifying the color of the justice-related words than the color of the other words. In addition, consistent with the prior literature on derogation of victims (Lerner, 1980), the extent of the interference caused by the justice content of the words was significantly correlated with the participants' subsequent evaluation of the innocent victim: the greater the interference the more negatively they portrayed her character. As expected, neither of these effects appeared when the participants believed the perpetrators had been apprehended and punished. When they believed that justice had been at least partially done, they had no need to be as concerned with finding or restoring justice.

The evidence clearly revealed that the vivid portrayal of the robbery and beating of the innocent student led the participants to be preconsciously concerned with justice, and the extent of these concerns predicted their automatically trying to reestablish justice by an assessment of the victim that implied he or she had, in some way, deserved a negative outcome.

Additional research inspired by Hafer's experiment contributed similar evidence of people preconsciously focusing on issues of deservingness and justice immediately after witnessing an injustice. Isabel Correia and her colleagues (Correia et al., 2007) presented their Portuguese participants with a compelling video of a boy who had lost both arms as a consequence of accidentally grabbing a live high-powered electric cable while trying to retrieve a ball. The researchers varied the degree of injustice of this terrible fate by informing some of the participants that prior to the accident the child had been warned about the presence and danger of the cable: the victimization occurred because the child had recklessly ignored the warning. That information was not offered to the other participants. In addition, the information given to some of the participants identified the child as either a member of a culturally devalued minority group (gypsies) or a member of the Portuguese majority.

The participants then responded to the color-identification task that employed justice-related and appropriate control words as the target stimuli. The findings revealed significant preconscious interference in identifying the color of justice-related words, but primarily when they believed the victim had not been forewarned, that is, was objectively innocent, and a member of their own group. The terrible suffering of either the careless or derogated minority child elicited remarkably less justice-based interference. Apparently the participants viewed the reckless or minority child as less worthy, and their sense of justice was measurably less threatened. Aguiar and colleagues (2008) confirmed that the victimized Portuguese child elicited greater preconscious concerns with justice. However, they also found that, along with this increased threat to their sense of justice, the participants revealed evidence of implicit derogation of the innocent Portuguese child who had lost both of his arms through no fault of his own.

Additional experiments employing the innocent victim of a vicious bullying incident (Callan, 2010) or of a sexually transmitted disease (Hafer, 2000b) yielded similar interference effects. These findings, taken together, provide strong support for the conclusion that people who become aware of actual or potential undeserved suffering automatically and preconsciously become concerned with issues of deservingness and justice: the greater the possible injustice, the greater the automatic preoccupation.

But what are the consequences of that concern with deservingness and justice? How does it influence what people think and do?

THE PRECONSCIOUS INFLUENCE OF COMMITMENT TO DESERVINGNESS ON MEMORY, RECALL, ATTRIBUTION, AND SOCIAL JUDGMENTS

To begin answering those important questions, one can turn to evidence concerning how people's commitment to deservingness, and their related need to believe they live in a world in which people get what they deserve, influence the way they comprehend, recall, and react to significant events. As studies show, the automatic preconscious focus on issues of deservingness and justice leads people to construe and remember events so that they support and confirm the fundamental belief that they live in a just world.

Mitch Callan and his colleagues conducted several experiments that reveal various preconscious manifestations of the themes of deservingness and justice on the way people process information. In his classic research on moral development, Piaget (1932) had documented young children's tendency to reason backward directly from the value of the consequences of someone's acts or of what had happened to them to their personal merit. He identified belief in "immanent justice" as the source of this rather primitive form of moral reasoning. Callan, Ellard, and Nicol (2006) not only documented this form of moral reasoning among adults, but also they clearly demonstrated the origins in the person's concern with finding that justice had occurred: that is, bad things happen to and are caused by bad people, whereas good things happen to and are caused by good people.

In one experiment, Callan et al. (2006) presented their participants with a scenario in which someone had a terrible automobile accident. The researchers also varied the character of the target person, who was portrayed as someone who previously had behaved either admirably or despicably in a context unrelated to the accident. Despite the remoteness and irrelevance of the prior event, the findings revealed that the participants were more likely to blame the despicable person's prior behavior for the accident (bad outcome) than the admirable person's prior acts. In a follow-up experiment employing the same scenario, Callan, Sutton, and Dovale (2010) demonstrated that the participants' attribution of the accident to the victim's prior immoral behavior was mediated by their belief that the immoral victim deserved his or her fate. Additional analyses revealed that these findings of deservingness and attribution were enhanced when the participants were given a simultaneous task that reduced their available cognitive resources: the immanent justice effects were primarily the result of preconscious processes that linked the victim's outcomes directly to his or her moral worth.

The results of a related experiment confirmed the role of the participant's concern with justice in attributing blame to the victim's prior acts. That experiment varied the intensity of the participants' concern with justice by having them watch a videotaped interview with a young woman who was either going to continue suffering from the effects of being accidentally infected with HIV (see Hafer, 2000b) or whose infection had been successfully controlled with drugs, that is, greater or lesser undeserved suffering. That video had been shown in previous research to reliably elicit greater or lesser preoccupation with justice using the Stroop color-identification task (a cognitive task that can measure people's tendency to focus on particular concepts; Hafer, 2000a). After generating greater or less concern with justice, the researchers predicted and found that those participants who previously had been exposed to the greater undeserved suffering were even more likely to blame the victim's prior immoral behavior for his or her accident. Apparently, those participants had a greater need to find that people deserve their fates.

The researchers found similar results when the participants were informed that someone who previously had behaved either admirably or despicably had won a large lottery. The participants were more likely to attribute responsibility for the fortuitous desirable outcome to the perpetrator of prior admirable acts than to someone who had exhibited undesirable previous behavior.

Callan, Kay, Davidenko, and Ellard (2009) demonstrated that this concern with justice also influences how people construe good and bad events that occur fortuitously in their own lives. They found that participants who had been informed that, by chance, either something good or bad just happened to them subsequently remembered having correspondingly done more good or bad things in their recent past. Apparently, their recall of prior behavior confirmed their belief that they personally – and, by extension, people in general – deserve what happens to them, even when the events are merely fortuitous. A related experiment also found that participants who first had been asked to recall either recent good or bad deeds that they had done, were subsequently also more likely to judge a chance-determined outcome (coin flip) as fair when the outcome (good or bad) corresponded to their recent behaviors that had been made salient.

A similar recent study (Gaucher et al., 2010) extended the evidence for how deservingness affects recall and expectation. In this study, researchers asked participants to remember either good or bad deeds they had done or good or bad "breaks" (twists of fate) they had experienced. People who had done good things, compared to those who recalled bad deeds, interpreted future events as more positive, showing that they expected to be rewarded for their past behavior. However, people who recalled good breaks, compared to those who recalled bad breaks, interpreted future events more negatively, showing that they thought justice required an even distribution of good and bad. In a second study, people who were led by the experimenter to experience a good or bad break also remembered more experiences of the other kind of event, that is, experiencing a good break led people to remember more previous bad breaks, so that they could maintain a perception that everything evened out: overall, people deserve what they get.

This tendency to construe people's fates as manifestations of their merit occurs along with, or possibly in spite of, a similarly motivated tendency to remember and recall events so that people's outcomes correspond to their merit: bad or good things happen to similarly bad or good people. People get what they deserve and deserve what they get. Employing the example of someone winning a large lottery, Callan and colleagues (2009) varied the moral worth of the winner, who was portrayed as either a good or bad person. After performing an unrelated task, the participants' subsequent recall of the size of the lottery prize was clearly influenced by the personal merit of the winner: they recalled a significantly larger prize for the good person than the bad winner. Apparently the participants' recall revealed their preconscious attempts to have the desirability of the prize correspond with the merit of the winner.

An additional experiment revealed that enhancing the participants' concern with justice, by having them witness a victim of greater rather than less undeserved suffering, increased the participants' subsequent preconscious efforts to recall that the size of the lottery winnings corresponded to the personal merit of the winners in order to affirm their belief that good things happen to good people. That is, this justice-based memory bias was stronger when justice was more salient to the participant.

Investigators have also found evidence that this process extends to evaluating someone's personal worth from the desirability of their appearance. Ken and Karen Dion (1987) reasoned that, in this society, physical attractiveness is highly desirable, and as a result people would be inclined, preconsciously, to believe that in a "just world" good character goes along with good looks. Their participants' ratings of people depicted in photographs revealed that more positive personalities were attributed to the more attractive photos. This tendency was stronger among those participants who also described themselves as having a greater belief in the justness of their world, as measured by the BJW scale.

Callan, Powell, and Ellard (2007) extended and built upon these findings by demonstrating that people tend to infer personal merit from the social value of someone's appearance. They presented their participants with the report of the tragic accidental death of a woman. The participants reported the event as more tragic if the victim was physically attractive rather than less attractive. Consistent with the inference that the participants' reactions were motivated by justice, they also assigned greater punishment to the negligent perpetrator when the victim was physically attractive. Additional evidence in a second experiment revealed that participants recalled the same victim to be less attractive when her undeserved suffering was greater rather than less.

In Summary

A wide range of studies illustrates a tendency for people to alter their cognitions in such a way as to bring their evaluations of the outcomes and personal merits of others into congruence. This tendency is strengthened among people who care about justice, either because it is a personality trait or because justice has been made situationally salient. The drive for justice can create beliefs that provide reassurance that justice exists.

EMOTIONAL RESPONSES

The personal contract theory assumes that witnessing an injustice challenges people's commitment to justice and threatens their confidence that they live in a just world. As a result they become emotionally aroused and experience an imperative to rectify the injustice. Greater, more vivid injustices elicit greater threats and arousal and stronger justice-restoring imperatives. Presumably, all of this occurs automatically without the person being aware of the processes underlying their experienced emotions and imperatives. They may be aware of an injustice having occurred as well as their anger and impulse to punish the perpetrator without any awareness of what is driving their reactions, that is, without being aware of why the injustice arouses their anger, for example, and/or their desire to punish the perpetrator.

Two experiments employing the videotape of a very moving bullying incident (Gross and Levenson, 1995) provided compelling documentation of the automatic reactions to witnessing an injustice: the emotion of anger directing the imperative to punish harm doers. Even more important, they vividly demonstrated the persistent preconscious influence of these initial automatic justice-driven imperatives on the person's behavior in a subsequent situation.

In these experiments, conducted by Jennifer Lerner, Goldberg, and Tetlock (1998) and by Goldberg, Lerner, and Tetlock (1999), participants rated their emotions and affect, including the extent of anger they were experiencing, after viewing the bullying tape. Following that, under the guise of a separate experiment, they responded to several incidents in which someone through various degrees of negligence had caused harm to others. The participants then rated the extent of the negligent perpetrator's responsibility and culpability for the harm as well as the amount of punishment the negligent perpetrator should receive. In both experiments, the participants' reported levels of anger at the first incident of injustice (the bullying) predicted the extent of punishment they assigned to the negligent perpetrator in the second situation. The angrier they were at the first injustice, the more punishment they assigned to the second negligent perpetrator of underserved harm. Apparently, to the extent that their sense of justice had been aroused and threatened, they maintained the impulse to punish harm doers. That impulse persisted until they reacted to the next, ostensibly unrelated, event involving a negligent perpetrator of an injustice.

The influence of the participants' commitment to justice is supported by an additional finding: if the participants had been informed at the outset that the bully in the first incident had been apprehended and punished, their anger was not reduced, but it no longer affected the punishment they assigned to the second negligent harm doer. It appears that if the participants believed that justice had been served, at least in part, they felt no need to express their anger at the injustice by subsequently punishing the second harm doer (Goldberg et al., 1999). This provides additional reason to infer that the participants' anger was elicited by and concerned with the injustice, not merely the suffering and abuse they had witnessed. Also, the participants were unaware of the source of their nonrational motivation to punish the negligent harm doer. As reported earlier, Callan and colleagues (under review) found that viewing this videotape elicited measurable concerns with justice in the color-recognition task: The emotionally aroused viewers became preconsciously concerned with justice and injustice.

In sum, the experiments described here provide considerable support for various aspects of the personal contract theory of when and how justice matters to people. The evidence confirms the prediction that, when confronted with an injustice, people are automatically impelled to reestablish justice through reinterpreting events and/or acting to reestablish justice. The greater the injustice, the greater those efforts. It is particularly important to recognize that these justice-restoring reactions are automatic and preconscious. Reactions that take place outside of conscious awareness are difficult to monitor and, thus, control.

SELF-EVALUATIONS

Though providing impressive illustrations of people's reactions to injustices experienced by others, none of the research described to this point directly examined how people react when critical events and justice imperatives threaten their own benefits, that is, are explicitly contrary to their own self-interest. If justice imperatives are an important influence in people's lives, it should be possible to demonstrate that people engage in justice-restoring reactions even when that requires losses in commonly desired resources, including their own self-esteem.

It should be noted at the outset that, according to the contemporary theorists cited earlier, there is no reason to investigate this because people's automatic, essentially irreversible, egocentric and egoistic self-benefiting reactions would preclude self-punitive or costly reactions from happening (see Moore and Loewenstein, 2004; Epley and Caruso, 2004, cited in the preceding text) unless one assumes the presence of some residual bad habits, masochistic pleasure, or incredible stupidity.

As illustrated by the examples with which we began the book and confirmed by considerable research, whether or not one chooses to define it as perverted or normal, justice imperatives can and often do take precedence over people's desire to benefit themselves. Consider, for example, the experimental demonstrations of an all-too-familiar event: what happens when people suddenly become aware that they accidentally caused harm to someone? They had no intention of causing the harm, nor could the accident be rationally attributed to their negligence of commission or omission. It was an unforeseeable accident. This automatic self-blame and self-punishment following the accidental infliction of harm can be easily illustrated by instructions to imagine the following:

> You are at a rather formal dinner party, the soup course has just been served, and a loud crash of falling plates behind you startles everyone at the table, some quite visibly. As a result of the crash your elbow jerks causing your plate of soup to spill on to the lap of the elegant woman sitting next to you. Then follow that with questions such as "how would you feel? What would you say?"

Virtually every "accidental harm doer" imagines feeling terrible and blaming themselves for being so clumsy. As a result, they profusely apologize and may offer to pay for cleaning and possibly replacing the dress. Then ask the person to take the role of the poor victim and ask her how she would react. She would tell the harm doer that it was not his or her fault. The "victim" tries to make the harm doer feel better and insists it was not their fault, and they need not pay for the cleaning, and so forth. It was just an accident. The important point is that accidental harm doers often blame themselves and offer to punish themselves and compensate the victim; while the victim, reciting the conventional norms for assigning culpability, explains that they need not feel guilty. As everyone but the harm doer seems to recognize, it was simply an unforeseeable uncontrollable unfortunate accident.

The important point is that for the accidental harm doer, even in role playing, something quite contrary to self-interest was automatically operative and primal. A good candidate for that can be roughly described as a vestigial form of the "moral realism" and "immanent justice" that Piaget (1932) found in the moral judgments of very young children. The automatic reasoning backward from the moral value of outcomes to the personal worth of an actor leads to the conclusion that bad things are done by bad people.

Although one cannot deny the immediate rather painful self-blaming reactions, it is possible to ascribe the subsequent behavior of the participants in this scenario to something like a required social "dance" that has its roots in cultural rituals designed to maintain social integration. To fend off retaliatory punishment the harm doer demonstrates his allegiance to the victim and the group by apologizing for what has occurred, and the victim, as well as the audience, then graciously assures the harm doer that his or her status in the group has not been damaged. But that subsequent ritual does not negate the immediate automatic self-punitive feelings of guilt, shame, and so forth from having been the patently accidental "cause" of an injustice.

Similar conditions were met in several early experiments (see, e.g., Freedman, Wallington, and Bless, 1967): participants were made to believe that by engaging in a typically innocuous act they had accidentally harmed someone. For example, by following their experimenter's instructions to take a seat they had inadvertently caused systematically arranged cards hidden on the seat of the chair to be spilled on the floor and thus seriously impeded someone's valuable research project. Following the accident, most participants automatically experienced a very unpleasant emotion – shame or guilt – that induced them to volunteer for relatively costly altruistic acts, possibly to regain their self-esteem (Meindl and Lerner, 1983).

The important point for present purposes is the automatic eliciting of relatively painful feelings of guilt for having accidentally caused harm. If self-interest was the invariably primal, automatic reaction, the participants would certainly not have experienced self-punishing feelings, especially because the easily accessible conventional rules for blaming would have completely exonerated such unforeseeable accidental harm doing (Shaver, 1985; Weiner, 1993). Nevertheless, further research revealed that after accidentally causing harm, participants automatically lowered, and subsequently engaged in measurable efforts to repair, their sense of self-esteem (Meindl and Lerner, 1983).

Miller and Gunasegaram (1990) conducted a delightfully simple thought experiment that, because of the explicit role of "chance," provided evidence of a fundamental and pervasive process eliciting self-inflicted blame. They asked their participants to imagine a situation in which two people are informed they would be given $1,000 if they flipped coins with matching outcomes: that is, both coins came up heads or both came up tails. Then, ostensibly, the first person, Sam, flipped his coin, and it came up heads. With both of them in great anticipation, the second person, John, flipped the coin, and it came up tails. They were then asked who would feel most guilty, or responsible, for their not winning the $1,000, Sam or John? As expected, the participants predicted that John, the second person, would be blamed the most and feel most guilty. Why? Why any blame or guilt at all? It was simply a matter of chance. Apparently, the participants must have reasoned backward from a chance-determined bad outcome to attributions of blame and guilt: bad outcomes are caused by bad people. Rather than engaging in a situation-specific cultural ritual, the participants automatically demonstrated and maintained rather primitive attributions of blame even when it clearly violated their own self-interest.

These reactions occurred in the context of highly educated people role-playing a reaction to a hypothetical event. A similar reaction, however, appeared in the other extreme of emotionally involving experiences with much more serious personal consequences. There was no role-playing or imagining a response to a hypothetical event in the fully engaging natural experiment conducted by Rubin and Peplau (1973). They obtained self-esteem ratings from young draft-eligible men before and shortly after they learned of their fates in the publicly broadcast draft lottery held during the height of the Vietnam War. As they listened to the lottery, the participants knew that those with birthdates that were among the first one-third drawn by chance would be certain to be drafted, while those among the last one-third would be assured they would not and could go on with their normal lives.

The main test of the hypothesis required comparing the before and after self-worth ratings of the "losers" in the lottery, those who had just learned they were virtually certain to be drafted, with the "winners," those who learned that chance had smiled upon them and they would not have to go to war.

The fortunate young men, lottery "winners," revealed a slight increase in their self-esteem after they learned about their very desirable fates. Most of the "losers," however, showed significant signs of having lowered their self-esteem. Those young men who were inflicted with a horrible fate, simply because of the order of selection of their birth date in the lottery, measurably lowered their ratings of their self-worth and thus added to their own miseries.

It would appear that the self-punitive reaction in these young men stemmed from their automatically applying a form of immanent justice rule to themselves. Any rational-thinking person would realize that their being drafted because of a lottery was just chance, bad luck of the worst sort, but apparently, these reasonably intelligent young men were influenced by the scripted response: bad things happen to bad people. It was as if their automatic and clearly preconscious reactions were "Something terrible just happened to me so I must be a bad person." Certainly, it would be extremely difficult to find any evidence of an initial, automatic, primal self-interest reaction in these irrational, self-punitive judgments.

Several investigators have described the appearance of similarly nonrational and apparently self-punitive reactions among objectively innocent victims of horrible crimes and tragedies (Alicke, 2000). According to these reports, not only do self-blaming and condemning reactions appear as an automatic response, but also they remain remarkably resistant to reality-based information that would reduce that pain. Efforts to explain these reactions in terms of some form of a "cognitive balance" mechanism operating in the victim's minds (Feather, 2006; Heider, 1958) or their motivation to maintain a sense of control (Janoff-Bulman, 1979) have not yielded persuasive results

(Meyer and Taylor, 1986; Zuckerman and Gerbasi, 1977). Suffice it to say, at this point, these tragic reactions reveal no sign of an automatic and influential form of self-interest.

AUTOMATIC PREFERENCES FOR FAIRNESS REPLACED BY THOUGHTFUL DECISIONS TO MAXIMIZE PROFIT

Although justice motives affect the initial response, other motives can complicate or override the initial reaction in subsequent, more rational processing. Bazerman, White, and Loewenstein (1995) produced rather compelling evidence for two processes that may be operative in the normal course of events with predictably different consequences: conscious, thoughtful application of conventional norms and the direct expression of automatic, preconscious, scripted reactions.

In several experiments they varied the alternative amounts of profit and unfairness so that the lesser but fair outcomes, in separate ratings of desirability, elicited higher ratings than the ratings of greater but clearly unfair outcomes. This occurred when the participants were role-playing their reactions to hypothetical events such as a job offer, as well as when they were reacting to actual offers. For example, participating in an experiment for a larger paycheck, but less than others were paid, was considered less desirable than an experiment in which they would receive a lesser but equal paycheck.

The findings revealed that, at least within certain parameters, people initially appeared to be more satisfied with fairness than with economic profit, or possibly that they were more upset by unfairness than by less profitable outcomes. The researchers also reported, however, that when similar participants were simultaneously presented with both the lesser but fair and the larger but unfair outcomes possibilities, and asked to choose between the two pairs of alternatives rather than sequentially rating the desirability of each set of outcomes, their preferences were reversed. They reliably chose the more profitable but less fair alternative. Participants' more complex decisions, when they were consciously comparing the two outcomes, revealed that the goal of maximizing their economic profit prevailed over their desires for fairness. But because the exact same amounts of profit and unfairness were involved in the separate ratings of desirability and the choice of the preferred pair of alternatives, what would account for the reversal in preference?

Unlike the act of directly expressing how they felt about particular amounts of money and fairness, having to make a choice between two sets of alternatives that involved trade-offs in profits and fairness involved a more complex comparison. As a result, they were compelled to consciously think about what factors were involved and find an acceptable reason for their choices. For most participants, such thought processes (not unlike having to think about what one would say in an interview, see J. Lerner et al., 1998) involved the application of conventionally predominant norms of rational self-interest that overruled their automatic preferences for fairness. Their automatic direct reactions revealed a preference of fairness over profit, while the consciously reasoned process led to the more normatively appropriate choice of profit rather than fairness.

These research findings suggest that when people spend the time and effort needed to think about their reactions they are more likely to employ conventional norms to determine their evaluations, judgments, and decisions than when they respond automatically to the salient cues. That does not mean that conscious considerations of justice and deservingness will not influence people's thoughtful reactions, but rather that they are much more likely to appear in the service of, and be shaped by, normatively appropriate goals. In economic encounters, or more generally competitive encounters over relatively scarce or highly desirable resources, the norms in this society typically sanction the rational pursuit of self-interest: economic gains, self-esteem, and public-esteem management (Bazerman et al., 1995; Lerner and Lichtman, 1968; Miller, 1999).

For present purposes, it is important to emphasize that the participants' initial intuitive reaction reflected their personal commitment to fairness. Self-interest appeared as the dominant theme only when the participants consciously thought about which was the "better," that is, more normatively appropriate, choice for them.

SUMMARY: EVIDENCE OF JUSTICE IMPERATIVES

The experiments described thus far have documented two important aspects of justice imperatives. The first, critically important one is the automatic appearance of the justice imperative that impels people to maintain or restore justice. These responses appear to be scripted, and as they increase in intensity they are guided by emotions such as anger or guilt to influence how the person reestablishes justice. The second is that the participants were often, if not invariably, unaware of the preconscious processes that were influencing their reactions. They had no awareness that their own commitments to justice and deservingness were generating their reactions to these injustices. If asked, they would have been unable to consciously retrieve these processes (Haidt, 2001). The strength of the emotional response to injustice is heightened by the fact that the assessment of justice is automatic and lies outside of conscious awareness.

Despite what we see as convincing evidence that assessments of justice are primary reactions, most justice researchers – along with a more general public – have asserted that justice functions in the service of self-interest. Before going on to a closer examination of the way people determine their own and others entitlements, that is, who deserves what, it is useful to attempt an understanding of how self-interest came to be portrayed as the dominant social motive. To understand and critique the basis for this perspective, we turn now to a critical review of a sample of the research that has typically been used to make the case.

4

Explaining the Myth of Self-Interest

It should be strikingly obvious at this point that the findings just reviewed are inconsistent with the prevailing contemporary view that manifestations of self-interested motives appear as the automatic response and shape subsequent judgments of deservingness and justice (see, e.g., Epley and Caruso, 2004; Moore and Loewenstein, 2004; Skitka et al., in press). The evidence is clear: justice imperatives in predictable circumstances automatically influence people's thoughts, feelings, and behavior. To put it baldly, there is clear and compelling evidence that egocentric and egoistic reactions are not invariably the primary automatic dominating influence. This raises the question of exactly when and how self-interested motives actually influence people's judgments of deservingness and reactions to injustice.

An important step in this ambitious project consists of critically reexamining examples of the kind of research findings that are typically employed to provide supporting evidence for these self-interest dominated theories. Do they confirm the central role of self-interest, or do they demonstrate certain methodological and interpretive shortcomings that undermine their conclusions? A reexamination of evidence that is typically cited to infer the effects of egoistic motives will be the first step in answering those questions. Upon closer examination, do those findings actually reveal people automatically and preconsciously framing, modifying, or biasing their judgments of deservingness and justice to fit their self-interested purposes?

We will not attempt an exhaustive review of the extensive array of experiments in the literature. The alternative adopted here will focus on highly cited or prototypical experiments for critical reevaluation. Do the findings of these experiments clearly illustrate the influence of self-interest? Our reexamination of the evidence will be guided by the question of whether or not there are actually more compelling explanations for the participants' behavior than the purported influence of self-interested motives. After suggesting other, more plausible explanations for those findings, we describe a few reasons why the self-interest–dominated view of human motivation has persisted in spite of the available evidence and become the unquestioned explanation of choice adopted by social and behavioral scientists.

PRECONSCIOUS BIASES: SELF-INTEREST OR SELF-CONCEIT?

The highly cited experiments of Messick and Sentis (1983) provide a good place to begin a reexamination of the evidence for the influence of self-interest. These studies had undergraduate participants describe fair pay distributions for themselves and others in hypothetical work situations. In essence, the critical findings in this research resulted from comparing participants' reports of what would constitute a fair payment for themselves with their assignment of a fair payment for another person when their relative contributions were equal in terms of productivity and time worked. Directly comparing the two amounts revealed that the participants reported they deserved considerably more pay than they thought was deserved by an equally productive other worker. According to Epley and Caruso (2004), these findings clearly demonstrate the influence of an egoistic self-benefiting bias.

Stillwell and Baumeister (1997) reported similarly self-benefiting biases. In their critical conditions, they assigned participants the role of imagining they were either the harm doer or the victim as they read a rather detailed description of a hypothetical incident in which a student harm doer had failed to repay the help previously received from a victim. Subsequently, the participants were asked to reproduce what they had read. As predicted, those reports were highly biased in ways that reflected the reader's assigned role. In their written descriptions, those who were instructed to imagine themselves as the harm doer while they read the story remembered or invented more details that exonerated the harm doer. Meanwhile, those taking the part of the victim produced a version with errors of invention or omission that portrayed the harm doer in a more negative light with greater harm to their imagined self, the poor innocent victim. They presented equally distorted mirror images of what had transpired.

Both of these experiments found clear evidence of systematically biased reactions, but it is less clear that these reactions resulted from self-interested motives. How is it possible to infer the influence of self-serving motivation given that these role-playing participants had to be fully aware that they had literally nothing to gain by generating biased responses? There was no money, prestige, self-esteem, or experimenter approval for them to gain or lose by biasing their responses to portray themselves as meriting more pay or in a more flattering light.

Certainly, the nature of the biases implied a favoring of the self as the imagined actor in hypothetical scenarios, but that occurred in the absence of any incentives, anything tangible or symbolic to be gained or lost for generating biased reactions. Actually, Stillwell and Baumeister (1997) found that these biases persisted even when their experimenters explicitly instructed the participants to be as accurate as possible in their recalled versions of what they had read. Apparently, the participants were unaware that they were generating biased reports. It seems necessary to look for an explanation for the systematically biased responses other than the participants' attempts to promote their self-interest.

Absent the possibility of anything to be gained, the crucial task is to identify an alternative motive or phenomenon that could have led to the participants' biased views of what transpired. One possibility may have been the participants expressing their preconsciously held self-conceit rather than a purposive act of self-interest. Taking the part of a harm doer or an employee, for example, may have automatically elicited preconscious beliefs such as "I am a good person" and "a good worker, better than others" (Epley and Caruso, 2004). Once salient, though still preconscious, those themes or schemas would automatically influence the processing of information as well as subsequent recall of events and subsequent judgments to be consistent with the self-conceited images of themselves (Epley and Caruso, 2004; Epley and Dunning, 2000). According to this analysis, the biased reports and judgments were not intended to be self-enhancing or self-benefiting. Rather, they were the automatic expression of typically unarticulated, preconsciously held beliefs of relative superiority.

There is some evidence consistent with the assumption that most people walk around with preconsciously held self-conceited beliefs of moral superiority. For example, Messick (reported in Messick and Sentis, 1983) asked participants to recall the things that they or others do that are fair or unfair. In describing each of them, they were to begin the sentence with "I," if they do them more than others, and "they," if others do them more. The remarkably easy-to-replicate finding is that people begin more sentences with "I" when they are listing fair things and more with "they" when depicting unfair acts that people do.

In several classroom demonstrations the students revealed that they were unaware that they were creating a biased favorable impression of themselves when they wrote their sentences. They were genuinely surprised when they each reported their responses and then saw the significant systematic discrepancies displayed on the board. The students were unaware that their preconsciously held assumption that they were more moral and less immoral than others affected their judgments.

This and similar self-conceited assumptions (I am a good/better person, good/better worker, etc.) may influence and bias social judgments in ways that appear to be self-serving, but it would be seriously misleading to construe those biased judgments as manifestations of self-interest or self-serving motivation. They are simply the expressions of preconsciously held beliefs concerning their relative superiority. One can argue that the origins of those beliefs may have been some form of self-interested motivation, but, even if that is the case, apparently once established the self-conceited beliefs operate independently and appear automatically in the absence of any immediate self-serving incentives.

There are also good reasons to believe that people's desires and motives as well as their self-conceited beliefs can influence their perceptions of events. Their salient motives and goals might shape the focus of their attention, which has been shown to affect the interpretation of a situation (Arkin and Duval, 1975), as well as the ease with which they encode and retain motivationally compatible information and the goal-relevant schemas with which they organize their perceptions. As a consequence of this self-conceited or motivationally influenced selection and processing of information, people may generate a biased representation of events that then leads to judgments of deservingness in ways that appear to be self-serving. The point to be emphasized here is that the biased representation of the relevant events, not the participants' self-seeking motives, determines their judgments of deservingness.

It is important to recognize that the preconscious influence of self-interested motives may not directly bias the person's judgments of deservingness or their selection of the particular rules applied in order to determine deservingness. Rather, this would occur indirectly: the person's motives would affect the acquisition and processing of the information that enters into their own assessment of relative deservingness. What is not clear at this point is the extent to which the person's self-conceit, that is his or her preconsciously assumed relative superiority, and the person's self-interest, desires, and wants, either or both contribute to the biased search, processing, and memory that generate the biased information employed in the judgments of deservingness (see Babcock et al., 1995). The evidence does indicate, however, as seen in the previously described experiments, that self–conceited beliefs without the presence of self-interested motivation can be sufficient to elicit biased judgments of deservingness.

The research of Babcock and colleagues (1995) clearly illustrates the process whereby the preconscious influence of self-conceit and self-interest biases the relevant information base and the effects of that biased information on the person's subsequent judgments of deservingness. Once the biased construction of deservingness has occurred, however, it can function in ways that are independent of and even impede the person's self-interested goals. In their experiment, participants played the role of legal advocates, for either the plaintiff or the defendant, in a previously adjudicated case involving liability and compensation for an accident. They were given economic incentives to arrive at an agreed outcome as early as possible while trying to maximize the negotiated award for their plaintiffs or minimize the cost to their defendants. To encourage the advocates to agree on a settlement, the role-playing participants and their hypothetical clients would incur an economic cost on each of the five opportunities they were given, if they failed to agree on a settlement. The costs to the role-playing participants were actual, nontrivial amounts of money.

After reading a full description of the details of the case, but before beginning the negotiations, all the participants were asked to rate the actual previous judges' assessment of the strength of several arguments for and against their clients, as well as the amount awarded to the plaintiff by the judge who had previously adjudicated the case. These two ratings revealed the participants' genuine beliefs concerning the merits of their client's case and the appropriate fair settlement. Fortunately for present purposes, the experimenters also varied when the participants learned of their roles: half of them were informed prior to reading the details of the case and half learned they were to represent the plaintiff or the defendant subsequent to the reading and just prior to making their ratings concerning the merits of their case.

It is most revealing that whether the participants learned of their roles before or after reading the details of the case had a remarkably strong effect on their ratings as well as their subsequent negotiations. Those participants who knew their role prior to reading the details of the case took considerably longer, and more of them failed to reach an agreement, than did those who only learned of their role after reading it. This bias incurred considerably greater real costs for themselves and, symbolically, for their clients.

Underlying this difference in costly behavior were comparable discrepancies in their beliefs before beginning the negotiations. Knowing their roles in advance of the reading led to dramatic differences in their beliefs concerning the objective merits of their clients' cases and the amount the judge had actually awarded to the plaintiff. By way of contrast, although the same self-interested motives were present during the negotiations, there were relatively few self-benefiting biases in the judgments of those participants who were informed of their role only after reading the case history. Though similarly motivated to gain the most for their clients and avoid a costly conflict, absent the preconscious generation of biased views that occurred while reading the case, they were able to come to the clearly more profitable, rather quick agreements on an appropriate settlement. As a result, the investigators concluded that:

> Perhaps disputants are not trying to maximize their expected outcome, but only trying to achieve a fair outcome. However, what each side views as fair tends to be biased by self-interest, reducing the prospects for settlement.
>
> (Babcock et al., 1995, p. 1342)

The authors may not have fully appreciated the important implications of their findings. Their participants' self-interest and self-conceit "I, we, are the good ones in this dispute" only affected their judgments and behavior when it had led to the biased assessments of the facts of the case! This is consistent with the hypothesis that the effects of self-interest were mediated by the influence on the participants' actual "views" of what occurred.

It is important to recognize that these biased beliefs about the merits of their case were not direct expressions of the participants' self-interested motives. That motivation was also present among those who learned their roles only after reading the case. Apparently the critical event was that their self-conceit, made salient while reading the case history, determined what they believed to be the relative merits of their case, and thus what would be a fair settlement (see Stillwell and Baumeister, 1997, cited in the preceding text). Though unintentionally biased in their favor, that information nevertheless shaped what the participants believed to be the merits of their client's case, that is, what they were entitled to receive according to the "facts" of the case, as evidenced by their prenegotiation ratings of the initial judges' assessments of the merits of their litigants' claims.

As the authors noted, the participants' judgments of what their clients deserved, not self-interest, were the primary source of motivation generating their extended and costly negotiation. The participants were willing to incur considerable actual and symbolic costs in order to pursue what they believed were objectively fair settlements for their clients. It is equally clear but not explicitly recognized by the authors that if self-interest had been the dominant motive the participants would have reached settlements much earlier in the increasingly costly negotiating process, regardless of whether they learned of that interest prior or subsequent to their exposure to the case information.

WHY RESEARCH FINDINGS MAY BE MISINTERPRETED AS EVIDENCE OF SELF-INTEREST

The evidence presented to this point suggests two important conclusions:

One recognizes the influence of automatic preconscious self-conceited scripts on people's judgments of their merit and thus what they deserve. The other indicates a tendency for investigators to misattribute the effects of these automatically elicited, preconscious, scripted reactions to the influence of self-benefiting motives. Apparently, investigators have offered such preconscious automatic judgments as evidence of purposeful efforts to serve self-interested goals.

This analysis also suggests that highly competent and experienced investigators may be inclined to see self-interested motives in their participants' behavior even when it is more plausibly explained by other processes. The next section will present research in which the assumption of omnipresent and dominant self-interested motives appears to have functioned as a much too readily available, virtually automatic, default explanation that may have precluded investigators' consideration of other, more plausible alternatives: If everyone knows that people are driven to get the best deal for themselves, why look for other explanations of their apparently self-serving behavior?

"SELECTIVE EXPLOITATION" OR MEETING OBLIGATIONS?

Research that purported to have found evidence of participants, acting as managers, sacrificing equity to exploit employees provides an intriguing example of this misattribution of motives. In a prototypical experiment the role-playing participants offered considerably smaller raises to a highly valued employee whose family commitments made it difficult to accept competing offers from other areas, compared with the raises offered to one who was similarly qualified but had no constraints on mobility. Rusbult and colleagues (1988) portrayed these findings as evidence that people, role-playing the part of managers, were willing to sacrifice equity and fairness for self-interested purposes. They termed these apparent violations of pay equity "rational selective exploitation."

That could be a valid description of the managers' motivation, but it seems equally plausible that the managers were not ignoring rules of fairness or equity in order to rationally exploit the vulnerable employee. On the contrary, offering lesser raises to the relatively immobile employee could have been the consequence of managers simply doing their jobs and trying to meet their conflicting obligations.

Managers have legitimate obligations to their employers and the corporate stakeholders, and primary among those is the responsibility to minimize costs in order to maximize profits. They are not permitted to violate rules of fair competition or basic morality, for example to cheat and lie, but they are expected to take advantage of every legitimate opportunity to benefit their company. Awarding the lesser bonus to the employee who was less mobile in comparison with one who could more easily have left for another job would not be unfairly exploiting that employee if he or she was already receiving a fair wage; whereas, awarding an employee a greater financial bonus than necessary would have unfairly reduced the profits for the corporate stakeholders. Parenthetically, some evidence suggests that if the transactions with the vulnerable employee had involved pay reductions rather than raises or a bonus added to their present salary, people would be more likely to consider that to be an unfair violation of a previous implicit contractual relation with the employee rather than a legitimate action to enhance the profits of the corporation (see Kahneman, Knetsch, and Thaler, 1986).

This alternative explanation could be viewed as a weak justification for the self-interested exploitation of vulnerable employees. But before accepting that possibility, consider what form or kind of "self-interested" motivation could have been driving the participants' apparent sacrifice of equity and willingness to exploit someone while simply role-playing the part of a manager. What did these role-playing participants' have to gain by reporting that they would have given a smaller raise to the hypothetical vulnerable employees? Conceivably, they could have been relying upon a stereotypic notion of a "manager" that included the willingness to take advantage of any opportunity to exploit a vulnerable employee, that is, rational selective exploitation. Such evidence speaks to the influence of stereotypes on people's judgments but does not indicate either signs of rational selective exploitation or acts of managerial responsibility. The main point here is that the authors, and possibly the participants, found it natural to assume motivated acts of corporate greed and employee exploitation.

Pointing to inconsistencies or failures to consider plausible alternative explanations in a few examples of the self-interest validating literature is only suggestive, at best. Persuasive evidence requires experimental testing of these conjectures. There are studies that have attempted to do just that, with illuminating results.

Role-Playing Greed

The theoretically impressive findings reported by Rivera and Tedeschi (1976) clearly merited experimentally investigating plausible alternative explanations. In their experiment, participants reported being considerably more pleased with receiving a larger rather than a smaller reward when attached to a lie detector, even when the greater reward was at the cost of another equally productive "employee." Without the lie detector, similar participants expressed the typical "equity" finding that being overrewarded was less pleasing, or more disturbing, than being given a lesser but deserved pay (Adams, 1963). These results allowed the researchers to conclude that people only pretend to care about norm of fairness in public situations, but in private they are primarily interested in maximizing their profits. One could not ask for clearer evidence of the fundamental role of self-interest. Or could one?

As it happens, there were good reasons to question the self-interest interpretation of those findings. Instead, the results suggest that participants understood the role demands of the situation.

For example, the participants' investments and rewards in this experiment seemed to be too trivial to elicit the reported large differences in either pleasure or distress. It is difficult to imagine that differences of twenty-five cents and fifteen cents would induce the reported measurable amounts of happiness or distress in university students. Also, it seems more plausible that after the participants had learned that they and the other participant had performed equally well, they assumed they each would receive equal pay. Then, after the participants learned that they had been given more pay than the other worker, the researchers' elaborate procedure for validating and employing the lie detector implicitly instructed the participants that the experimenters wanted them to respond in some way that they would have not divulged.

It had to be obvious to the participants that equal performance deserved equal pay. In that case, the counternormative response that someone would want to hide would have to be "greed." So the introduction and supposed validation of the lie detector, in effect, instructed the participants to confess to being "greedy." That was the obvious counternormative reaction. In this case, having understood the message they went along as good participants and pretended to be "greedy": they "confessed" being much happier with receiving ninety cents than seventy-five cents, and happier with seventy-five cents than fifty cents.

Following these hunches about the participants playing their parts as good, helpful participants, we reasoned that changing the norms in the situation to justify the employees trying to maximize their pay, by making them competitors rather than co-workers, would lead the role-playing participants to publicly express greater pleasure with the same trivially greater rewards, while hooking them up to the lie detector would make them "confess" the counternormative response: in this case, that the greater pay made them less happy. The findings confirmed those predictions (Ellard, Meindl, and Lerner, 2000).

There was no reason to believe that realistically trivial differences in economic rewards elicited any self-interested or equitable motivation. Apparently, however, it was natural for the investigators to assume that people only give lip service to following rules of fairness and decency while they are driven by self-interest. But that was probably not a valid interpretation of what their participants' reactions had revealed.

Portraying Fairness as Self-Interest

Another early example of investigators too readily finding evidence of self-interest in other people's behavior appeared in an experiment with young children. After all, doesn't everyone know that children are selfish?

Leventhal and Anderson (1970) reported that children generally kept half of the rewards earned by their partner and them for themselves, even when their teammate had contributed twice as much as they did to earning the rewards. The investigators portrayed those allocations as evidence that the children allowed their self-interest to influence their allocations. Having noticed that these investigators had referred to the two children as "partners" and "teammates," it seemed equally plausible, if not more plausible, that the children were simply applying the appropriate rule of fairness. Again, the children may have understood the roles they were asked to play in the situation, that of equal partners. Even very young children may know that partners and teammates deserve equal shares.

To assess whether or not the children were responding to self-interest or the appropriate rules of deservingness, in a subsequent experiment (Lerner, 1974) employing essentially the same procedures the children were referred to as either partners or co-workers. Also some of the children were led to believe they had been twice as productive while others thought they had produced only half as much as the other child. The results were fairly clear. The children's allocations to themselves and their "partners" were close to equality regardless of their relative contribution. The children divided the rewards between themselves and a "co-worker" according to their relative productivity, even when that meant that, as the less productive worker, they kept considerably less than half for themselves.

These findings provide rather clear evidence for important inferences. Even at an early age (4–6) children knew that there were two different rules for allocating jointly earned rewards: equal for partners and according to contribution for co-workers. Furthermore, they automatically applied these rules without regard to their own self-interested share of the rewards. It appears that it was the investigators, not the children, who were focused on self-interest rather than fairness.

Understanding the Limits of Self-Interest

It is worth noting that many experiments that have reported clear evidence of self-serving biases in evaluations and behavior often contain additional evidence documenting the limits of these reactions. For example, the most common finding is that self-serving, biased reactions appeared primarily when the participants believed they were in parallel or direct competition with the others, as in most economic encounters. Those biased and self-serving reactions disappeared, however, when the others involved in the encounter were friends, very similar to them, or people toward whom they felt close (Austin, 1980; Benton, 1971; Loewenstein, Thompson and Bazerman, 1989; Mikula, 1998; Van Yperen and Buunk, 1994; Wicker and Bushweiler, 1970).

Although those findings document an important contextual limit on the appearance of self-serving biases, in actuality, that should not be surprising to most people on the basis of their own experience in competitive and cooperative or friendly encounters. Ironically, it is not uncommon, however, for investigators, when confronted with such findings, to view the self-serving reactions as the "normal" response that may be temporarily modified in some "special" noncompetitive encounters (Mikula, 1998). A closer analysis of how considerations of deservingness and justice appear in various social contexts, however, suggests that judgments of "normality" must be viewed as context-specific: "Normal" conduct between competitors is predictably different from the "normal" interactions between cooperating partners. We know from other research that the norms of justice vary in different contexts, with equity sometimes dominating but equality, need, or "winner-takes-all" expected to predominate in other contexts (see Deutsch, 1975; Lerner, 1974).

If it is true, as the selected evidence presented here suggests, that investigators are inclined to see a self-interested motive in their participants' behavior – even when it is not there – that raises another intriguing question: what might lead investigators to make this erroneous assumption? Two good candidates as possible answers to that question have origins in the sociocultural system of norms shared by investigators and their research participants.

THE SELF-PERPETUATING MYTH: THE NORMALITY OF SELF-INTEREST

The most obvious norm-based explanations for the prevalence with which investigators assume that self-interested motives are responsible for their participants' behavior begin with the commonly accepted belief that promoting one's self-interest is the "normal" way to behave. Dale Miller (Miller, 1999; Ratner and Miller, 2001) conducted a series of imaginative experiments to demonstrate how that commonly accepted norm of conduct could, and does, lead people to act in ways that would support its validity. The dynamic underlying this self-fulfilling and socially maintaining process arises from people's desire not to be viewed as abnormal.

Acting in ways that appear to contradict that which is normal or customary makes one vulnerable to being viewed as a "deviant." As a result, people may comply with, or at least avoid appearing to violate, the expectation that everyone is supposed to be motivated by self-interest. Although altruistic behavior may eventually be judged to be virtuous, or better than normal, it begins with the risk of being viewed as deviant, even devious in some respect, or at the minimum reflecting some form of ultimate self-gratification. If we assume that people are acting in order to serve their own interests, an action with no obvious attribution to self-interest makes us suspicious that there is a "hidden" motive. Ironically, in order to avoid possible public sanction people often feel impelled to explicitly "justify" their generosity as motivated by self-interest. "It gives me a great deal of pleasure. . . ."

If people wish to avoid being viewed with suspicion they must feel constrained either to avoid acting in ways that are inconsistent with self-interest or to provide a normally self-interested public cover for their actions, regardless of what their true motives might be. That is, if you simply want to help someone in need at some cost to yourself, either you must effectively resist that impulse because of not wanting to give rise to the question, "what's in it for her?," or in anticipation you denature that potential suspicion by offering a self-interested explanation in terms of what benefits you derive from helping that person.

The unintended but very important consequence of this is that whether by making people reluctant to engage in altruistic acts or by leading them to publicly frame their acts as self-interested, the normatively held belief that everyone is driven by self-interest becomes a self-fulfilling prophecy. Though not an accurate portrayal of what actually motivates many people's behavior, it acquires the status of a truism in our lay psychology.

The research generated from these insights by Miller and his colleagues (Ratner and Miller, 2001) clearly demonstrates the processes whereby the pervasive norm of self-interest insidiously influences people's behavior and impressions of one another. Initially, they demonstrated that people, when asked to predict the behavior of others, reliably underestimated other people's willingness to do the right thing, for example, give up smoking in public places or donate blood, unless it supported their own self-interested goals. Additional research found that participants anticipated eliciting confusion and negative reactions from others if they publicly supported causes that would not directly benefit themselves (Ratner and Miller, 2001), for example, men and women publicly supporting a policy that would primarily benefit members of the opposite gender. Other experiments yielded evidence that these trepidations were well founded: similar participants described their own confusion and negative reactions in response to people who publicly supported causes in which they had no obvious vested interest (Ratner and Miller, 2001).

Disguising the Attempt to Help Innocent Victims as an Economic Transaction

An early experiment by Holmes, Miller, and Lerner (not published until 2002) provided compelling evidence that people may often require that their altruistic acts appear to be driven by economic incentives rather than by the desire to help innocent victims. In that field experiment, people, when solicited for donations in their homes, were very reluctant to give any money either to benefit neighborhood children's athletic programs or to help emotionally deprived children in critical need. However, when similar residents from the same community were approached with the opportunity to buy rather expensive decorator candles with the profit going to provide needed help for the emotionally deprived children, they bought the candles at a remarkable rate. The opportunity merely to buy the candles, however, provided no similarly effective appeal when the people were told the profits were to go to benefit the neighborhood children's leisure activities. These potential customers were unresponsive, in stark contrast to their neighbors' willingness to buy multiple candles to benefit the innocent victims.

It is important to emphasize that the opportunity to simply donate, and thus to portray oneself as a generous altruistic person, was ineffective in inducing or enabling the people to help the same innocent victims. In addition, the candles were not an attractive purchase on their own. As expected, however, the candles provided participants with the opportunity to portray their helping donations as a self-benefiting purchase, and thus allowed them to express their impulse to help the victims. That is, the candle purchase, a "normal economic exchange," enabled them to disguise for themselves as well as others the troublesome fact that they felt impelled to help innocent victims. They, as most people, had learned that if they reacted every time they experienced the imperative to help an innocent victim, they would be unable to maintain their own personal contract: to get and keep what they deserve. More about this "prepared solution" to maintaining one's personal contract will be described in Chapter 8.

Taken at face value, these findings stand in stark contrast to the assumption that people are exclusively driven by self-interest rather than by other motives such as trying to do the "right thing." It is important to recognize that if the investigators had attempted to get money to benefit the innocent victims only by asking for donations, they would have generated further evidence confirming the image of people as primarily governed by self-interest and thus indifferent to the undeserved suffering of innocent victims.

The Legitimate Pursuit of Self-Interest as a Rule of Deserving

A second norm-based explanation suggests that inferring the influence of self-interest is not invariably an error. In certain encounters, participants intentionally manifest self-benefiting responses, but they are motivated, or at least justified, by social norms of appropriate behavior. To understand the role self-interest plays in shaping how people treat one another, it is important to recognize that the pursuit of self-interest is legitimized, even condoned, by an important and rather ubiquitous rule of deservingness. Self-interest is an important motivator, and there are circumstances in which it is consistent with a justice principle.

In our society a normatively supported rule of "justified self-interest" appears in those situations in which more than one person desires the same indivisible resource to which no one has a greater or exclusive legitimate prior claim (Lerner, 1975; Lerner, Miller, and Holmes, 1976). Without any recognized basis for making a definitive prior claim for the resource, all the participants can attempt to "win" that resource by following legitimate rules of parallel or direct competition. When this occurs, regardless of the participants' relative needs, efforts, contributions, and general merit, the one who comes out ahead, reaches the defined goal first, or is the last one standing is deemed the winner and thus deserves the "prize": that can be a fair maiden, the fellowship, the promotion, the million dollar lottery, or the best seat in the house. In these normatively sanctioned competitions, all the participants are expected to do whatever they can using any and all resources they have available to "win," as long as they do not violate the prescribed rules of "fair" competition: they do not cheat. As a result of those competitive efforts, the winner and the losers have gotten what they deserved. Justice has been served. Virtually every culturally conversant person knows and regularly applies this rule of deservingness.

The Luck of the Draw

A common and easily recognized form of this rule of deservingness appears in the use of the principle "first come, first served": "I saw it first; if someone else had seen it first they would have grabbed it," "Lady Luck smiled on me," or "the gods picked me, this time."

In one experiment (Lerner and Lichtman, 1968), for example, young women were recruited to participate in a study of human learning. When they arrived they learned that in each pair of participants, one would have to be the experimental subject and receive electric shocks while learning pairs of nonsense syllables, while the other in a separate room would be the control subject, doing the same task but with no punishment for erroneous responses. There was one task that was much more onerous than the other. Some of the participants were then informed that for scientific purposes the table of random numbers was consulted and, based upon the chair they happened to occupy, they would be given their choice of condition. In this case, the other participant's role would be determined by default. Under those circumstances, and to no one's surprise, the vast majority of these young women selected the control condition for themselves. Their subsequent ratings, including those of the other participant's character as well as their rating of their responsibility for their own and the other participants' fates, revealed no signs of guilt for having made a choice that would require another person to suffer electric shocks.

When interviewed about their reactions, the participants readily stated that they felt no guilt. Why? Because she, the other participant "would have made the same choice if she had the opportunity." They readily pointed out that anyone would have chosen to avoid the electric shocks. The reactions of their coparticipants confirmed that prediction. The participants intuitively knew that the "table of random numbers," or chance, had given them the perfect right to choose the desirable condition for themselves.

Because these young women wanted to avoid the electric shocks, one could argue that they used the contemporary norms of justified self-interest in order to justify doing what they preferred. Or, is it the case that, regardless of their preferences, the choice of the desirable condition for themselves appeared as an intuitively appropriate way to behave? Were they trying to get the best deal for themselves or doing what intuitively seemed to be fair – the right thing? Would those participants, given the opportunity to choose their condition, have sought out and used some other excuse to benefit themselves?

Evidence for the intuitive deservingness-driven explanation was generated by giving the participants the same power to choose their conditions while the appropriate rule of deservingness would require them to elect the shocks for themselves. In one such condition, the participants learned that they and the other participant did not have equal prior claim to the desired resource: avoiding the shocks. The other participant, because of being severely traumatized by an electric shock while a young child, was exceptionally fearful of them, actually phobic. In that case, because the other participant had a greater legitimate need to avoid the electric shocks, the norms of justified interest would not apply. The participants, preferring to avoid the shocks, could have ignored that claim and taken the desirable condition for themselves. That would clearly have been in their best self-interest. As we expected, however, the large majority of participants elected to respond to the legitimate needs of the other participant who had previously been inflicted with a phobic response to electric shocks. As expected, they assigned themselves to the shock condition.

An even greater proportion of the participants elected the painful shocks for themselves in another condition in which the relationship between the participants had been altered by the other participant: the other participant refused to be a "competitor." That occurred when the participants learned that the random process had initially given the choice to the other participant, and she had chosen to allow the participant to make the decision. By using her opportunity to choose in order to allow the participant to have the choice, the other participant had refused to compete over the scarce resource while empowering the participant. Because by that act their relationship was changed, they were no longer competitors but simply two paired participants. Thus, the appropriate response for the participant was to reciprocate generosity with generosity (cf. Gouldner, 1960) by electing the shock condition for themselves – as 90% of them did.

The essential point is that the vast majority of the participants in the three experimental conditions intuitively felt justified in their decisions. They understood when it was appropriate to take the desirable condition or elect the painful shocks for themselves instead of assigning them to the other vulnerable or generous participant. In either case they believed they were doing the "right" thing. Is it possible to rule out an underlying self-interested motive in those decisions? No, but it is also most important to recognize there is no need or reason to infer its presence or influence.

BY WAY OF SUMMARY

The evidence described here focused on instances in which highly competent investigators apparently may have misattributed their participants' behaviors to the influence of self-interested motives. In these well-known investigations, the effects of either of two different processes were misidentified as evidence that the participants were trying to unfairly benefit themselves.

One of these involves participants acting in compliance with societal norms that prescribe and sanction various behaviors including, at times, acting on one's own behalf. Investigators have inferred the influence of self-interested motives when acting to benefit oneself was actually the normatively appropriate way to behave in situations of parallel or direct competition for desired resources (Lerner et al., 1976).

The second process consists of investigators implicitly assuming that the pursuit of self-interest is the "normal" way to behave. This assumption led them to find self-interest in the manifestations of self-conceited cognitive themes or schemas that portray the self and one's behavior as essentially good, better, or more, that is, relatively superior to others, regarding the dimensions that matter. When made salient, these schemas preconsciously direct the processing of information, facilitating attention to and memory for information that is thematically consistent with the self-conceited evaluative assessments. The information base resulting from that preconsciously biased processing, as has been shown, influences the participants' subsequent judgments of relative deservingness that to the observer appears intended to serve self-interested goals. The participants, however, unaware of their biased information base, are convinced they are acting upon "objective" assessments with no underlying self-benefiting intention or self-interested motives (see, e.g., Babcock et al., 1995; Stillwell and Baumeister, 1997). The preconscious biasing influence of these self-conceited assumptions of relative merit often generalizes to include those people perceived to be similar on situationally salient dimensions. They, too, are automatically judged to be relatively "better," less culpable, and more deserving (Hastorf and Cantril, 1954; Valdesolo and DeSteno, 2007).

The processes involved in erroneously inferring the influence of self-interested motives in the experiments cited here may be reasonably generalized to other experiments that purported to find self-interested behaviors by using similar research situations. Whatever that proportion of the published research might be, what remains, however, is the indisputable fact that most people are frequently aware of their own intentions to get what they want, and they can recall that they have been tempted, sometimes successfully, to ignore considerations of fairness or morality in order to gratify those desires. On other occasions they have been willing to manipulate others to benefit themselves and consciously sought ways to excuse and justify their acts in order to avoid sanctions.

Without attempting to report research that documents the occurrence of these all-too-familiar self-interest–directed acts, recognizing their occurrence should be sufficient to proceed with the next important task: using the information we now have available to articulate hypotheses of when and how justice imperatives and self-interest appear in people's lives. In that vein, it is worth noting that in experiments that have reported clear evidence of self-serving biases in evaluations and behavior, one often finds additional evidence pointing to important limits of these reactions.

For example, apparently self-serving, biased reactions appeared in separate experiments using several different paradigms but primarily when the participants believed they were in parallel or direct competition with the others, as in most economic encounters. More consistently, in those contexts when the others involved in the encounter were friends, quite similar to them, or people toward whom they felt close, those biased self-serving reactions disappeared (Austin, 1980; Benton, 1971; Loewenstein et al., 1989; Mikula, 1998; Van Yperen and Buunk, 1994; Wicker and Bushweiler, 1970). Actually, when one simply thinks about it, this should not be surprising to most people on the basis of their own experiences. Finally, it should be no surprise that much of the evidence of self-interested behavior has been generated in experimental situations in which the participants were implicitly and often explicitly instructed to attempt to maximize their own outcomes (Frohlich, Oppenheimer, and Moore, 2001; Konow, 2005). Let's take a closer look at the experimental contexts.

COMMON ERRORS CONTAMINATING THE RESEARCH LITERATURE: BIZARRE EVENTS AND BARREN CONTEXTS

Having considered evidence describing conditions under which people directly express their commitments to deservingness and justice and when they apply their understanding of conventional rules of justified self-interest, it is time to return to two related and important questions: why has so much published research failed to confirm the influence of the justice motive, and how could published research have repeatedly demonstrated the importance of self-interested motives?

The first part of the answer focuses on the research participants for two possible explanations. One is that when participants are induced to engage in thoughtful considerations, having internalized societal norms, their subsequent behavior, decisions, and social judgments will typically reveal the influence of self-interest. They believe that being guided by self-interest is "normal": how they are expected to behave (Miller, 1999). Similarly, they will consciously attribute their own and others' behavior to some form of self-interest. Also, these norm-based influences will be most evident when participants' justice imperatives are minimally aroused and their evaluation apprehension, that is, their desire to be a good cooperative participant, has been heightened by the experimenters' bizarre behavior or confusing instructions.

What this points to is the need to consider and examine the nature of the situations in which research participants perform in order to arrive at a valid interpretation of their behavior. The evidence presented here suggests that when participants respond to a hypothetical event portrayed in a vignette or while role-playing a part in a simulation, they may reveal the influence of justice imperatives when directly expressing their immediate thoughts and feelings. If, however, they respond after being induced to thoughtfully consider their responses, for example to make a decision, their views of the normatively appropriate, rationally self-interested way to react will shape their reports or behavior (see Bazerman et al., 1995; J. Lerner et al., 1998; Miller, 1975, 1999). Considerations of deservingness or justice, if they appear at all, will often be incorporated in the service of self-interested motives just as predicted by the early theorists: enlightened and rationally executed self-interest is considered to be the normal way to behave and is particularly likely to influence participants who are sensitive to the need to create an acceptable impression of themselves; that is, that they are not "deviant" (Ratner and Miller, 2001).

An examination of some of the prominent research situations that have been generating the recent published evidence about justice and self-interest yields very revealing insights into how the research literature became contaminated. The basic question is: what are the motives and cognitive processes that have been elicited in these situations commonly used to study social motives and decision making? Of particular concern is whether the research participants were directly or indirectly induced to be thoughtfully concerned with acting in ways that are socially appropriate, that is with "impression management," rather than directly expressing their thoughts and feelings and behaving as they would during the normal course of events.

By using research strategies that heighten their participants' concerns with impression management, the experimenters inevitably arrive at inferences that inflate the importance of self-interest (see the discussion of the myth of self-interest, Miller, 1999; Ratner and Miller, 2001) and portray people's concern with justice as an instrument employed to maximize self-interested outcomes. During the normal course of events that instrumental application of justice may naturally occur, but only under those special and limited circumstances when people feel impelled to carefully construct and monitor their public behavior.

Unfortunately, the methods some investigators have employed that compel their participants to thoughtfully manage their responses, cannot capture the influence of justice motivation that is operative as people more mindlessly go about their lives and preconsciously cope with the important decisions of who deserves what from whom. It seems likely, rather, that some of the most commonly used methods actually heighten participants' efforts to consciously shape their responses.

Unexplained and Odd Events Elicit Heightened Impression Management

A good place to begin this section is "inside the heads" of the participants in an experimental situation that has been used to generate the findings for several major publications (see, e.g., Van den Bos et al., 1997; Van den Bos et al., 1998, 2006; Van den Bos, Wilke, and Lind, 1998). Your task here is to imagine what the participants were thinking and feeling at the time they generated responses that were interpreted as revealing their concerns with justice.

To begin, imagine that you have been recruited to participate in a psychology experiment and promised a reasonable pay for your time. When you arrive for your appointment you are seated in a cubicle in front of a keyboard and terminal and informed that, for purposes of the research, you and another participant seated at a terminal in another room will be judging the number of target elements in a series of complex figures that will appear on your monitor. You are given no reason why you have been paired with another participant or why you were given that information. But that is only the beginning of a series of unexplained events. Each of these unexplained events invites, and in some cases virtually impels, you to wonder about "what is going on here?" and "how am I supposed to react?"

After a few practice trials you perform the task for approximately twenty minutes and, after you finish, you are informed that you and the other participant did equally well at the task. Again, there is no explanation as to why you were given the information about the performance of the other participant.

You are then informed that you will receive three lottery tickets and also told, with no explanation as to why, that the other participant will receive, one, three, or five lottery tickets. The condition in which you are informed that you both received the same number of lottery tickets (3) makes some sense, especially because previously you were told that you both performed equally well. But the conditions in which you are informed that you and the other participant receive unequal rewards (other received 1 or 5), after previously being gratuitously informed that you both performed equally well at the task, must seem strange if not bizarre. "Why did the other participant not get the same as I?" and "why am I being informed about all of this?" might be the thoughts that cross your mind.

Partial answers to those questions may emerge for you when you are then asked to complete a number of rating scales assessing your view of the fairness, desirability, and so forth of what has occurred, again with no explanation as to why you were being asked to do that or the use to which your ratings would be put. By this time, whatever your feelings were you must be concerned with "why does the experimenter care about my reactions?" and then "how am I supposed to feel . . .?"

The key question is: given that context, what could your or anyone else's ratings possibly reveal about justice and deservingness, other than the common understanding that people who performed equally might deserve the same outcomes?

In their efforts to be cooperative, the participants probably suspended disbelief sufficiently to surmise that the number of lottery tickets they and the other received were either more or less than would be appropriate (5-3 or 3-1) given that they had just been told they performed equally well at the task and that was one of the few pieces of information they were given.

Would you wonder why, if the experimenter wanted you to know about your relative performance (you both did equally well), then the experimenter did not do the obviously fair thing and allocate the same number of lottery tickets to both of you? When, in one study, they were asked, virtually all the participants subsequently reported they and the other equally performing participant deserved the same number of lottery tickets (Van den Bos et al., 1997, p. 1040-1). Because the appropriate allocation was so obvious, how, absent any other possibly relevant information, would the participants make sense of the experimenters' patently bizarre behavior: with no accompanying explanatory information, after informing you that you and the other participant did equally well at the task, and then giving you more or fewer lottery tickets than the other. With only that information available to you, how would you respond to the questions asking you to rate the fairness and desirability of the experimenter's allocation?

It would be natural for the participants to wonder why the experimenters were asking those questions. Why would the experimenter, who clearly allocated the lottery tickets unfairly (by giving you more or less than the equally performing other participants), then ask those questions about desirability and fairness? All of this strange, unexplained behavior would almost certainly require that you engage in some problem-solving thought processes in order to generate a response.

The crucial point is that any response to those questions generated after such implausible circumstances would inevitably be greatly shaped by your thoughtful concerns about how you were supposed to respond as a good participant and/or a good person. As the literature demonstrates, your decisions would reveal your understanding of the appropriate norms (see, e.g., Bazerman et al., 1995; Hessing, Elfers, and Weigel, 1988; Simons and Piliavin, 1972) and how you are supposed to feel rather than your own desires for fairness or maximizing your rewards.

At a minimum, the experimenters' strange, unexplained behaviors must have created some degree of confusion and evaluation apprehension. Even in the conditions in which the participants are led to believe they are both given three lottery tickets, they had to wonder, if only half-consciously, "what is going on here, what does the experimenter want from me, expect me to do?" The rating scales that the experimenter put in front of them would have provided sufficient information for the participants to make some reasonable guesses as to what the experimenter was looking for. Then, they would try to generate the responses they believed were expected of them. "Ah ha, regardless of how strange all this is, I am obviously supposed to evaluate how pleased I am with the tickets they gave me, and how fairly I was treated, etc. That must be what this is all about. But, since it must be equally obvious to the experimenter that I and the other participant deserved the same amount, I wonder how I am supposed to complete these ratings so I don't disappoint him or look like a fool?"

In that state of experimenter-induced evaluation apprehension, the participants may then have sought to generate a response by recalling how one is supposed to feel about such events – getting more or less than someone else who is equally deserving. That may have recalled familiar feelings about deservingness and justice but only in the context of being primarily concerned with appearing to be a "good participant" and not making a fool of oneself.

The essential point is that regardless of how much participants might actually care about justice and the allocation of the lottery tickets, the procedure is much more likely to elicit the participants' attempts to generate normatively appropriate responses, rather than reacting directly to their experiences. That may explain why the investigators typically found essentially no differences between the behavior of their experimental participants and those who were explicitly role-playing their reaction to hypothetical situations portrayed in brief vignettes. The same norm-generated psychological processes were elicited in both contexts.

There can be scientific and practical value in assessing people's understandings of the appropriate ways to act, or the norms they believe apply in various contexts. Often, however, participants who are role-playing their reactions to hypothetical events do not – actually cannot – directly express their intuitive, automatic commitments to deservingness or justice. Those commitments typically appear in the relatively seamless course of events in daily life or in the heightened arousal associated with critical situations (see e.g., Lerner, 1971; Miller, 1975, 1977). Instead, as consciously cooperative participants they become aware of, and allow themselves to report, what they believe are the normatively appropriate ways to react (Aronson et al. 1990; Miller, 1975). Some participants may try to react on the basis of their reconstructed memories of how they behaved under similar circumstances, but if their evaluation concerns are heightened, for example, by the experimenters' bizarre behavior, the participants will be additionally motivated to shape their responses to fit normatively appropriate expectations (Bazerman et al., 1995; J. Lerner et al., 1998).

There is ample reason to believe that the participants' desires for justice and deservingness had little if any influence on their reactions, except as they "thought" they were supposed to act as if they cared: Why did the experimenter tell me the other participant and I performed equally well? Why did he not allocate the same lottery tickets to both of us? Why would he ask me what I thought about the obvious way to react? Why would he then ask me how satisfied I was?

Those who are not familiar with the justice-related research literature may have wondered, at this point, why so much time and space was devoted to discussing the problems associated with this one experimental situation. The simple answer is that several articles based upon the findings generated in this experimental context appeared in the most prestigious journals as studies of justice motivation. The prestige of these journals is based, at least partially, on their use of extensive editorial and peer reviews. The publication of these manuscripts in preference to many others suggests that the editors and reviewers may commit the same or similar errors in their own research, or at least that the errors are pervasive enough to be unrecognized. But those are not the only errors.

Inadvertently Instructing Participants How to Behave and Then "Discovering" Self-Interested Motives

EXAMPLE 1. CONCEPTUALLY STERILE "GAMES" WITH MYSTERIOUS INSTRUCTIONS

The copious research relying upon participants' reactions to "ultimate" and "dictator" games contains the same serious, typically unrecognized limitations (see Konow, 2005). There is good reason to believe that the social psychological architecture of these games dramatically limits the participants' ability to reveal useful information about their concerns with deservingness and justice. The information provided to the participants in the basic situations employed in these "games" includes none of the familiar cues required for them to either automatically or thoughtfully recognize their own or the other participants' entitlements. The one common exception is that the basic experimental instructions appear to empower and legitimize the participant's pursuit of self-interest.

Typically, in the dictator and the ultimate games the initial information indicates to the participants that they are in an experiment in which the experimenter has given them the power to divide money between themselves and another participant and thus legitimized the pursuit of self-interest.

> You have been arbitrarily [*sic*] chosen to decide how the total (amount of money) will be distributed.
> This decision is completely up to you and is confidential: only the experimenter will know who made this decision.
>
> (Konow, 2005, p. 103)

The lack of a reasonable explanation for why the participant has been chosen, "arbitrarily," to do what the experimenter would normally be expected to do, would naturally elicit the participants' evaluation apprehension and desire to perform in a way that would not reflect negatively on themselves and be of help to the experimenter (see Aronson et al., 1990). The assurance of confidentiality also clearly conveys the message that the experimenter expects and legitimizes the participants' use of their arbitrarily acquired power to do something that would displease the other participant, such as seeking to maximize their own outcomes.

That is all there is to the basic architecture of the dictator game. Other elements are added that are expected to influence the participant's decision (Konow, 2005). For the most part they do not eliminate the participant's concerns and suspicions. In any event, it should be no surprise, for example, to find that a significant number of participants in this literally bizarre situation often suspect that the experimenter is deceiving them about important elements of what is to take place (Frohlich et al., 2001).

Some investigators are impressed with the findings indicating that dictator participants will modify their allocations if given the kind of information that several previous experiments have shown to have an effect. Such information could include relative merit or the amount of contribution a participant has made to earning the total pay to be allocated. Dictators are inclined, other things being equal, to keep more of the money for themselves than would have been allocated to them by the uninvolved allocators, who are simply dividing the pay between the two participants (Konow, 2005). After all, norms of justified self-interest would define fortunate allocators as "foolish" or as pretentiously posturing if they did not take advantage of their "luck" to benefit themselves.

Although these apparently self-interested allocations have been attributed to a form of "self-deception" (Konow, 2005), there is even more reason to believe that the participants have no reason to "deceive" themselves but rather are simply trying not to make fools of themselves while doing what is expected and appropriate for them in this context. One can easily imagine a participant thinking: "After all, if I weren't allowed, expected, to keep 'more' for myself why would the experimenter have given me the power to allocate the pay and then promise to keep my decision confidential? But, of course I don't want to appear to be too greedy, because I don't quite trust that experimenter, whatever s/he says."

In any event, it would be difficult to have any confidence in assessing to what extent the participants' reactions were influenced by considerations of deservingness, desire for the pay, or simply their attempts to generate an "appropriate" response under the scrutiny of the strangely behaving and possibly untrustworthy experimenter.

Similar concerns arise when attempting to understand the findings generated by the ultimatum game. In this game the participants who are assigned the task of allocating a sum of money are led to believe that the other participant with whom they are paired has the ability, by refusing the allocation, to cause the allocator as well as themselves to end up with nothing. Again, what could this possibly have to do with the participants' concerns with justice? Absent any other relevant information, what deservingness or entitlement-based claim does either of the participants have to the money? They are strangers to one another who volunteered to participate in an "experiment" for money or course credit. Conceivably, the norm of justified interest may enable the allocator to keep all the money. But that may be nullified by the recipients' veto power so that neither of them gets anything. As a result the participants are, in effect, left with the instructions to strategize, or scheme, in a game with the goal, legitimized by the experimenter, of maximizing their shares. Again, what does all that have to do with justice?

The allocators may realize that the safest allocation to avoid ending up with nothing is to offer the other participants half of the money that, in truth, neither of them could claim to deserve. In this context, giving any amount, including half, to the other participant is probably not an act of fairness or generosity, but it must be recognized by both participants as a self-interested strategy. The participants must realize from the outset that, for the purposes of this game, their goal is to keep as much money as possible for themselves, or possibly, the game is a test to reveal something about themselves to the experimenters: their intelligence or character. They realize that any money is better than none, but as the evidence indicates, the recipients often prefer to cause them both to have nothing rather than accept a share that is less than 30 to 40 percent. Does that form of self- and other punishment represent a reaction to being treated unfairly or simply frustration over the other participant's lack of empathy, "caring," or just plain selfishness?

Mainly, it is difficult to imagine what rules of fairness or deservingness are involved in this situation, other than possibly the implicit contractual agreement with the experimenter to be a good research participant and follow the explicit rules of the game, for example, not walk out, punch the experimenter, or shout obscenities at the other participant.

If they are presented with a scale for rating the "fairness" of a particular allocation or the other participant, as cooperative participants they would make a mark on a scale, but that would not negate the bald fact that no culturally available rules of deservingness or justice would obligate the allocators to give any of the money to the other recipient. Although giving money may be laudatory, wise, or foolish, no one is obligated to be generous, and there is no amount that would be "deserved."

The closest consideration might be the allocator's concern about appearing to be greedy or stupid in the exercise of the arbitrarily assigned power or the recipient's desire not to be insulted by the inferred allocator's belief that they would be so money hungry as to accept any offer. "Do I want people to think I won't stand up for myself?" Under these bizarre circumstances, the participants' cannot forget that this is an experiment designed to find out if they will do "X" or "Y" and thus reveal something about themselves that is of interest to the experimenter! Under these circumstances, they must be mostly concerned with what would make them look good, bad, or at least acceptable in the eyes of the experimenter.

As it happens, Bazerman and colleagues (1995) found that presenting the recipients in the ultimatum game with an array of divisions and asking them to designate the amount they would accept elicits acceptance of a significantly smaller share than if they were simply given a single offer to accept or reject. Why?

If participants respond after being induced to thoughtfully consider their responses, for example to make a decision, there is a higher probability that their responses will be influenced by what they think is the normatively appropriate way to react (see, esp. Bazerman et al., 1995; J. Lerner et al., 1998). Apparently, as with the findings in other experimental contexts, the thought processes involved in making comparative choices make the norm of self-interest more salient and compelling.

Participants' thoughtfully considered responses could provide valuable information concerning the situational cues that elicit various normative expectations. If interpreted, however, as revealing something about human motives beyond impression management, that information will generate a misleading norm-dominated portrayal of how people's concern with deservingness and justice appear in the normal course of their lives as well as in critical situations.

EXAMPLE 2. INSTRUCTING PARTICIPANTS HOW TO BEHAVE AND THEN DESCRIBING THEIR COOPERATIVE BEHAVIOR AS "MORAL FAILURE" AND "HYPOCRISY"

The considerable research on hypocrisy conducted by Batson and his colleagues (Batson et al., 1997; Batson et al., 1999; Batson, Thompson, and Chen, 2002) is based upon presenting their participating students with instructions similar to those described in the preceding text. They tell their participants that they were arbitrarily selected to assign themselves or the other participant (whom they have not met) to the desirable or undesirable task. The students are assured at the outset, and once again at the end of their instructions, that they are free to make whatever assignments they wish, in private. In addition, the experimenter assures them that they will tell the other participant that the assignments were made on the basis of random procedure. These instructions reinforce the social norms (justified self-interest) that legitimize the contestants' use of every opportunity to acquire an indivisible (zero-sum) desired resource (see, e.g., Lerner and Lichtman, 1968; Lerner et al., 1976).

After the initial, but prior to the final, explicit assurances of the participant's complete freedom of choice, the experimenter gratuitously informed them that most participants feel that the most fair way to decide is by flipping a coin or the most moral way is by assigning the other to the desirable condition. (When asked, approximately a third of the participants stated that flipping a coin is most moral, whereas slightly more believed that assigning the other to the desirable task is most moral, and slightly less that there is no most moral way to make the assignment.) Batson et al., (1997, 1999, 2002) claimed that those instructions were intended to make the most moral alternative salient for the participants.

Given the context in which the participants were given that information, however, there are reasons to believe that it was perceived by most of the recipients as an implicit but clear instruction as to what their experimenter believed they should do. Why else would the experimenter have brought it up? If that is true, then the experimenter's instructions to the participants would have initially and subsequently legitimized their doing what anyone would do: take the desirable condition for themselves. Contradicting that, however, the experimenter also recommended that they should choose a random assignment by flipping the available coin.

How would the participants respond to the experimenter's two clearly contradictory instructions? If they took the desirable condition for themselves in private, regardless of the outcome of the coin flip, as many of them did, Batson and colleagues (1997, 1999, 2002) labeled that as a "moral failure." In addition, most of them publicly rated their task assignments as relatively moral, even after they had described random assignment, which they had ignored, as the most moral way to make the assignments. In this manner, a remarkable number of those who exhibited moral failure also earned the label of "hypocrites" by claiming that their behavior had been relatively moral. Obviously, that is what Batson and his colleagues had expected to find. Previous research on norms of justified self-interest (e.g., Lerner and Lichtman, 1968), however, suggests a radically different portrayal of the participants' behavior.

The findings of four experiments employing the same basic procedures conducted in three countries, the United States, Spain, and Argentina (Dols et al., 2010), clearly supported an alternative interpretation of the participants' private and public behaviors. How would cooperative participants react privately and publicly when they were instructed to follow their own justified self-interest and take the desirable condition for themselves, and additionally instructed to be "moral" and use random assignment as decided by the coin flip?

Among the various ways they might have considered to resolve this conflict, it appears that most participants simply adopted the strategy suggested by their experimenter's behavior. Their experimenter not only explicitly legitimized their taking the desirable condition for themselves, but also arranged for the participant to make that choice in private, and showed that she or he was willing to protect the participant by deceiving the other participant into believing their undesirable fate was decided by random. The experimenter clearly modeled following justified self-interest in private and publicly giving allegiance to the morality of fair, random assignment. That was the message available to the participants. Were the participants revealing moral failure and hypocrisy when they adopted the experimenter's instructions, or were they merely being good cooperative participants?

The experiments designed to test these conjectures employed a direct replication of Batson's basic condition, for purposes of comparison. To test the alternative interpretation, additional conditions left out one of the conflicting instructions. For example, the condition in which the participants were informed about the moral norm with no mention of their being explicitly empowered to make any choice they wished, elicited relatively few moral failures or hypocrisy.

Another condition was designed to assess whether Batson and colleague's instructions simply made the moral norm salient or, rather, actually instructed the participants to use random assignment. In this condition, the participants were accurately informed that some participants had used the coin flip, had assigned the desirable condition to themselves, and had assigned the other to the desirable condition. Obviously, random assignment was now salient but without an implicit recommendation from the experimenter. In this condition virtually all the participants elected the desirable condition for themselves, and they did not publicly rate their decision as particularly moral or immoral: no hypocrisy?

When they had been instructed that random assignment was required for purposes of the experiment and left alone to make the assignments, there were no moral failures. Virtually all the participants' assignments followed the outcome of the coin flip, and once again, absent the experimenter's instruction to be moral, the participants did not rate their assignments as particularly moral or immoral. They were merely doing what was appropriate. There are good reasons to conclude that Batson and colleagues did not reveal their participants' moral failures, but rather created a normative conflict for their participants and then modeled how they could resolve the contradictory demands imposed upon them by the experimenters' instructions. Rather than being hypocrites, the participants may have primarily been trying to be cooperative and behave as they were instructed.

SUMMARY

The studies we have reviewed are typically cited in support of the hypothesis that self-interest trumps and employs the desire for justice. A critical review and examination of their methodology generates serious doubts about the validity of their conclusions. The experiments employed confusing or contradictory instructions, or no compelling justice-eliciting cues, thus enabling the intrusion of other motives, particularly the participants' concerns with meeting the experimenter's expectations.

Several factors converged to make these particular experiments worthy of special attention. Along with similar others, they were authored by experienced and well-known psychologists who were leaders in the field. They were published in the most prestigious journals after a thorough and critical review process. Most important, the critical analyses presented here strongly suggest that they conveyed misleading conclusions about human motivation, especially the appearance of justice motivation in people's lives.

5

Defining the Justice Motive: Reintegrating Procedural and Distributive Justice

Having established the importance of justice, in this chapter we further explore its definition. In particular, we will review the relatively recent history of "procedural justice" as a form of justice that is distinct from the earlier focus on "distributive justice." After carefully examining some of the prototypical and most highly cited research that illustrates the unique status of procedural justice, we will make the case that the distinction between procedural and distributive justice does not "carve nature at its joints"; that is, divide two things where they ought to be divided: it is a confused and confusing distinction. The only reliable difference between these two types of justice is in the desired resources involved. Procedural justice refers to the acquisition and distribution of "symbolic" resources, while distributive justice research and theory typically includes both symbolic and concrete resources. The available evidence confirms that, when we attempt to explain and predict how the concern with justice and deservingness appear in people's lives, the same social psychological processes apply to the acquisition and distribution of both essentially fungible and interchangeable kinds of resources, symbolic or concrete. In essence, justice consists of people getting what they deserve, or what they are entitled to have on the basis of who they are and/or what they have done. We close with a discussion of the relationship between justice and other moral mandates.

THE "DISCOVERY" OF PROCEDURAL JUSTICE

In the mid-1970s, Thibaut and Walker (1975) published an impressive series of studies that clearly confirmed their hypothesis that people from all walks of life and diverse cultures prefer to be involved in a formal adversarial process rather than one of magisterial fact-finding in litigating their rights and obligations. That preference for adversarial procedures even appeared among the majority of their European participants, whose prior experiences and traditions were based upon a magistrate directing the gathering of information in order to arrive at a decision. The evidence also revealed that the psychological underpinnings of this preference stemmed from the participants feeling that the adversarial process gave them more control over the litigation and its outcome.

In addition to identifying this preference for procedures that allowed people greater control over the outcomes, Leventhal (1976) and Deutsch (1975, 2000) noted that people employ various criteria in evaluating the fairness of procedures for allocating desired outcomes. Relying essentially on anecdotal evidence, they suggested that people expect allocators to be objective, impersonal, unbiased, accurate, and so forth in assessing who deserves what. That made good sense because the failure to meet those criteria would easily lead to unjust allocations. Nevertheless, these authors, and many others since, emphasized the fairness of the procedures as being distinct from the fairness of the outcomes they produced: thus, the concept of procedural justice was launched as an important and relatively unrecognized central component in people's judgments of fairness and satisfaction with their outcomes.

This argument may have encouraged Allan Lind, one of Thibaut's students, to do research directed at demonstrating the distinct importance of procedural justice. His important experiments showed that procedures, that is, procedural fairness, mattered to people even when outcomes and control were not directly involved. Some studies, for example, denied participants their deserved outcomes but subsequently gave them the opportunity to voice their opinion about what occurred. This respectful treatment successfully mollified the participants' feeling of being treated unjustly (e.g., Lind, Kanfer, and Earley, 1990). This led Lind and Tyler (1988) and many others to do several studies (e.g., Brockner and Weisenfeld, 1996) revealing the importance of "voice," by giving people the opportunity to express their opinions, preferences, and so forth over denying them that opportunity. In a multitude of those experiments, those given voice were much more satisfied than those denied voice even when the eventual outcomes were equally undesirable.

By 1996, there was a sufficient number of published studies for Brockner and Weisenfeld to publish a meta-analysis leading to a description of how people's outcomes, and the procedures employed in arriving at those outcomes, influenced their reactions to their fates. This analysis led Brockner and Weisenfeld to conclude that if people's outcomes were sufficiently desirable, the fairness of the procedures that led to the outcomes was virtually inconsequential. If, however, the outcomes were relatively undesirable, then the procedures that led to those outcomes appeared to matter. If the recipients judged the procedures to have been relatively fair, they were less likely to be upset over their undesirable outcomes.

Many investigators came to be persuaded that the procedures employed to distribute desired resources matter, and influence people's satisfaction and feelings of fairness in spite of the outcomes they receive. A host of studies, too numerous to mention, subsequently confirmed this general proposition in a variety of settings, both in the field and laboratory. However, Tom Tyler (1994) published the most seemingly definitive and hence influential research that explicitly purported to establish procedural justice as a distinct and dominant form of justice: "Psychological Models of the Justice Motive: Antecedents of Distributive and Procedural Justice."

The research reported in that article led Tyler to conclude that:

the results supported a model in which relational issues dominate definitions of justice. Whereas distributive justice judgments are shaped by both resource and relational judgments, procedural justice judgments are shaped by relational concerns. The findings suggest two distinct justice motives. (Tyler, 1994, p. 850)

Obviously the discovery of two distinct justice motives and the singular importance of "relational issues" had major theoretical implications. As such, it merited and received special attention by social scientists who study human motivation and especially those who had studied justice motivation for several years without having reached the same conclusion.

As aspiring investigators learn, it is necessary first to return to the data that were collected and critically examine how the participants' responses were analyzed in order to distinguish the findings from the interpretation and to get an adequate picture of the research findings leading to this important discovery of two distinct justice motives. To accomplish that it is often necessary, as it was in this case, to go beyond the published report of the methods and data analyses and conduct some secondary analyses. As will be revealed in the following discussion, those additional efforts yielded very illuminating results that raised serious questions concerning the validity of the initially reported findings and provided a radically different set of conclusions.

A Close Look at the Research

Now, with apologies for presenting the considerable but required details at various points, this is what was found about what Tyler (1994) actually discovered.

The reasonable assumption underlying this research is that people's feelings about an encounter with someone in authority, especially how angry, frustrated, or pleased they feel, will directly reflect the extent to which they believe they were treated justly or unjustly: to what extent they did or did not receive the outcomes and treatment they felt they deserved. The specific purpose of the research was to assess the relative importance people attached to various aspects of their treatment, an assessment of procedural justice, versus their outcomes, an assessment of distributive justice. By separating people's feelings about the justness of how they were treated versus the justice of the outcomes they received, Tyler proposed to assess the relative importance of these two distinct forms of justice on people's resulting satisfaction.

To test their hypotheses, the investigators conducted telephone interviews with people who were asked to recall a recent encounter with a legal authority such as a police officer or a judge in Study 1, or with a work supervisor in Study 2. The respondents answered a series of questions about the recalled event. These questions focused on their memories of how they were treated and what the outcomes were; how they felt about the treatment and the outcomes they received in terms of satisfaction and fairness; and their present feelings (how angry, pleased, or frustrated they now felt) about their experience with the authority figure. (It should be noted at this point that an extensive analysis of the data for Study 1 had been reported in at least one prior major publication: Tyler, 1990. The appendix in that volume, which contained the actual questions employed and how the responses were scored, provided extremely important information for evaluating the findings reported in Tyler, 1994.)

As is common in survey research, the investigators used the respondents' answers to those questions to create several measures that they treated as independent, intervening, and dependent variables (see Table 5.1).

LISREL analyses (Joreskog and Sorbom, 1986), which compared the ability of alternative theoretical models constructed from these variables to predict the results, supported the hypothesis that people's reports of how fairly and respectfully they were treated had considerably more influence on their present feelings about their encounter

TABLE 5.1. *Sample variables from Tyler (1994)*

Independent variables	
Outcome favorability	How favorable was the outcome to you?
	How much influence did you have over the decisions made by the police/judge?
Process control	How much opportunity were you given to describe your problem before any decisions were made about how to handle it?
Neutrality	Did the methods used by the police/judge favor one person over another, or were they equally fair to everyone involved?
Trust	How hard did the police/judge try to be fair to you?
Standing	How politely were you treated?
Dependent variables	
Procedural justice	How fair were the procedures used to handle the problem?
	How fairly were you treated by the police/judge?
Distributive justice	How fair was the outcome you received?
	Did you receive more than you deserved, what you deserved, or less than you deserved?
Affect	Do you feel angry at the police/courts?
	Do you feel frustrated?
	Do you feel pleased?

with the authority than did the extent to which they reported having received the outcomes they believe they deserved.

But how confident should one be in arriving at conclusions based upon those data and their analyses? At the outset, it is important to recognize that all the causal models tested in the critical LISREL analyses assumed that the respondents' reports of how they were treated and the outcomes they received (the independent variables) determined their present reported feelings (the dependent variables: angry, pleased, or frustrated) about their recalled encounters with the authority figures.

Unfortunately, the LISREL analyses did not include a theoretically important alternative causal model. Given the survey methods employed to generate the data in this study, one must seriously consider the possibility that the respondents who, at the time they were being interviewed, disliked (or liked) the authority figure, for whatever reasons, would be more likely to recall, reconstruct, and report attitude-consistent details about their encounter with the authority (Hessing et al., 1988). The respondents' present feelings and attitudes toward the authority figures could well have been the "independent variable" influencing their reports of what had transpired: how fairly the judge or their supervisor had treated them. They would attempt to give a coherent and essentially univalent response to all the questions that they were asked.

The possibility that the respondents' attitudes were shaping their reports of what had occurred in their encounter gains credence from the fact that in both surveys the respondents' attitudes and feelings about the relevant authorities were made highly salient before the interviewers asked them to recall and discuss their own encounters. It is well recognized that people's salient attitudes influence their memory and reports of important events in their lives (see, e.g., Ross, 1989). In the process of recall and reflection, people tend to construct a normatively coherent narrative of what transpired, especially when they are questioned about the events in a public context (J. Lerner et al., 1998).

The impact of attitudes on the generation of attitude-consistent responses becomes particularly likely in this study because virtually all of the questions subsequently asked of the respondents included a rather obvious evaluative component. That is, rather than asking for specific descriptions of what had or had not occurred, the researchers asked for responses that explicitly included a positive or negative judgment about the authority figure. For example, consider the procedural justice questions: "Were the police/courts honest in what they said to you?," "How hard did the (police/judge) try to be fair to you?," and "Did the police/judge do anything you thought was dishonest or improper?" (Tyler, 1994). Remember that there were no independent assessments of what had actually occurred in the recalled incident.

Added to that is the fact that, prior to being asked to select a recent incident involving their contact with police or the courts, which was to be the focus of their responses for this research, participants had answered more than fifty questions that assessed and made salient the extent to which they trusted, and how they evaluated, the police, the courts, and so on (Tyler, 1990, App.). Prior to selecting the particular incident, participants had been amply primed to respond to the specific questions that provided the data for this research in terms of making their attitudes toward the police and the courts vividly salient.

Both the evaluative aspects of their questions concerning prior treatment, and the extensive questions eliciting evaluative reactions before the participants responded to the specific selected incident, suggested the need for additional analyses.

Those analyses of the original data point to a radically different interpretation of the Tyler (1994) findings. Evidence suggests that the respondents in that study had reacted to all the questions on the basis of their salient attitudes, or how positively or negatively they evaluated the police or the courts. For example, treating all the variables in the study as items comprising one evaluative attitude scale yields a Cronbach's alpha of .87 for Study 1 regarding legal authorities and .89 for Study 2 regarding work supervisors. (Cronbach's alpha is a measure of the extent to which scale items are consistent, i.e., related to each other. A value greater than .70 is considered acceptable, and 1.0 would be the theoretical maximum value.) As most psychological researchers know, that kind of assessed consistency would be considered an exceptional accomplishment for any multi-itemed scale or measure intended to assess a single attitude or trait. Similarly, a principal component factor analysis of the intercorrelations among all the variables indicates that in Study 1 and Study 2 all variables load .54 or higher on the first unrotated principal component. According to the two most common criteria (eigenvalues and scree test) all the variables have only one common factor in Study 1 (legal authorities), and in Study 2 (managerial authorities) there is a small second factor on which all the "outcome" variables load. These additional findings are most consistent with the hypothesis that one common evaluative attitude, made salient by the interviewers' prior questions, accounts for and shaped the largest part of the participants' responses to virtually all the questions they were asked. Those findings leave little room to make any assertions about how justice considerations, of any kind, influenced the respondents' reports of their feelings. Certainly one could not hope to make any kind of case for finding two distinct justice motives.

That leaves one potentially important unanswered question. If all the responses were determined by the same salient evaluative attitude toward the authority figures, how can one account for the fact that a higher empirical association was found between the relation measures, that is, fair procedure, and the participants' reported present feelings, compared to the association between those feelings and the measures of the participants' reports of the fairness of their outcomes, that is, distributive justice? There are several components to the answer.

First of all, the justice models the researchers employed in their LISREL analyses were theoretically inappropriate. Their models treated the respondents' reports of "outcome favorability" (e.g., "how favorable was the outcome to you?") as the independent variable that ostensibly influenced the intervening variable of "distributive justice" that in turn influenced the dependent variable "reactions to the experience." Whereas, to be consistent with the most recognized theories of distributive justice (Adams, 1963; Walster et al., 1978), Tyler would have had to portray the participants' reports of the fairness and justice of their outcomes (distributive justice) as influencing the participants' evaluations of the "favorability" of their outcomes. Adams (1963) would have treated the fairness of the outcomes as the determinant of favorability, and Walster et al. (1978) would have required adding their coequal influence in determining the favorability of the person's resultant affect.

An even closer examination of the questionnaire and its scoring (see Tyler, 1990, App.) helped account for the reported lack of a significant direct relationship between the respondents' reports of distributive justice and the dependent variable of reported affect. The fact that, in the path analysis, the response to the question "Did the methods used by the police (judge) favor one person over the other or were they equally fair to everyone involved" had no significant relation to the "distributive justice measure" (fairness and deservingness of outcome) raised a large bright red flag. How could that be?

Let's go back to the appendix (Tyler 1990) for the answer. It appears that the responses to two items were used to construct the distributive fairness measure: "How fair was the outcome you received?" and "Did you feel you received the outcome you deserved?" The former was scored correctly, from 1 (very fair) to 4 (very unfair). The scoring of the responses to the deservingness item, however, confounded favorability with deservingness (distributive justice): better than deserved was scored as a 1, deserved outcome as a 2, and worse than deserved as a 3 (See Tyler, 1990, App., item 61, p. 203, 211). "Better than deserved" was considered to be more fair, in calculating distributive fairness, than "deserved." So a measure of fairness was combined with a measure of favorability rather than deservingness. If the responses had been scored 1 = deserved, 2 = more than deserved, and 3 = less than deserved, that would have been consistent with the Walster et al. (1978) theory. In actuality, an even more valid assessment would have scored both more and less than deserved as equally lower than deserved. In either case, according to theories of distributive justice, within predictable parameters getting more than one deserved typically elicits a relatively negative response in comparison with getting what one deserves.

If the data used in Tyler (1994) were scored as indicated in the appendix of Tyler (1990), then the "mysterious" failure to find a significant relation between the item assessing their having been treated as fairly as similar others and the item assessing their having gotten the outcome they deserved (the measure of distributive justice) can be easily explained: the distributive justice measure employed by Tyler (1990, 1994), having confounded favorability with deservingness, was not a valid measure of the participants' assessment of the distributive justice they received.

In short, there is every reason to conclude that the research reported in Tyler (1994) was fatally flawed by its conception and methods. The results of this study of attitudinally consistent responses to telephone interviewers concerning respondents' contacts with police, the courts, or one's managers does not speak at all to the question of how the justice motive in any form appears in people's lives.

As for the discovery of "two distinct justice motives," in order to arrive at that most ambitious conclusion one would have had to ignore the simple finding that, as in most studies, the participants' procedural and distributive justice ratings were highly correlated with each other (Study 1, r = .77; Study 2, r = .64), certainly approaching the reliability of each measure. In this case that was easily attributed to the fact that they were both measures of the same attitude.

Conflating Generosity and Kindness with Fair Treatment

More recently, Tyler and Blader have continued to describe *procedural justice* as the wave of the future and of unique importance in people's lives. According to Tyler and Blader (2003, p. 350), "Justice research has followed the path outlined by this evidence because it finds that the primary impact [of justice concerns] on people's lives comes from their judgments about the fairness of procedures." They cite earlier publications by Tyler and his students (see e.g., Tyler et al., 1997) in support of that assertion. But then they go on to state:

> This does not mean, of course that people no longer study distributive justice, but that there is a particularly strong focus in current research on issues of procedural justice. This focus is embodied in the group engagement model by the key role it accords to procedural justice.

The "group engagement model," introduced by Tyler and Blader, establishes fair treatment – procedural justice – as the key element in leading employees to identify with and voluntarily benefit their employers. In support of their theory, Tyler and Blader reported evidence purporting to demonstrate, first, that treating employees fairly will naturally lead to their identifying with that organization, and, second, that as a consequence of that identification they will voluntarily engage in cooperative and self-costly efforts to benefit their employers (Blader and Tyler, 2003; Tyler and Blader, 2003). Procedural fairness is the key to creating ideal, highly valued, self-sacrificing employees who are fully identified with the company. If true, this discovery would have enormous theoretical and practical implications.

It is easy to imagine a stampede of corporate executives and managers rushing to learn the magic formula ... now that the word has gotten out! Before the hordes of managers line up and compete to get to the front of the line, they should stop to consider. First of all, it would be no surprise to discover that employees who report feeling disrespected or humiliated by their organization or who believe their company mistreats other employees would probably be reluctant to identify with, and voluntarily engage in self-sacrificial efforts to benefit, their employers (see, e.g., Brockner and Wiesenfeld, 1996). Secondly, it is probably true that employees who have fully identified with their organization will be more likely to engage in relatively costly efforts to benefit the organization. But what is the relationship between being treated fairly and identification?

Being treated fairly, or not being treated unfairly, either distributively or procedurally, is simply equivalent to receiving the treatment to which one is entitled, or deserves. At the same time, it is difficult to imagine how fair treatment, by itself, would provide any incentive or reason to generate affection for or sense of identity with the organization. After all, the company is merely fulfilling its contractual obligations. Early research by Nemeth (1970) demonstrated that participants who had been helped by someone who was mandated to provide that help felt no subsequent obligation to voluntarily benefit that person. Only completely voluntary, freely given, help elicited reciprocal benefits. Treating employees fairly, giving them a fair day's pay for a fair day's work and not mistreating or insulting them at the same time, is nothing more than an organization meeting its obligations. Such familiar forms of economic exchange between employers and employees are commonplace and not intended or experienced as something especially ingratiating, much less endearing.

If fair treatment, by itself, does not alienate employees but at the same time does not lead to identification and the willingness to incur costs to benefit their employers, how were Blader and Tyler (2003) able to report empirical relationships that clearly confirm their theoretical hypotheses, that procedural fairness leads to identification with the organization, which then elicits voluntary cooperative behavior? To answer that question one needs to look no further than the unique way they defined and measured procedural fairness in their research.

Their participants responded to several items assessing fair treatment in traditional forms, but the key element involved enlarging the concept of procedural fairness to include items pertaining to the "quality of treatment." That was assessed by their participants' responses to the following items (see Blader and Tyler, 2003):

- I trust (the organization) to do what is best for me.
- (The organization) really cares about my well-being.
- (The organization) cares about my satisfaction.
- My supervisor takes account of my needs when making decisions.
- I trust my supervisor to do what is best for me.
- My supervisor really cares about my well-being.
- My supervisor cares about my satisfaction.

The content of those quality of treatment items would be normatively appropriate when assessing the relationship between close friends, or family members, that is, what Clark and Mills (1979) would term "communal relationships"; however, it is difficult (impossible?) to see how they reflect procedural fairness occurring in an organizational context characterized by the normatively appropriate exchange relations (see also Buunk et al. [1993] for the different norms elicited by communal and exchange relations).

More to the point, positive responses to those items clearly indicate the kind of personal emotional attachment that would elicit or reveal an identification and voluntary cooperation with any person, group, or organization. If you are "identified" with someone or an organization for whatever reason then you would both agree with these items and probably reveal voluntary efforts to benefit them. But prior fair treatment, by itself, is not one of the ways of eliciting that identification. Certainly prior mistreatment or unfair treatment would inhibit identifying with the organization or supervisor, but that is beside the point.

It is probably a matter of common knowledge that most people will identify with others who they believe are identified with them and promote their welfare: who would not identify with those who seem to care about me, care about my well-being, needs, and satisfaction, and try to do what is best for me (Clark and Mills, 1979)? That is hardly a new or surprising discovery, but claiming that responses to those items have anything to do with fairness, procedural or otherwise, is misleading. Rather, given what is already known, it seems highly probable that fair treatment, or at least not being treated unfairly, may be a minimal but clearly insufficient basis for inferring that a manager or organization "really cares about me and my welfare."

In this society, good friends and family, but not your employer, are expected to "really care about" you. But if employers demonstrate that they go out of their way to care about your needs and welfare and what is best for you, then most people would want to reciprocate. They are treating you as a family member. But, contrary to what Tyler and Blader would suggest, simply treating you fairly, or not unfairly, might be a minimal condition but would not be at all sufficient to reveal or create such beneficent intentions. It appears that Tyler and Blader were able to confirm their hypotheses by simply redefining procedurally fair treatment to include acts of generosity and kindness that, as everyone knows, can elicit identification with the benefactor.

Hopefully, having carefully examined the demonstrably flawed efforts that purported to demonstrate that procedural justice is not only a distinct form of justice but also the most relevant form of justice motivation in people's lives, the reader will recognize the need to consider the following more fundamental, basic issue.

IS PROCEDURAL JUSTICE A DISTINCT FORM OF JUSTICE OR MERELY ANOTHER VERSION OF THE EMPEROR'S NEW CLOTHES?

One answer to that question points to the obvious difference between how people treat someone and the outcomes they each receive. Everyone can recognize that, at some level, procedural justice and distributive justice are distinct. But to accept that conclusion merely perpetuates a particular kind of theoretical myopia that erases the familiar recognition of the various desired resources involved in human exchanges and their relations to one another.

Procedural justice theorists seem to have ignored some familiar aspects of what people value for themselves and others. These commonly desired resources come in various distinguishable forms that can be roughly, but meaningfully, categorized as symbolic and concrete. Concrete resources include pay and other resources that can be easily seen and quantified. Respect and social esteem are obvious examples of symbolic resources. For various purposes, it makes sense to recognize differences within each of these large groupings that have distinct implications for specific interpersonal and psychological events (see, e.g., Foa and Foa, 1976). In addition, Tetlock and colleagues (2000) have provided compelling evidence for an important distinction between what they term "sacred" and "secular" resources. Sacred resources include such things as control over a person's body (e.g., as evinced in surrogate motherhood) and individual rights (e.g., to citizenship or to a jury trial), whereas more mundane secular transactions can include the purchase of housing, cleaning services, or food. For many people, the former, in concrete and symbolic forms, have singular value that must be protected from contamination by secular values or devaluation. Secular symbolic and concrete resources are fungible and may be included in the normal courses of making trade-offs. These are the resources most typically involved in issues of deservingness and justice in both interpersonal and commercial encounters.

The case can be easily made that those events that have been labeled procedural justice involve the acquisition and transfer of symbolic resources; whereas distributive justice focuses on the acquisition and transfer of symbolic and concrete resources. For example, the opportunity to have voice, as a sign of respect, can itself be a resource to be distributed (e.g., Klein and Azzi, 2001). Beyond the recognition of differing composition – symbolic versus concrete, intangible or tangible – further distinctions become trivial for most intents and purposes. The important point is that symbolic and concrete resources are fungible and substitutable. A clichéd example consists of a successful employee being awarded signs of enhanced status, such as the key to the executive bathroom or a title on the door, in lieu of an increase in economic compensation.

It is well recognized that symbolic resources, such as signs of deference, rank or status, and acts of approval or disapproval, can be exchanged or traded for desired goods and services. The courts may, in the name of justice, require someone judged to have intentionally defamed and damaged someone's reputation to provide appropriate amounts of economic compensation to their victim. Not only does it seem just for the courts to require economic compensation for loss of social esteem, most undergraduates exposed to a course in anthropology or sociology learn that in a vast array of cultures, the failure to reciprocate someone's gift-giving elicits the loss of relative status. Similarly, the recipient of an economic benefit can respond with public displays of gratitude and deference, thus acknowledging their benefactors' relatively superior status. There do not seem to be exact metrics for calculating how much of a symbolic resource such as social esteem is equal to how much of a concrete resource, but it is clearly understood that, except for sacred resources, they are interchangeable in arriving at judgments of fairness and justice.

The Importance of Voice or Deservingness?

Consistent with this recognition of essential similarities between different types of resources, a few investigators have demonstrated that the rules of deservingness and justice that apply to the exchange of concrete resources also hold true for the symbolic resources involved in "procedures": the manner in which people are treated, like the outcomes they receive, is assessed and judged. Probably the most researched aspect of procedural fairness concerns whether or not authorities allow people who will be affected by their decisions the opportunity to have voice. A marker of respect, *voice* is the term procedural justice investigators give to the occasion when authority figures either ask (voice), do not ask (no voice), or explicitly refuse to ask (voice denied) their constituents' opinion about what should take place. A relatively recent and growing body of research (Brockner et al., 1998; Gilbert et al., Experiment 6, 1998; Heuer et al., 1999; Sunshine and Heuer, 2002) has investigated when the salutary effects of fair procedures, for example, voice, will or will not occur. The findings of these studies effectively incorporated the beneficial effects of perceived procedural fairness (voice) within very familiar and well-understood social psychological processes that determine people's judgments of deservingness and justice with regard to the distribution of any desired resource.

Heuer and colleagues (1999), for example, demonstrated that participants who were led to believe they had little of value to contribute were not particularly bothered by authorities ignoring their opinions and were not upset by disrespectful treatment from the authorities if they believed on that occasion that their unacceptable prior behavior did not entitle them to be treated respectfully. Brockner and colleagues (1998) demonstrated similar results and reported that in several field studies the half of the employees who were assessed to be below the median in self-esteem did not respond positively to respectful treatment from authorities. Apparently, they felt unworthy of, and thus did not consider themselves to merit, the respect. Those with relatively high self-esteem reacted positively to the respectful treatment they believed was deserved. These findings were confirmed in three studies reported by Sunshine and Heuer (2002) in which people judged the appropriateness of whether or not others received respectful treatment.

The research program by Van den Bos and colleagues (1997) described in the last chapter also examined the effects of voice. In some experimental conditions, the experimenter, without any explanation concerning why, either gave or refused to give the participants voice about the allocations of the lottery tickets. In this experiment, voice allowed participants to indicate how many lottery tickets they and the other should be allocated. As it happens, the experimenter gave the participants no reasonable or even plausible explanation for why they were asked or not asked their opinion about something that under normal circumstances would have been decided by the experimenters: mysterious, puzzling, maybe silly?

It should be no surprise that if the only information was whether or not they were given voice, the participants would guess they should rate themselves as happier and having been treated more nicely than if they were ignored or denied the opportunity to express their opinion. But what could those ratings possibly mean in that context? Did the participants actually care one way or the other, or did they think the experimenter thought they should care? The answers to those questions become clearer when one considers two additional pieces of information that directly point to the issue at hand: were the participants consciously attempting to arrive at a normatively appropriate response rather than express their concerns about fairness or deservingness?

One of these is the consistent finding across at least four experiments that when the participants had any additional information about what transpired, including the relative number of tickets they and the other participant were awarded, the effect of the voice procedure entirely disappeared. Whether or not they were given voice did not add or detract from the participants' satisfaction with being given the same, less, or more lottery tickets than the other participant whose performance was equal to theirs (Van den Bos et al., 1997, 1998b). Apparently it was an irrelevant piece of information for the participants who were relatively under- or overbenefitted. That is an important finding because it directly contradicts one of the more stable findings in the procedural justice literature. Brockner and Wiesenfeld (1996) concluded, after reviewing the available procedural justice research, that procedural fairness, that is voice, typically does not affect people's reactions to highly desirable outcomes, but it reliably lessens people's dissatisfaction with having received undesirable outcomes. People who receive less than they desire or deserve are relatively satisfied if they were allocated the desired resource of being treated with respect, or given voice. But that did not occur in this experimental situation.

The failure to reproduce the highly stable effect of voice on people's reported satisfaction in this situation when the participants have other relevant information is consistent with the possibility that the unexplained strange procedures employed in these experiments had the predictable effect of raising the participants' evaluation apprehension, and in so doing the participants were less likely to experience or directly express their concerns with deservingness or fairness. Instead, motivated by evaluation apprehension, they focused on generating the normatively appropriate reactions to the most obvious cues.

It is also significant that the participants' reactions in this experimental situation closely matched those given by similar participants who were role-playing their part in explicitly hypothetical events involving greater or lesser outcomes and being given or denied voice (Van den Bos et al., 1997, 1998b). They were asked to imagine how they might, or would, actually respond if it were real and then, for some unknown purpose, report their imagined reactions to the experimenter.

It is not our goal to identify and reexamine every study that claims to report unique and singularly important effects of procedural fairness. The presently available evidence leads us to the important conclusion. In understanding how considerations of deservingness and justice appear in people's lives and how much and in what ways people care about justice, there is nothing unique or particularly important about the phenomenon of procedural versus any other form of justice. Justice consists of people getting what they deserve, or what they are entitled to by virtue of who they are and what they have done.

THE JUSTICE MOTIVE AND OTHER MORAL IMPERATIVES

We have devoted a fair amount of attention to the question of whether voice and fair treatment constitute a different and particularly important form of justice as part of our larger goal, which is to describe the phenomenology of justice. What kinds of evaluations and imperatives should qualify as justice-based? Having given detailed consideration to what justice is, it is important to recognize that justice imperatives are not the only ought imperatives that people commonly experience. Although there are sufficient reasons to identify justice imperatives as pervasive, compelling, and central in people's lives, it is also important to recognize the important influence of moral norms and cultural values: the person's desire to be, and appear to be, virtuous and to avoid self- and social condemnation while gaining approval and public esteem. These judgments may be expressed as assessments of fairness and deservingness; that is, immorality may be condemned as "unfair" and injustice experienced as immoral. These judgments, however, are not experienced in the same way as justice imperatives. Several kinds of moral injunctions and admonitions have been identified and studied, and certain forms of expected interpersonal treatment, such as respect for elders or parental care for children, may be described as rooted in morality as well as justice. According to the early descriptions of "moral relativism" by anthropologists (e.g., Benedict, 1934; Mead, 1939), the experiences of "moral" evaluations and judgments, such as desirable/undesirable, good/bad, or virtuous/evil conduct, are the product of the psychological internalization and representations of societal mores and norms, that is, the terms of the "social contract" passed on from generation to generation.

More recently, Jonathan Haidt (2001) documented the important fact that once the cultural rules and values are adopted and internalized they automatically influence people's judgments as intuitive, morally objective truths. Although it is possible for those who are at all culturally conversant to describe the content of the major moral rules in their society, once internalized as their own the resultant moral judgments often appear as automatic intuitive responses. As a consequence, people are often surprised and confused by a request to explain the basis of their intuitively expressed moral judgments. For example, for most people the moral condemnation of a brother and sister who had a sexual encounter would be automatic and seemingly obvious. Haidt (2001) has demonstrated, however, that if then requested to justify or explain the basis of their condemnation, they would literally be unable to retrieve the actual origins of their automatic intuitive response. Because the origins of what actually led to their judgments are "introspectively opaque," or not subject to conscious retrieval (Shweder and Haidt, 1993), people typically rely on whatever acceptable moral norms that happen to come readily to mind to justify their condemnation.

What is the relationship between justice imperatives derived from the commitment to the personal contract and the moral imperatives derived from the social contract? A considerable body of literature associated with the concept of altruism has explored when and how these moral imperatives appear in apparently costly behavior (see, e.g., Kurtines and Gewirtz, 1991). Linda Skitka (e.g., 2002) has generated evidence for the importance of a person's "moral mandates," their strongly held convictions concerning what is right and wrong, in shaping their social judgments and evaluations.

These important sources of motivation and evaluative judgments can contribute to the preconscious generation of justice imperatives by providing evaluations of people and their actions (positive or negative, good or bad, desirable or undesirable) and therefore the value of the outcomes they deserve (bad people deserve bad outcomes). Similarly, when individuals subsequently engage in conscious cost-benefit analyses of various alternative courses of action they often will automatically include the morality-based benefits and costs: How will others evaluate me? How will I evaluate myself if I do X or Y? As affirmed by Baumeister (1998), justice reasoning may be used to affirm the morality of the self. Although Skitka (2002) has identified and studied strongly held moral convictions, Tetlock and colleagues (2000), as described earlier, demonstrated the important distinction between some moral values that people consider to be sacred and other, essentially secular values that are fungible in making rational trade-offs. The sacred values must be protected even against implicit or symbolic violations and therefore cannot be compromised by rational cost-benefit considerations.

HOW DO MORAL VALUES AND JUSTICE INTERSECT AT THE INDIVIDUAL AND SOCIETAL LEVELS?

It would make sense to assume that rules of justice and deservingness, as articulated in the norms of the social contract that have been filtered through individuals' particular socializing agents, would enter into the development of their moral mandates and sacred values. What, however, about the personal and social dynamics associated with these related but different sources of motivation and moral dynamics? Although no easily identifiable research literature directly speaks to these issues, it is possible to offer some reasonable beginning observations.

It is easy to demonstrate that people often have differing moral mandates and sacred values (Skitka, 2002), and these may appear in public debates and often-intractable conflicts over what is evil or morally required (see, e.g., Lerner and Torstrick, 1994). Consider public discussions about abortion or women's rights. Not surprisingly, issues of deservingness and injustices are often marshaled in support of and as accusations by the contestants, but they appear to be easily ignored or redefined as being supportive so that each contesting party insists that it has justice on its side. It is not clear how people would respond to a direct conflict between justice and sacred values, for example, irrefutable compelling evidence that their moral mandates are the cause of terrible undeserved suffering and harm. Conceivably, that would not be possible because most people would be compelled to reinterpret or deny such "compelling" evidence, for example, offering justifications or denials associated with intentional killing of obviously innocent people in the service of a "sacred" cause. Skitka (e.g., Skitka et al., 2009) argues that moral mandates represent one type of justice judgment, with self- or socially interested motives providing alternative judgments, and suggests that the operative principle for an individual results from the perspectives, needs, and identities that are currently salient – although moral mandates will typically override judgments based on wants or needs.

What is clear, however, is that in essentially secular societies people who commit crimes while acting on their moral mandates or sacred values are treated as ordinary criminals (and maybe even worse, e.g., in the case of "hate crimes") and appropriately punished for the injustices inflicted on individuals and against the social order. Believing that God's decree, one's moral mandate, requires you to kill a physician who conducts legal abortions will not prevent your prosecution and punishment. Believing that God's decree requires that you withhold appropriate medical treatment for your sick child will not exclude you from criminal prosecution. At the societal level the unchallenged consensus insists that justice, not moral mandates or "sacred" values, must prevail.

In Summary

In this chapter we have examined some of the different concepts that appear in the research literature on justice in order to bring clarity to what is often conceptually clouded. The emphasis on the difference between procedural and distributive justice attributes too much significance to the distinction between symbolic and concrete resources. Symbolic resources can be distributed and traded off against concrete ones; concrete resources can reflect the extent to which someone is valued by a group. Both types of resource are evaluated and assessed to determine whether or not people are getting what they deserve, and the violation of either fair procedure or fair distribution can threaten confidence that justice will prevail. Morality, however, can be distinguished from justice by its emphasis on individual character. Witnessing an immoral act doesn't necessarily shake our faith in the social system, but it does taint the actor. Whereas morality refers to the evaluation of individual behavior, justice describes the appropriate relationship between people and their fates.

6

How People Assess Deservingness and Justice: The Role of Social Norms

The main function of presenting the evidence for the personal contract theory of justice imperatives and then critically examining the relevant self-interest literature was to set the stage for a theoretical model that attempts to describe how justice and self-interest appear in the normal course of people's lives and influence their reactions to critical events. Before embarking on that it is important to bring some clarity to the essentially important matter of how people assess who deserves what from whom. What rules and standards underlie or are revealed in their judgments of deservingness and justice?

Considerable research, as described in the preceding text, supports the hypothesis that people automatically seek out and respond to familiar cues that define who is entitled to what from whom as the primary and initial task in each encounter. The what in this context refers to forms of treatment and ways of interacting as well as to concrete and symbolic outcomes. As discussed in Chapter 5, interpersonal considerations and respect also represent resources that may be allocated (Clayton and Opotow, 2003). Unless and until modified by subsequent events, the automatically generated definition of the encounter provides the basis for what transpires. Having committed themselves to maintaining their personal contracts, people will naturally experience imperatives to comply with the preconsciously and consciously held rules that provide the structure and more or less specific guidelines for their daily activities. But what do we know of these rules?

Some investigators have suggested that there are inexhaustible lists of fairness rules that people can refer to or invent in order to promote their own interests. As noted earlier, they propose that people's inevitable egocentrism combined with their egoistic motives naturally lead to the insistence that "I have a right to have whatever I want," and "whatever I can do to get what I want is fair" (Epley and Caruso, 2004; Moore and Loewenstein, 2004). The result is an endless invention of self-promoting and self-justifying rules of deservingness and fairness.

Without denying that under certain specifiable circumstances, for example, hostile-competitive-combative encounters, people can be induced to act that way, closer examination, however, clearly reveals the appearance of relatively few rules of deservingness and justice, and they fall into a few meaningful categories based upon their social psychological origins. In addition, it is possible to specify the circumstances in which they become salient and operative for most people and some of the most familiar complexities that inevitably arise in the natural course of events.

What then are these rules: what are their origins, when do they appear, and how do they influence people's behavior?

CULTURAL VALUES DEFINE GENERAL ENTITLEMENTS AND OBLIGATIONS

The most obvious origins of these rules include general cultural mores and codes of conduct. The common culture provides well-understood general rules of deservingness and entitlement that have a great influence on people's daily lives. These rules, though typically tacit, define the treatment individuals deserve during virtually any encounter: what any and every person deserves. For example, most culturally conversant individuals naturally assume they are entitled to be treated with respect and allowed to maintain their dignity even in encounters with those in authority (Tyler, 1994). Another general rule that has been identified is a general norm of reciprocity (Buunk et al., 1993; Gouldner, 1960), which requires that in order to be considered someone of equal worth, receiving a favor or gift requires returning one of similar value. Another manifestation of the entitlement to be treated with equal respect requires that people meet their prior obligations and promised commitments (Kahneman et al., 1986): "A promise is a promise."

Though these rules are generally unspoken, most culturally conversant individuals would provide remarkably similar completions to the statements: "Every citizen is entitled to ..." or "every human being deserves ..." and would reveal similar reactions if those entitlements are violated (e.g., Huo, 2002). The growing body of research focusing on what has been termed procedural and interactional justice has documented the influence of these rules in shaping people's reactions to their treatment by authority figures, for example, police, courts, and supervisors (see Lind and Tyler, 1988; Tyler, 1994).

These rules are not identical from one culture to the next. Evidence of the cultural influence on justice-related norms can be seen in cross-cultural research that has, for example, indicated a greater emphasis on equality rather than merit as a distributive rule in less hierarchical societies (Fischer and Smith, 2003) and a greater emphasis on need-generated entitlements in collectivist cultures as compared to individualistic ones (Murphy-Berman and Berman, 2002). In addition, the actual level of treatment or resources that is considered fair is relative: what counts as respectful treatment in one culture may be insufficient or downright rude in another, and the amount of money or other resources that are considered "fair" compensation depends upon what others are receiving. As Crosby (1976; Zanna, Crosby, and Loewenstein, 1987) has persuasively described, a perception that one's salary is fair or unfair is determined by, among other things, one's standard of comparison. The effects of history and culture can be seen in whether, for example, women choose to compare their treatment to men or restrict their comparisons to other women.

JUSTICE AND DESERVINGNESS

Social scientists have provided excellent documentation of the institutionalized and general norms describing the prescriptive and proscriptive rules that generate the objective (in the sense of being identifiable), normative context in which encounters unfold. Ample evidence reveals that the initial framing provided by the social context includes descriptions of familiar cues that introduce justice imperatives, which will in turn influence the subsequent assessment of what is fair and what is deserved.

Of particular importance are cues that elicit general scripts based upon early experiences that have been repeatedly associated with interpersonal encounters and with the acquisition and distribution of resources. These typically appear in the initial automatic preconscious reactions as well as in the system of conventional norms. For example, one of the most prevalent forms of entitlement emanating from developmental processes (see Chapter 2) and confirmed by societal norms associates deservingness with merit. People will generally agree that good people deserve good things, bad people deserve bad outcomes, and better people deserve more than people who are not quite as worthy. Although typically left unarticulated, there is a strong tendency for people to infer a person's merit directly from the desirability of what they are experiencing or the consequences associated with their behavior. It is as if knowing the desirability of an outcome preconsciously elicits the assumption that bad (good) things happen to bad (good) people, and bad (good) outcomes are caused by bad (good) people. In addition, the perception of merit can be elicited by a variety of familiar cues indicating relative accomplishment, as well as membership in various categories of socially defined merit. The most familiar of these include ethnic categories; age, gender, and socioeconomic statuses; physical characteristics, speech patterns, clothing, and names; and so forth.

Evidence described earlier confirms the influence of these merit-bestowing evaluative beliefs. For example, as described in the preceding text, physically attractive people were judged to deserve better outcomes than less attractive people, who were considered to be less worthy because of the preconscious association of attractiveness with virtue (Callan et al., 2007; Dion and Dion, 1987). Similarly, the tendency for people to assign better outcomes to themselves than others, even when those outcomes have no extrinsic value, that is, the participants are role-playing a reaction to a hypothetical event, may be traced to their tacitly assumed more virtuous character or behavior. As described earlier, Messick (in Messick and Sentis, 1983) has documented the self-conceited tendency for people to automatically assume they are generally more fair and less unfair than others.

Status Roles

In addition to the culturally based general rules of entitlement, the institutional context of every encounter gives further specification of who deserves specific outcomes and treatment through including more or less explicitly defined roles associated with particular statuses in various social contexts: mother at home making breakfast for her family, driving to work, conducting a graduate seminar, buying groceries at the supermarket, representing a client before the court, or being stopped by a patrolman for speeding. As symbolic-interaction–trained sociologists have repeatedly demonstrated, much of what occurs in these contexts can be described as essentially automatic and preconscious. People respond to highly scripted cues, including commonly understood obligations and entitlements, that define how they will behave. Every socially recognized status implies more or less specific obligations and privileges with regard to socially defined occupants of other statuses, such as the reciprocal but distinct obligations of a mother and a child.

Professors, for example, are as highly influenced by their obligations with respect to the students in their classes and their colleagues as they were of the rules they followed when they drove to their offices. Most of the time, they respond automatically to the familiar cues and would notice any significant deviation from these obligations. Because these are highly institutionalized activities that typically require that more than one participant play their parts, if called upon, people can consciously retrieve and describe with considerable accuracy the prescriptive and proscriptive norms that are appropriate for each encounter. During the normal course of events, however, absent any surprises, they are not consciously aware of how those normative expectations influence their interactions (Haidt, 2001).

The Basic Templates: Identity, Unit, Nonunit

There are some reasons to suggest that early repeated experiences around events of consequence generate "templates" or "scripts" that persist and tend to organize cue-elicited reactions into familiar patterns. The earliest such template, developmentally, begins in infancy before the ego becomes differentiated. It links cues of dependency, vulnerability, and need with activities of vicarious experiences and succorance and, crucially, the perception of identity or belonging (see Hoffman, 1970). Once someone is identified as one of mine in need, in the absence of other more compelling cues, the person experiences the imperative to satisfy those needs.

As children develop a sense of their own separate identity, the perception of similarity and differences with others becomes a major template for organizing their experiences and activities. The origins of this may be the repeated occasions in which they are treated as similar to some others and different from others, by virtue of their age, gender, classmates, neighborhood, or ethnic category. Those experiences typically include allocations of the same desired outcomes, privileges, and obligations, as well as cooperative shared activities with those who are "similar"; while cues of difference are associated with a history of competition and even conflict over desired resources, leading to differing, greater or lesser, outcomes. Although individual contributions are irrelevant under a cooperative script, they become key to allocations under a competitive script. Evidence described earlier (Lerner, 1974; Leventhal and Anderson, 1970), revealed that five- and six-year-old children shared jointly earned outcomes equally with another child whom they had not met but believed to be a "partner" or "team member," regardless of who contributed more or less to earning those outcomes, whereas they followed rules of relative contribution when allocating the jointly earned outcomes with others who were not team members but were merely "other workers."

Considerable evidence, some of which has been described in the preceding text, confirms the persistent influence of the residual effects of these repeated experiences in the form of templates for organizing contemporary experiences. Cues of similarity including attitudes and values, social category, language, or geography – even arbitrary designations when salient – elicit preferences for those who share such attributes over those who are perceived to be different on virtually any salient dimension (Tajfel and Turner, 1986). In addition, there is evidence confirming that the residual effects of those repeated early experiences include not only greater preference and liking for those who are similar compared to those who are different, but also, consistent with the scripted nature of the organizing template, the tendency to link the recognition of similarity with the preference for cooperative activities and equal outcomes.

Continuing into adulthood, people find the early associations of cooperation with similar people and competition with those who are different as the preferred arrangements. For example, early research found that although participants preferred to interact with someone similar to them under relatively pleasant circumstances, they clearly preferred to compete over scarce resources with someone whom they believed was different rather than similar to them. That was most evident when the outcome of the competition had relatively serious consequences (Lerner and Becker, 1962).

In another experiment (Lerner, Dillehay, and Sherer, 1967), participants who anticipated a competitive encounter with someone they heard being interviewed tended to perceive their competitor to be significantly different from them on various personal dimensions; however, the anticipation of cooperative interaction led participants who heard the same interview to perceive that person as rather similar with positive attributes. Apparently, anticipating the cooperative or competitive interaction that was about to take place led the participants to process what they heard in ways that conformed to their cognitive template or script, which specified cooperation with similarly good people and competition with those who are different (Lerner et al., 1976). Similarly, several studies confirm the tendency for people to prefer equal sharing of desired outcomes, regardless of relative contribution, when interacting with friends or "teammates" (Austin, 1980; Benton, 1971; Lerner, 1974; Lerner and Grant, 1990; Loewenstein et al., 1989; Wicker and Bushweiler, 1970).

The perception of another person as similar or dissimilar can be described as assigning him or her to a category: s/he is in the same category as I (a unit relationship) or s/he is in a different category (a nonunit relationship). More rarely, a person can even be described as functionally identical to me when the boundaries between self and other are dissolved (an identity relationship). In each encounter, when a situation is being evaluated in terms of its justice or injustice, the justice script that is evoked will depend on the relationship of the perceiver to the affected party, as illustrated in Table 6.1. If the person perceives an identity with the affected party, the script elicits the obligation to satisfy that party's needs. If the affected party is perceived to be similar, the person will expect cooperative interactions and strive to achieve equal outcomes. If the affected party is perceived to be different, or one of "them," the perceiver will expect competition leading to outcomes that are appropriately different.

TABLE 6.1. *Justice scripts based on perceived relationship to other*

	Basic Scripts		
	Perception of Other	Interaction	Outcome
Identity	Me, mine	Vicarious shared experiences	Meet needs/welfare
Unit	Similar/us	Cooperation	Equal outcomes
Nonunit	Different/them	Competition	Differing outcomes

RELATIONSHIPS AND JUSTICE PRINCIPLE: ALTERNATIVE THEORIES

Investigators have recognized and attempted to organize the appearance of various distributive justice rules: equity or relative merit, equality, winner-take-all, and need are the most prominent (Greenberg and Cohen, 1982; Lerner, 1974, 1975). The important question is what determines which rule is operative in a given encounter. Some have proposed that the degree of interpersonal intimacy will determine which of these forms of justice will appear (e.g., Greenberg and Cohen, 1982). The most intimate relations involve need-based, equality, equity, and finally winner-take-all appearing in the least intimate relations. Deutsch (1975), instead, in a highly cited article, employed a functionalist-implicit "rational" model. For example, to explain how a justice of equity, distributing desired resources in proportion to relative contribution, often appears in economic encounters, he describes it as promoting the value of increasing productivity. Equal allocations promote the value of friendship and harmonious relations because they remove the opportunity for invidious comparisons and envy. Finally, allocating desired resources to family members as needed is functional for promoting the welfare of those family members who are too young or vulnerable to fend for themselves.

Although it is easy to recognize some rough ecological validity to the appearance of a justice of need in families, equality among friends, and equity or relative contribution in the business sectors (see also Skitka et al., 2009), a closer examination of the easily available evidence reveals fatal problems with the exclusive association of those contexts with particular forms of justice and with their assumed functional determinants. For example, it is easy to point to common occasions in most families in which desired resources are distributed not according to need but rather according to equality, for example, respectful treatment or waiting in turn; merit, for example, punishing rule breaking or awarding money for chores; and relative status, for example, older children given more privileges.

Although societal norms often require parental responsiveness to their children's needs, most people experience a similar imperative when confronted with signs of need elicited by the recognition of vulnerability and suffering of others who are essentially strangers to them. For most people, the specific eliciting cues appear to be indications of need and undeserved suffering; this automatic response appears very early in their lives and persists into adulthood (Aguiar et al., 2008; Callan et al., 2006; Correia et al., 2007; Hafer, 2000a; Hoffman, 1970). As a result, although action may not be required by societal norms, signs of vulnerability or suffering are sufficient to be the eliciting cue of the identity relation, including the imperative to come to the aid of the deprived or innocent victim in order to eliminate the injustice (see Batson, 1991, 1998).

It is also possible to point out that allocating desired resources equally rather than according to relative contribution is often considered to be functional for promoting coordinated efforts among interdependent team members. In sum, these, and many other equally accessible observations make it clear that predicting people's judgments of what is fair and just requires a more explicit understanding of the cues that elicit specific imperatives: those cues elicit a definition of who deserves what from whom in what context.

Justice as Balance

Feather (2006) offered an alternative to this theory of how people decide issues of deservingness and justice and why they care. Relying heavily on Heider (1958), he proposes that justice-related judgments and behavior occur as people seek to create "balance" among their evaluations of the worth of social actors, the behaviors of those actors, and the outcomes accruing to those actors. Balance in this case consists of univalent associations in which positively evaluated outcomes belong with positive behaviors and desirable people. For example, justice is satisfied when people perceive undesirable people doing bad things and receiving negatively valued outcomes. According to Feather, people experience some form of injustice-related emotion if any of those elements (person, action, or outcome) are not of corresponding value.

Setting aside for the moment the question of whether seeking balance is a sufficient explanation of the justice-relevant psychological processes, Feather has certainly demonstrated the relevance of people's "cognitions," that is, conscious preferences for univalent matching of actions, outcomes, and people. By relying exclusively on presenting participants with "vignettes," often no more than a sentence or two, and asking them to imagine how they would react and then express their preferences by completing an appropriate set of scales, he has generated copious amounts of confirming data. According to the results of several of Feather's vignette-based studies (e.g., Feather and Nairn, 2005), the participants predict they would have various injustice-related strong emotions, rage, anger, outrage, envy, and so forth, depending upon the particular sort of imbalance with which they were presented.

Hundreds of participants generally imagined and predicted that they would react to these briefly sketched events just as Feather's theory predicted, preferring cognitively balanced scenarios and considering unbalanced events as relatively unfair. These findings, however, need to be viewed in the light of considerable evidence suggesting that participants' predictions of how they would react are systematically biased. Though sincerely generated, they are typically unreliable predictors of how the participants would actually react if the events were real, compelling events. Certainly, if Milgram's (1974) research documenting the systematic gross discrepancies between participants' predicted reactions and their actual behaviors were not enough, many other studies (e.g., Gilbert et al., 1998; Hessing et al., 1988; Lerner, 1971b; Miller, 1975; Nisbett and Wilson, 1977; Simons and Piliavin, 1972) have subsequently provided more than ample reason to question the ability of people to accurately predict their morally relevant judgments and behaviors.

In brief, the available evidence suggests that most often investigators' hypotheses will be supported by the participants' responses to the extent that the investigators and participants both rely on the same norms and lay psychological theories in order to generate the hypotheses and subsequent confirming behaviors. When the relevant psychological processes occur preconsciously and are not consciously retrievable, that is, they are "introspectively opaque" to the participants (Shweder and Haidt, 1993), or the resultant predicted behaviors of interest are counter to the normative expectations for the situation (Milgram, 1974; Nisbett and Wilson, 1977), then there is a high probability that the use of role-playing and vignettes will generate invalid evidence (Hessing et al., 1988). If both are present, then it is a virtual certainty (Milgram, 1974).

For example, participants who were instructed that they were watching someone who was role-playing being inflicted with painful electric shocks in order to study how people react to "innocent victims of natural disasters" were unable to predict the derogating reactions of similar observers who believed that they were watching the actual suffering of an innocent victim (Lerner, 1971b; Simons and Piliavin, 1972). Participants can only tell you what they can remember and then apply to the event of interest. Whatever they are able to recall, they will most often predict a response based upon their notions of what is a sensible and morally acceptable (normative) way to behave (see esp., Hessing et al., 1988). As a result, most people believe, or at least would publicly report, that they or anyone would react with compassion and caring to the suffering of an innocent victim rather than the defensively generated derogation of that victim. The evidence, however, reveals that when the sense of injustice is aroused, and the imperatives are very compelling, people's emotion-directed reactions are often neither the most rational (Meindl and Lerner, 1983, 1984) nor normatively most appropriate (see, e.g., Goldberg et al., 1999; Lerner, 1971b; Lerner et al., 1998; Lerner and Simmons, 1966).

In all probability, Feather's role-playing participants thoughtfully generated ratings of expected anger, resentment, and so forth in response to the vignettes, which reflected the fact that they were all, including Feather, relying on common understandings of how people are supposed to behave in various contexts. Everyone who is culturally conversant recognizes that when someone obtains a desirable (good) outcome through undesirable (bad) means that is not just, deserved, actually not even nice. But there is no need to invoke cognitive balance or anything beyond societal norms and conventions to predict that: people are supposed to be entitled to the outcomes they receive. It is unlikely that any amount of cognitive imbalance or inconsistency is sufficient by itself to generate significant amounts of emotion, beyond surprise, amazement, or consternation. Typically, other motives, for example self-esteem, threat, and maintenance, need to be engaged by the content and implications of the imbalanced or dissonant cognitions in order to actually generate measurable amounts of emotion-directed reactions (Scher and Cooper, 1989).

All of the preceding discussion inevitably leads to the critical question of whether or not participants who believe they are responding to an actual compelling incident, when something more or less terrible or desirable has happened to someone, would reveal the same commitment to cognitively "balanced" cognitions as those multitudes in Feather's studies who were confronted with brief vignettes of hypothetical events. As it happens, there is at least one published experiment that speaks directly to and offers an answer to that question. Stokols and Schopler's (1973) participants believed they were being confronted with an actual victim: the report of a young woman supposedly victimized by an unwanted pregnancy, the effects on her life of which were vividly portrayed as either rather disastrous (bad outcome) or relatively benign (good or acceptable outcome).

According to cognitive balance (Feather, 2006; Heider, 1958), the relevant cognitions linking the victim to her outcome would involve the causal responsibility for her pregnancy; either she was the innocent victim of an accident (weak personal causal relation) or she had been recklessly careless (strong responsibility). The findings revealed that the participants' evaluations of the victim's character were strongly influenced by the outcome of the pregnancy: the more personally disastrous it was, the more negatively they viewed the victim. Contrary to the theory of cognitive balance, however, the differing cognitions linking the victim's behavior either weakly (an accident) or strongly (irresponsibly culpable), though recognized in the participants' explicit ratings of her lesser or greater responsibility, had no relation to their negative or neutral rating of her character. Their evaluations of her character were only affected by the severity of her victimization.

It is not readily apparent how "cognitive balance" would be able to explain why the participants' cognition of the victim's personal responsibility for her negative fate (accident vs. reckless) was not the necessary cognitive link between the participants' evaluations of the victim's fate (positive-negative valence) and the evaluation of her character (positive or negative). Achieving balance among the participants' cognitions would have required that essential cognitive link between their cognitions of responsibility and evaluation, and that did not happen among these participants who were reacting to a victim and not role-playing their predicted responses to a brief vignette. It is also worth noting that the responses of these fully engaged participants were entirely consistent with the effects of a motivated belief that people deserve their fates by virtue of their behavior and/or their character but not necessarily by virtue of both (Hafer and Begue, 2005).

More importantly, the theoretical value of Feather's theory, focusing exclusively on balance among cognitions, is seriously limited by the fact that it is essentially empty of content in the portrayal of the nature of justice-related reactions. All that is needed for the experience of justice being maintained is that the person's evaluations – varying from very positive to very negative – of someone, their actions, and their fates correspond: what determines the evaluation of a person, and constitutes desirable actions and fates, are issues, though obviously central to the understanding of justice reactions, that are left to theories other than cognitive balance.

The version of justice-motive theory offered here to explain how people judge who deserves what suggests that, on each occasion in which such a judgment is made, three basic scripts preconsciously function as templates that organize cues into familiar patterns and generate imperatives that typically include emotions and courses of action leading to expected outcomes. The recognition of any of the cues – who the person is, the nature of the interaction, or the outcomes – tends to elicit all the others in that script. Although the scripts represent the effects of early repeated experiences, once established they function as ought imperatives so that cooperating with someone similar not only seems natural but also is experienced as appropriate, fair, and deserved. Considerable evidence confirms the proposition that the association of appropriate outcomes with cues of similarity and/or cooperation is experienced as a justice imperative: similar others deserve equal outcomes, cooperating teammates are entitled to equal outcomes, and so forth. Corresponding imperatives are elicited by cues associated with each of the scripted elements in the identity and nonunit imperatives (Lerner, 1974, 1975, 1977, 1981; Lerner et al., 1976). But there is more that needs to be discussed.

THE APPEARANCE OF MULTIPLE IMPERATIVES

It is a common fact of contemporary life that very often more than one script is elicited in the same encounter, with each script eliciting an imperative. Some of the most familiar and often-complex circumstances have been termed *moral dilemmas* or *role conflicts*.

Often, conflicts are resolved when the multiple scripted imperatives become merged into a culturally familiar form. For example, when the situation requires that people engage in cooperative efforts (Unit) with one of "them" (Nonunit), the emergent response often is shaped by elements of both the Unit and Nonunit scripts. This merging of Unit and Nonunit imperatives leads to engaging in cooperative efforts (Unit activity), but the outcomes, rather than being shared equally, are distributed according to relative contribution, investments, or costs (Nonunit outcomes). Or, the imperatives elicited by having to compete with "similar" others (Unit) in a winner-take-all situation (Nonunit), for example, competition among friends for scarce fellowships, friends wanting the same romantic partner, or simply contestants for the same prize, may lead to relatively well-recognized rituals to reestablish and demonstrate before and after the prize has been awarded that the winner and the other competitors deserve equal respect and status (Unit). Such demonstrations may include ritualized hand shaking or equalizing statements: "Next time it will be your turn," or "I was just lucky, it could have gone either way."

We were struck by evidence of this while watching the 2010 Winter Olympics, as competing skiers on the U.S. team went out of their way to stress the normality of intrateam competition at the same time that they emphasized that what was really important was for the United States to win as many medals as possible. These and similar statements are intended to minimize the threat of the drastically different outcomes to maintaining a Unit relation based upon the recognition of similarity and equality.

Not all conflicting imperatives, however, are amenable to merging into culturally appropriate forms. It is very important, for theoretical and practical reasons, to recognize that people often feel compelled to develop defenses or procedures for screening or controlling the appearance of conflicting imperatives that would threaten their ability to maintain commitments to their personal contracts. A common example of this defensive-screening process is intended to prevent the intrusion of newly experienced imperatives that would, if acted upon, prevent people from fulfilling prior or anticipated commitments to deserve their desired, needed resources. A sad fact of life in this complex society is that by adulthood many of these defenses have become automatic responses to particular familiar cues, often defining others so as to exclude them, or their cues of similarity, suffering, and deprivation, from eliciting the imperative to come to their aid or to share one's resources equally.

Deservingness vs. Entitlements?

Feather recently highlighted a form of conflicting multiple imperatives when he proposed a clear distinction between the social psychologies of deservingness and entitlement (see, e.g., Feather, 2003. Earlier investigators (Lerner, 1977; Major, McFarlan, and Gagnon, 1984; Mikula, 1998) had emphasized the common social psychology of all justice imperatives by subsuming them all under the generic term of *entitlements*. People are entitled to specific outcomes if, by virtue of who they are and/or what they have done, they have met the qualifications for acquiring the outcome. According to Feather (2003), however, the earlier investigators had failed to recognize an essential difference between the social psychological processes involved in deservingness and entitlements. Judgments of deservingness are based upon the assessed correspondence between the value of people's actions and personal qualities and the value of the outcomes they receive, or their earned outcomes. Judgments of entitlement, however, are derived from applying the "external framework of laws, rights, and social norms." Those include the normative requirements specified in the social structure, for example, legal statutes, status-roles, social categories, and the application of more informal societal norms.

Feather offered several studies to demonstrate the relevance and importance of this distinction between judgments based upon deservingness and entitlement. In these studies, participants typically reacted to hypothetical incidents described in brief vignettes that were meant to independently vary entitlements and deservingness and the value of the associated outcomes (relatively good vs. bad). After reading a vignette, the participants were asked to express their reactions, or how they would respond to such an event, on a series of scales. Those ratings were intended to assess the extent of their preferences and judgments of the deservingness and entitlements, as well as the sense of legitimacy, resentment, and so forth that they (believed they) would experience in regard to the event portrayed in the vignette. In this manner, presumably, Feather could precisely answer important questions such as "Do people express more or less resentment or satisfaction, or differing emotions, when an entitlement versus a person's 'deservingness' is met or violated?" These findings would demonstrate the validity and importance of distinguishing between the dynamics of deservingness and entitlements.

As it happens, even setting aside the insurmountable problems with deriving and generalizing inferences from the use of vignette methodology, as previously described, an examination of the actual contents of the vignettes employed in these studies reveals the conceptual flaws in the proposed distinction between deservingness and being entitled to an outcome. It becomes apparent that Feather failed to recognize that judgments of deservingness and entitlement, as he portrayed them, rely on formal and informal norms in order to determine what kind of person and what kind of behaviors entitle someone to what particular outcomes.

For example, Feather, in a recent study (2008) ostensibly varied deservingness for a job promotion by having one candidate portrayed as having performed very well, a "top performer" working very hard, with a top-quality application, and having completed all training, whereas the other candidate performed simply adequately on all those criteria. Entitlement was supposedly varied by having one of the candidates be of the appropriate gender in order to meet a government affirmative action criterion for promotion. The other candidate was not. At that time the company did not have a sufficient number of executives of the appropriate gender to fully comply with the government's directive. The person in question was either promoted or not. This is an obviously familiar event in contemporary public dialogues, but what could one learn from this study about deservingness and entitlement?

The fundamental problem for Feather's theory is that only his special view of entitlements would apply at all in this event. Certainly, the minority candidate was not "entitled" to the promotion unless one judges his or her status as actually meeting the requirements for promotion, because the firm was not under any compelling obligation to promote that particular minority candidate, although it would have helped them meet their obligations to the government. According to the previous definition of *entitlement*, only if the firm had actually promised this or any other minority candidate that he or she would receive the next promotion, would she or he be fully entitled to it (e.g., Lerner, 1977; Major et al., 1984; Mikula, 1998). Such a candidate would have fulfilled the requirement for the promised promotion simply by staying with the firm until the opening for promised promotion appeared, and would then be and could feel legitimately entitled to the promised promotion. Similarly, the company's explicit and implicit norms had not promised the top performer that he was "entitled" to the promotion by virtue of his performance.

In brief, this was not a study contrasting degrees of entitlement and deservingness, merely the agreement or disagreement with emphasizing the value of one or another form of relative eligibility for a promotion. As portrayed in this experiment, neither candidate was fully entitled to the promotion by virtue of either gender or prior performance. It is important to remember that codified rules and context-specific norms (external entitlements according to Feather) defined what specific behaviors and personal qualities were relevant to the acquiring the desired outcome: promotion.

Virtually identical conceptual problems involved in maintaining the distinction between personal effort-based deservingness and external norm-based entitlements are highlighted in Feather (2003), in which the participants are given the task of deciding the appropriate relative amounts of money an ailing elderly man should bequeath to a son, good friend, or neighbour. The recipients' relationship to the donor was supposed to determine the various degrees of entitlement. Presumably, deservingness was varied by their behaviors: whether the potential beneficiaries had provided either a fair amount of help for the ailing man or had spent most of their time furthering their own careers.

To begin with, most social scientists would find it incomprehensible that Feather had construed the deservingness manipulation in this context (prior aid) as different from, and not involving, entitlements. Social scientists as well as culturally conversant citizens would have no trouble recognizing the ubiquitous and compelling "norm of reciprocity" (Gouldner, 1960) as providing an entitlement based upon how much help the elderly man had received from the potential beneficiaries. The helpful son, neighbor, or friend may be judged to have "deserved" (be more entitled to) compensation from the elderly man, but the elderly person was also constrained by the culturally familiar norm of reciprocity to repay them appropriately for their help. Why is that form of entitlement portrayed as importantly distinct from the recognized entitlement of a son for a father's financial legacy, unless his behavior had negated his rights and entitlements as a son?

Feather offers no theory-based reason to predict whose outrage over not receiving that to which he was entitled, his "fair share" of the legacy, would have been more or less, or of different quality: a disinherited son or a disappointed caregiving neighbor? They might point to different criteria to justify their entitlements, but it boils down to the argument that they had or had not met the requirements to acquire the legacy. Either it was merited by virtue of birth, or it was merited because of prior aid – the appeal to the norm of reciprocity. The priority of or preference for one rule of entitlement or deservingness over the other may reflect personal ideological differences, but it is not relevant to understanding how and why justice imperatives influence people's behavior and social judgments.

In a second experiment reported in Feather (2003), the participants responded to very brief vignettes concerning the justness of winning or losing an election. Entitlement was presumably varied by having the candidate be older than eighteen, the required age to be eligible, or the candidate was only seventeen. Deservingness was varied by amount of effort exerted to be elected. The outcome was the candidate was either elected or not. How fair, just, or deserved was the outcome for that candidate?

In the first place, typically neither the candidate who expended great effort nor the one who was eighteen were entitled to be elected. The most that can be said in that vein is that the older person was eligible to be a candidate but not entitled to the outcome. It is commonly recognized that, regardless of efforts, personal qualities, and so forth, the only consideration that entitles someone to be elected is getting the most votes (legally). Putting in great(er) effort and failing is very common and may elicit some pity, but it has nothing to do with deservingness or entitlement, unless the "efforts" involved cheating or some form of violation of the rules of fair competition – but that brings up the relevance of norms again.

Finally, Feather and Johnstone (2001), in probably the most mystifying study, confronted their participants with a vignette concerning a nurse's response to a psychiatric patient who had acted out, causing a ruckus. She then either had the patient put in isolation or offered him extra personal attention and help with the crisis. Presumably, those were supposed to be recognized as an undesirable versus a desirable outcome. The patient's deservingness was varied by the diagnosis of either a schizophrenic or personality disorder. That was supposed to represent either an innocent victim of his psychosis or a rather nasty person who could have chosen to behave otherwise.

As it happens, the patient's entitlements had been met. Both outcomes represented normatively appropriate ways for the nurse to handle that kind of incident. One may have seemed more pleasant or generous, but both were equally appropriate. Depending upon one's convictions concerning the effectiveness of certain kinds of therapeutic interventions with certain kinds of patients, one response may have seemed preferable but not more just or unjust. Deservingness was also not varied by the diagnosis, except for the assumption that the personality disorder patient was personally culpable for his bad behavior. But, if that is true, then one has to construe being removed from the area as a punishment rather than, as is commonly understood, an appropriate way to manage patients acting out. To be sure, the nurse was more generous with her time and effort with the schizophrenic, but at this point it also seems appropriate to stop and reflect: what kinds of theoretically interesting inferences about justice imperatives – entitlements or deservingness – could one possibly draw from the ratings generated in this "experiment"?

SUMMARY

If the available evidence does not link rules of justice to a single dimension of intimacy, nor exclusively to a particular social or economic context, such as family or marketplace, that leads us back to the initial basic question of what does elicit particular justice imperatives? What are the specific cues, and what is the nature of the experienced

7

Integrating Justice and
Self-Interest: A Tentative Model

Up to this point the focus has been on three tasks. The first involved explaining how justice imperatives become a pervasive and important source of human motivation. Our second task was to critically reexamine the evidence for how self-interest appears in people's lives. That reanalysis of available evidence persuasively described how preconscious self-conceited beliefs, rather than self-serving motives, biased judgments of deservingness; that does not negate the common observation that people may, at times, intentionally manipulate rules of fairness or ignore them to justify benefiting themselves. Finally we described, with supporting evidence, how people arrive at judgments of deservingness and justice.

The important task now is to understand when and how self-conceited beliefs, and motivations based on self-interest, might interact with the important influence of justice imperatives in order to guide emotional and behavioral responses. We will begin by examining a few experiments that provide examples in which justice imperatives appear along with motivations based on self-conceit and self-interest as alternative and/or conjunctive influences in people's lives.

Persistent Influence of Initial Automatic Imperatives

One set of studies illustrates the way the preconscious effects of the justice motive can override self-interest. Apparently, when people are highly aroused by the initial recognition of an injustice to themselves or others, they will often ignore or at least be relatively unaffected by the dictates of conventional rules of rational judgment (Simons and Piliavin, 1972). In addition, they may ignore considerations of self-interest, as they automatically engage in emotion-directed justice-restoring reactions. These nonrational reactions may include the decision and appropriate efforts to reestablish justice by punishing the harm doer (Meindl and Lerner, 1983) or compensate deprived innocent victims (Miller, 1975, 1977) even at substantial costs to themselves. Additional evidence suggests that while preoccupied with intense justice imperatives, the person has neither the incentive nor cognitive capacity to engage in additional norm-directed thoughtful processing of the available information (Goldberg et al. 1999; J. Lerner et al., 1998).

In other cases the person's thoughtful efforts to promote their rational self-interest are actually hampered by an assessment of their own deservingness that is biased by self-conceit. In the study by Babcock and colleagues (1995) described in Chapter 4, biased processing and recall of information about a claim for damages meant that participants were less likely to reach a settlement with their opponents, with costly results for both sides. Their preconscious biases led the participants to measurably overestimate what they believed they deserved, and their subsequent efforts to gain what they believed they were entitled to have – that is, to achieve a just outcome as they perceived it – inevitably elicited their own and others' costly punitive reactions.

Automatic Reactions to Innocent Victims Replaced by Normative Compassion

Early research examining observers' reactions to innocent victims yielded two rather distinct reactions. Participants who believed they were witnessing the serious and continuing suffering of an innocent victim were inclined to find ways to condemn and derogate the victim's character if they were unable to come to her aid and also believed she would not be appropriately compensated for her suffering (Lerner, 1971; Lerner and Simmons, 1966). That is, when they were unable to restore justice through their own behavior, they were motivated to restore justice cognitively by reevaluating the victim as having deserved his or her outcomes. Similar participants witnessing the same victimization reacted quite differently if they were instructed to view the victim as comparable to someone who had been victimized by an uncontrollable natural disaster. These participants did not derogate or condemn that victim (Simons and Piliavin, 1972). Apparently, the unprepared automatic response to the suffering innocent victim involved derogating her character, but the prior availability of a salient alternative normative framework, such as that provided by a natural disaster, eliminated this tendency. Considerable additional evidence (e.g., Aguiar et al., 2008; Correia et al., 2007; Hafer, 2000a, b) identified the derogation as a rather primitive preconscious way for the participants to minimize the injustice they had witnessed. That obviously nonrational, preconscious automatic reaction, however, could be prevented by previously reminding the observers of societal norms that require responding to truly innocent victims with sympathy and compassion. As everyone knows, according to the norms of this society no sane, decent person would derogate the character of an innocent victim, at least not consciously.

For the task of constructing theoretical hypotheses, it is important to note that, a) the initial reaction reflected an automatic preconscious reaction to an injustice, and b) that automatic reaction was different from, and amenable to being replaced by, the normatively prescribed conventional reactions to innocent victims. The perceiver's reliance upon and/or desire to uphold well-learned social norms generated a different assessment of the situation.

Alerting Witnesses of an Injustice to be Rationally Thoughtful

The research of Jennifer Lerner and her colleagues (1998) provides an example of a more subtle but equally effective introduction of societal norms in people's responses to an injustice. In this case conventional rules for finding blame and assigning punishment effectively trumped and radically modified the automatic preconscious justice-motivated punitive response. As previously described, Lerner and colleagues' participants initially observed the very moving depiction of a bullying event. Witnessing that event elicited considerable anger as well as automatic preconscious concerns with justice and deservingness (Callan et al., 2006; Goldberg et al., 1999).

Those clearly detectable concerns were manifested in the participants' subsequent punitive responses to a negligent harm doer portrayed in the next situation: the greater the participants' residual injustice-induced anger from the first situation, the more punishment they assigned to the next negligent harm doer. That direct correlation between residual anger and punitive reactions did not appear, however, if the participants believed that the initial bully had been caught and punished, that justice had been reestablished (Goldberg et al., 1999). That is consistent with the injustice-based explanation for the anger-induced punitive reactions.

In a further twist, it is important to note that this direct relationship between the participants' anger and their subsequent punitive response did not appear among participants who were previously led to anticipate an interview with a graduate student at the end of the experiment concerning some of their reactions to the bullying tape (J. Lerner et al., 1998). The subsequent punitive reactions of the participants anticipating the later interview did not directly reflect the extent of their anger. Instead, their punitive reactions were related to their own ratings of the negligent harm doer's culpability and blameworthiness. Having the participants think about their reactions in anticipation of the interview was sufficient to trump and replace the primitive automatic anger-induced punishment reaction with conventionally accepted norm-based rules for assigning blame and punishment.

Clearly, the anger evoked by witnessing the injustice persisted into the next situation, but if the participants' conventional thought processes were also engaged, their expression of that anger was mediated by conventional norms: punishment should be proportional to blameworthiness. Without the extra inducement to think about what they were experiencing in preparation for a discussion, the participants' preconscious processes led them to directly express their earlier injustice-induced anger by punishing a subsequent harm doer. Even though this was irrational and in violation of conventional norms they punished the next available harm doer, who had no relation to the initial injustice.

Summary Hypotheses

Though a fully specified theory does not appear attainable at this point, there is sufficient evidence to provide a tentative working model of the way in which self-conceit as well as self-interested motives and justice imperatives appear in people's lives. The model, illustrated in Figures 7.1 and 7.2, recognizes that the process of

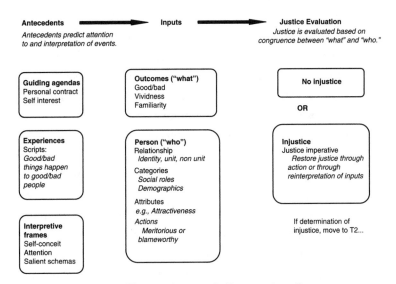

FIGURE 7.1. Time 1: Automatic Preconscious Processes

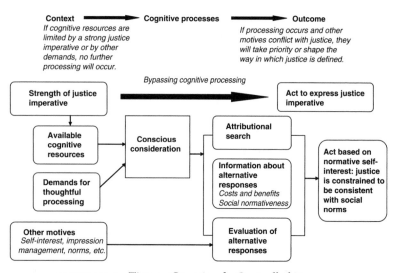

FIGURE 7.2. Time 2: Consciously Controlled Response

evaluating and responding to important events typically occurs in two stages, each with distinct cognitive-affective processes.

The evidence suggests an initial stage (Time 1, Figure 7.1), in which automatic processing of cues elicits a preconscious recognition and comparative evaluation of what has occurred, which is then experienced as a justice imperative. If the initial imperatives are relatively weak, with sufficient time and incentives for further information processing the thoughtful employment of societal norms will guide the expression of the initial imperatives as they are integrated with other salient motives. Those norms typically legitimize and often require acts of enlightened rational self-interest (Miller, 1999). When that occurs, self-interested motives, including the desire to appear reasonable and socially appropriate, will influence, often decisively, how people decide issues and how justice imperatives are expressed. The distinct influences of these two stages are most clearly demonstrated by evidence that, following conscious deliberation, people's responses will be more normatively appropriate whereas the immediate, automatic, response will more directly express the feelings and intuitions of the initial imperatives.

Considerable research and theory have examined the nature of these two contents and processes: those that occur preconsciously and appear as implicit agendas and the more explicit and thoughtful controlled shaping of intentional reactions (see, e.g., Bazerman et al., 1995; Haidt, 2001). The point at which the person's subsequent conscious processes – their thoughts, judgments, decisions, and intentions – become operative will be considered Time 2 (Figure 7.2). In the next chapter, we will also discuss a Time 3: justice-motivated interpretations of events that generalize beyond a single incident to comprise pervasive ideologies and worldviews.

TIME 1: THE INITIAL RESPONSE

The first stage, Time 1 (Figure 7.1), occurs preconsciously, instigated by automatic responses to cues that become salient as the perceiver initially attempts to assess whether or not someone's outcomes correspond to what they deserve. The assessment process begins with the recognition that something of consequence (good or bad) is impending or has happened to someone. Although that recognition may involve processing several cognitive elements, relatively simple cues such as a person crying or grimacing with pain, or even a facial expression indicating sadness or happiness, may be sufficient to automatically elicit the processes of concern here. In general, the salient prior agendas, though not necessarily consciously represented, will interact with the familiarity and vividness of the situational cues in order to determine the specific cues that are attended to and processed.

That initial recognition automatically elicits more or less elaborately scripted preconscious processes that typically include evaluations, thematic organization of reactions, associated affect, and propensities to act. The important initial cues in the situation indicate what has occurred, including its value – more or less desirable or undesirable outcomes – and the person who is the focus of attention. The relevant dimensions of this recognition are derived from familiar identifying features and invariably include evaluations of greater or lesser merit and the person's scripted entitlements based upon cues of identity, similarity, or difference. Cues of familiar social categories and identities can elicit social evaluations of good, bad, better, and worse. These cues may assign a personal social value to the recipient. Evidence also indicates that the recognition of similarity or difference with the target person, along with eliciting the relevant unit or non-unit scripts, often preconsciously elicits the self-conceited positive evaluation of the similar target individual or negative evaluation of those who are different (Epley and Dunning, 2000; Tajfel and Turner, 1986; Thornton, 1984; Towson, Lerner, and de Carufel, 1981).

The evidence suggests at least two preconscious reactions to the initial assessments of outcomes and persons. In one, the value of the outcomes generalizes to the value of the target person: "bad things happen to bad people," "bad people do bad things," and "bad people deserve bad things." In addition, the preconscious processes include the comparison of the outcomes with the target person's entitlements (deservingness) based upon the assessment of the person's merit and the recognition of a unit, nonunit, or identity relation. The preconscious commitment to deservingness then automatically impels the observer to act on the basis of the generalized evaluation (Apsler and Friedman, 1975; Rubin and Peplau, 1973; Simmons and Lerner, 1968; Stokols and Schopler, 1973; Thornton, 1984) and script-based entitlements. Perceived discrepancies result in an emotion-guided imperative to reduce the remaining discrepancy between entitlements and outcomes, for example by punishing harm doers (Goldberg et al., 1999; J. Lerner et al., 1998) or compensating victims (Simmons and Lerner, 1968).

In essence, the recognition of a positive or negative outcome automatically elicits preconscious simple scripts of social evaluation and judgment: "bad (good) things happen to bad (good) people" or "bad (good) things are caused by bad (good) people." Similarly, the recognition of cues indicating who is the recipient of the outcome, automatically elicits scripted entitlements (e.g., identity, unit, or non-unit), as well as self-conceit–based scripted evaluations and judgments. These may include evaluative responses to similarity and difference cues. "I, and people like me, are good, better, more deserving, than others. Different people are worse than I and people like me."

Affective-Evaluative Reactions

Of particular importance in shaping what emerges from the implicit preconscious processing of cues are affective-evaluative values associated with the outcome and the person of focus. As for the outcome – the "what" that is being experienced – this value appears as degrees of good/desirable or bad/undesirable. The affective consequence of the evaluative assessment, for example, someone grimacing in pain, is greatly influenced by the stimulus value and vividness of those cues, from vaguely discernable to "in your face" cues that demand all of the observer's focus of attention.

These same dimensions appear in the affective impact of the responses to the question of "to whom": who is experiencing the event. The person cues can range from barely noticeable, commanding little attention, to the extreme of appearing overwhelmingly vivid. The intensity interacts with the evaluative valence of the person cues to determine the affective consequences. The target's acts, if discernable, will elicit evaluations, as well as the value of their identifiable social category. Any or all of these may be salient and contribute to the perceiver's overall initial automatic affective-evaluative reaction to the target person.

Considerable experimental evidence suggests that the more intense the outcome evaluations and the more extreme the evaluation discrepancies between the outcome and the target's entitlements, the greater the affect and imperative. More specifically, early research found that participants were more aroused by and personally condemning of an innocent victim whose suffering was more severe and of longer duration than an identical victim whose suffering was relatively minimal, was of shorter duration, or would be appropriately compensated (Lerner, 1971b; Lerner and Simmons, 1966). Although it is well recognized that people are more upset if an innocent or good person is deprived or harmed rather than one of "them" or a bad, culpable person (Aguiar et al., 2008; Correia et al., 2007; Meindl and Lerner, 1983), some evidence also found that when the participants were unable to rescue or compensate the victim, their condemning reactions, which attributed justice-restoring negative attributes, were even stronger for a victim whose suffering resulted from altruistic motivations (Lerner and Simmons, 1966).

More recently, several investigators have employed ingenious methods to find more direct evidence of the automatic preconscious processes assumed to be generating these reactions. Thornton (1984), for example, reported persuasive evidence of the preconscious influence of emotional arousal directing the person's evaluative reactions of the suffering victims. As the experimenter induced greater or lesser arousal, the participants manifested greater or lesser blame and condemnation of the victim, while retaining the overall more positive reactions to a similar versus a different victim. In addition, the evidence previously described in Chapter 2 (Aguiar et al., 2008; Callan et al. 2006, 2007, 2009, 2010; Correia, et al., 2007; Hafer, 2000a, b; Hafer and Begue, 2005) documents the nature and occurrence of the preconscious processes that shape the participants' memory and reconstruction of events to correspond with justice imperatives.

The Nature of the Interaction

As described in the previous chapter (see especially Table 6.1 and following), it is most common for people to be affected by cues concerning both who the other participants are (e.g., identity, similar to me, or different from me) and the nature of the interaction (e.g., dependently in need, cooperative, or competitive) (Lerner et al., 1976). There are reasonably well-understood cues that elicit particular rules of entitlement: everyone who is culturally conversant or fully socialized recognizes the obligations, privileges, and general rules of conduct that apply to the salient status roles in each encounter. Among the most prevalent and important are the normative as well as internalized and scripted expectations associated with competitive and cooperative encounters. Although there are recognized variations within these general contexts, for example, rules that apply to competitive encounters that are specifically contests, competitions rather than conflicts, or "fights," there are some important commonalities. For example, there is a general recognition, conscious and preconscious, that each participant is expected to pursue the desired outcome in any way that is not specifically prohibited. In this manner, the successful competitor is recognized as being entitled to the "fairly" or not illegally achieved outcomes, and need not be concerned with the fates of the other contestants or competitors.

The most familiar cues for eliciting competitive relations involve scarce and commonly desired resources. For any of various commonly recognized reasons, the desired resources cannot be shared: there must be a winner, who successfully acquires the resources, as well as losers. It is all fair: everyone is judged to have received what they deserved, if the specified rules for acquisition were not violated. At the same time, however, it may not be that simple. As discussed in the preceding text, people tend to evaluate others on the basis of their "outcomes." As a result, winners not only get the desired resource, but also preconsciously held scripts may lead to their being personally evaluated as "better" or relatively superior, and losers may be personally evaluated as "worse" or inferior.

The unrecognized preconscious scripted processes may have pernicious effects on the nature and consequences of these encounters. It has been proposed here that these scripted accompaniments are derived from repeated early experiences, for example on the playground in early childhood, and interactions with family members. Commonly, children compete with others who are categorized as one of "them," as defined by age, gender, household, neighborhood, or social category, and cooperate with others who are defined as one of "us." Unfortunately the tendency to categorize others as belonging to "us" or "them" typically elicits additional self-conceited evaluative scripts, such as "we are better," that can, again preconsciously, influence competitors' evaluations of relative deservingness and merit: because we are better we deserve more. The consequences of those preconscious assumptions can be compounded and escalate when, apparently, "they," who are vulnerable to the same preconscious processes, not only do not concur with our greater deservingness, but also "they" inexplicably act as if their merit is greater than ours.

Ingroup and Outgroup

There is evidence that the insidious effects of these processes may actually begin simply with awareness that a competitive encounter will occur. In an early experiment described in the preceding text (Lerner, Dillehay, and Sherer, 1967), the participants were either initially instructed that they and another participant would attempt to "trap or maneuver the other subject into making an error, and that the participant who trapped the other the greatest number of times would be the winner and receive a substantial amount of money," or that the "object of the task was for the participants to help each other to collect as many points as they could" (p. 482). They were also told that the subject and his or her partner would be given some money for each point the two of them were able to collect and that there was a fairly good chance that each of them would be able to earn a substantial amount of money. In this manner, both their relation to the outcomes, which were either gained by joint action or zero-sum at the cost of the other, as well as the nature of the interaction, combative or cooperative, created a clear conflictual or cooperative encounter. The participants were then given the opportunity to hear a four-minute interview with the "other person" so that they could gain an impression of him or her. (Two different interviews were employed: one contrived by a grad student and one an actual interview of another participant.)

The results confirmed the hypothesis that the nature of the encounter anticipated by the participants would lead them, without their awareness, to perceive the other subject in ways that would conform with the preconscious script: if I will compete with the other participant he or she is different from me, one of "them"; if I will cooperate with the other participant he or she is similar to me, one of "us." Despite the fact that the two interviewees (that is, the tapes of the purported interviews) created distinct impressions, when the participants anticipated competing with them, the participants rated one of them as relatively different and the other was perceived as a measurably less desirable person. In either case, anticipating a competitive encounter led participants to perceive the other as one of "them," either through distancing or through devaluing the potential partner. It easy to imagine how two participants holding mirror-image negative perceptions of one another leading to distrust would have exacerbated the devaluing and distancing during the course of a competitive encounter and thus provided self-fulfilling prophecies for their initial false impressions.

Competitive encounters, in which the participants are clearly defined as belonging to or representatives of different groups, may also elicit efforts to maintain or express the self-conceit–based relative superiority of the ingroup over the outgroup. Hastorf and Cantril (1954) demonstrated that, after observing an important football game, fans seemed to have been watching two different events depending on whether they supported the home team or the visitors. Whichever team they associated themselves with, the observers reported having seen events that portrayed the other side as having committed considerably more fouls than their own.

The evidence provided here suggests an important revision to the processes that account for this repeatedly confirmed biased recall of important encounters between us and them. As described in the preceding text, one common explanation has been simply that people need to feel superior to them, and that need extends to individuals or groups with whom the person identifies (see, e.g., Tajfel and Turner, 1986). But is it all that simple: an extension of the individual's egocentric and egoistic needs to others with whom the person sees a relevant "similarity"? The illuminating research by Babcock and colleagues (1995) described earlier revealed that it is unnecessary, and may be inappropriate, to invoke a self-interested motivation. Self-conceited biases, the perception held by most people that they are basically good or better than others, are sufficient to elicit cognitive processes of attention, interpretation, and recall that automatically lead us to represent events in a way that favors us and the people who are similar to us.

Research with children sheds additional light on the development of these biases and when they influence behavior. Shelagh Towson and colleagues (1981) observed the reactions of fifth- and sixth-grade children who were assigned the role of supervisors or "bosses" in order to evaluate and ultimately provide rewards to two other children, one of whom was a boy and one a girl. They observed the two competing children attempt to make towers by stacking shoe boxes from a common pool. During the course of the interaction the workers "inadvertently" bumped into one another and their respective towers in such a manner that after viewing the same video the outcomes of the contest could be credibly manipulated at the very end: one of the children, the winner, had two remaining towers while the other, the loser, had only one. The male and female supervisors subsequently rated the two workers on many dimensions and then assigned them each a share of the total pay earned by their combined efforts: twelve nickels.

On average, when described as an individual competition male and female supervisors assigned the winner just slightly less than two-thirds of the payment. When, however, the workers had been described as representatives of their competing boys' and girls' teams, a different pattern emerged but with the similar outcome of relative superiority. The male supervisors awarded significantly less of the payment to the winning female competitor, whereas the female supervisors greatly increased the payment to the girl who won the competition against the representative of the boys' team.

It is not clear whether these children realized they were tailoring their payments in order to maintain superiority of one of their own over one of "them," or whether they believed they were merely doing their job and assigning the pay according to what they actually believed the workers deserved. What is clear is that the combination of recognized similarity and difference to the others in a context of competing teams was sufficient to elicit important efforts to maintain the superiority of us versus them, even though the person would not be directly affected by what transpired or the outcome of the competitive encounter. The participants believed they were witnessing a real competition and assigning actual payments, but for them the meaning of the event was entirely symbolic and representational. It seems most plausible that the biased assignments of pay were the result of their preconscious self-conceited beliefs about the relatively superior performance of one of "us" versus one of "them" (see Messick and Sentis, 1983).

Lerner and Grant (1990) provided an interesting confirmation and elaboration of these findings with another set of social categories. They had third- and sixth-grade children from the majority white ethnic group respond as supervisors with the task of evaluating and assigning payments to two workers, one of whom was from the majority category while the other had features common to the

East-Indian minority group. The scenario was essentially the same as in Towson and colleagues (1981), with one of the workers ending up having produced two towers while the loser had only one. In addition, they had been either competing as members of the same or competing teams. When the winner and loser were portrayed as members of the same team the younger children tended to divide the payments equally, but when they were representatives of competing teams the winner was allocated considerably more than the loser. In either case the payments of the younger children were unaffected by the ethnicity of the winner.

The children who were on average three years older reacted differently. Generally they gave more to winners regardless of whether or not they had been portrayed as members of the same or different competing teams. But in addition, they tended to give more to the majority group member, especially when they were representing a team that looked like ingroup members competing with a representative of their teams. It is worth noting that, although other evidence revealed that the younger children held the same relatively negative stereotypes about "them" as the older children, they did not feel compelled to express those stereotypes in their allocations of pay to the workers. Something happened in those three additional years that led the older children to express those stereotypes in clear discriminatory behavior against "them," especially when they were in a competitive relationship.

Again, in trying to understand the social psychological processes elicited by ingroup-outgroup competition, it is important to remember that none of the events directly, concretely impinged upon the lives of the participants; nevertheless they were sufficiently affected by the symbolic meaning of the encounter to affect the pay they awarded to the ethnically different competitor. A sense that "they do not deserve and thus should not get as much as one of us" drove the eleven-year-old children to allocate relatively less to actively discriminate against another child with whom they had no personal contact, nor could expect to, but who merely looked like one of "them" and was competing with a team member who looked like one of "us." Their allocations of pay reflected the theme: "They are not as 'good' as we are and therefore do not deserve as much as we do."

Generating the Justice Imperatives

Guided by the commitment to the personal contract, the two primary evaluations – of the person and of the outcome – are automatically compared and processed. Any affective-evaluative discrepancies automatically elicit emotion-directed imperatives to eliminate the injustice. These evaluative discrepancies, however, are merged with the imperatives elicited by the perception of who the other is: Greater and lesser discrepancies between the target's "outcome" and the scripted outcomes merited by the perception of the target as one of mine, similar, or different. Presumably, the larger the discrepancies, the stronger the emotion and resultant imperative will be. How the preconsciously elicited imperatives are expressed may initially be influenced by the person's habitual modes of responding. The evidence suggests that the imperative will generate the person's reaction if or until the person's focus of attention is shifted and more consciously controlled processes occur.

Although the documentation of the nature of the preconscious process provides an excellent beginning, actually predicting the manner in which justice imperatives influence people's behavior is complicated by the fact that, as described in the previous chapter, more than one rule of deservingness may be operative in each encounter. The participants' initial goals may direct their attention and thus influence the cues they are most likely to attend to and process, but, with the availability of adequate cognitive resources, highly familiar and accessible cues will provide additional justice imperatives. As described earlier, some theorists have proposed that when more than one rule of deservingness is available, people will adopt and try to persuade other participants to accept the rules that allow them to maximize their own share of desired resources (see, e.g., Walster et al., 1978). A typical example of this occurs when research participants who are given the opportunity to allocate jointly earned outcomes ignore relative contribution in favor of more equal shares when they have contributed less but allocate more to themselves when they are the major contributor (see Messick and Sentis, 1983). There is additional available evidence, however, that this will only occur under limited predictable circumstances, for example, explicitly economic or competitive encounters in which participants recognize that they and the others are expected to maximize their own outcomes within the rules of the "game" (see Konow, 2005) or when interacting with a member of an outgroup.

The available evidence indicates that, in most circumstances, all the salient cues will have an effect, usually resulting in some form of compromise or blended response. As the encounter continues, if the person has sufficient time and cognitive capacity, additional incentives and motives may influence how the person responds through thoughtfully constructed social judgments and decisions. Conceivably, rather than the influence of preconscious beliefs of self-conceit, it is under these circumstances, at Time 2, that the normatively supported motivation to maximize one's profit may shape and at times consciously dominate the influence of justice imperatives. That is, the competitors may try to use rules of justice to maximize their preferred outcomes.

TIME 2: THOUGHTFUL AND CONTROLLED RESPONSES

If the expression of the justice imperative is impeded, or when the initial imperative is relatively weak so that competing attractive opportunities become salient, the person's remaining available cognitive resources will become involved in consciously arriving at a decision concerning how to react. Unlike the person's initial preconscious reactions, the controlled processing of information and decision will be guided and ultimately constrained by salient societal norms that define conventionally accepted thought processes, socially desired goals, and rules of conduct (see Figure 7.2). The evidence suggests that the most prevalent norms can be subsumed under the general category of "enlightened self-interest" (Bazerman et al., 1995; Miller, 1975, 1977, 1999); that is, a behavioral choice that encompasses self-interest as constrained by social norms, including norms about justice, in order to avoid self- and social sanctions. To arrive at a decision, the preconscious input and conscious assessment of the contextual cues – the opportunities and constraints – will be processed according to familiar norms that can easily be paraphrased as, "I would like to be a nice person and meet my obligations, but first and foremost I must take care of myself and those who depend upon me," and to do that I will use the conventional rules of thought and decision making to "make the most of the opportunities to do what is best for me, us."

There are reasons to propose that, if the initial emotion-directed imperative is sufficiently strong and compelling, the person may have neither the cognitive resources nor incentive to attend to or process interrupting cues. Observers' intuitively experienced imperative will direct their reactions with little or no concern for the personal costs and benefits, as in the top line of Figure 7.2 (Babcock et al., 1995; Meindl and Lerner, 1983). When the experienced initial imperative leaves sufficient cognitive resources available and the interrupting cues are sufficiently vivid to make alternative incentives salient, then the initial imperatives will persist but be incorporated into the norm-constrained and legitimized subsequent response (Babcock et al. 1995; Goldberg et al., 1999; Holmes et al., 2002; J. Lerner et al., 1998; Meindl and Lerner, 1983; Simmons and Lerner, 1968). Justice will be pursued in ways that do not violate societal norms concerning the appropriate way to behave.

Weaker initial imperatives may be ignored or set aside when confronted with more attractive vivid alternatives during the conscious decision making (Bazerman et al., 1995; J. Lerner et al., 1998). When the implicit threats to the commitments to deservingness and justice are discernibly present but are relatively trivial, the subsequent norm-directed decisions will reflect the most beneficial or least costly way to respond, that is, "rationally self-interested" as defined by the relevant social norms. This is typically the case when research participants are asked to respond in simulations and role-playing contexts. In these contexts, it is possible to elicit judgments of fairness and deservingness but with little if any emotional involvement. Other incentives, including the desire to maintain a favorable public image, can easily lead the participants to replace or ignore these considerations of deservingness and justice with those of rational self-interest (Bazerman et al., 1995; Miller, 1999).

Basically, at Time 2 people employ culturally familiar concepts and rules of inference in order to arrive at a meaningful understanding of what is occurring and the most sensible (profitable) and appropriate way to respond. During the process they can be expected to adopt conventionally accepted rules of inference for assigning causality, responsibility, and blaming as well as normative rules of conduct (Weiner, 1993). Generally speaking, in evaluating what has occurred and deciding how to react they employ and reflect their beliefs that people are supposed to be good and decent while meeting their obligations to themselves and others and promoting their own welfare – that is, rationally pursuing what they want and attempting to meet their desires. Failure to meet those obligations or violations of rules of decency and fairness automatically incurs (preconscious script-based or normative) negative evaluations, bad feelings, and the desire for rectification. Otherwise, people are expected to be rational actors in pursuit of generally valued outcomes. It is commonly expected that those outcomes, desired and undesirable, should be distributed by parents, employers, fate, laws of nature, or god, according to entitlements with special praise for those who demonstrate noble, altruistic motives above and beyond the call of duty (Dols et al., 2010).

At Time 2, people consciously achieve an evaluation of what has happened or may happen and decide who has done what to whom and, through some conventional form of cost-benefit analysis, calculate how to best pursue their own self-interest while not violating their obligations. All of this takes time and sufficient incentives to engage people's attention and concerns.

EVIDENCE FROM FIELD EXPERIMENTS DISENTANGLING NORMS, JUSTICE, AND SELF-INTEREST

Several previously discussed experiments provide direct comparisons of participants' immediate intuitive responses and their more thoughtfully generated reactions to the same events. Bazerman et al. (1995), for example, reported several experiments in which participants' immediate evaluations indicated clear preferences for fair rather than more profitable but less fair outcomes. Those preferences were reversed, however, among similar participants who were induced to engage in more thoughtful decision making. Presented with the same pairs of alternatives, they revealed the more normatively appropriate preference for increased profit over the desire for fairness (Miller, 1999).

Miller (1975, 1977) reported even more dramatic differences between the relatively automatic, "intuitive" justice-seeking reactions and more thoughtfully generated profit-oriented reactions to the same event. Those participants who were asked to imagine how they would respond to an opportunity to help a particular family described as being in desperate need predicted that they and most people would ignore the family's suffering if offering financial aid would interfere with normatively justified efforts to increase their own profits. Similar participants, however, when confronted with the actual opportunity to help that same family, immediately offered the needed assistance even at considerable personal cost to themselves when offering that help did not interfere with the participants' own deserved pay. As expected, the compelling recognition of the family's undeserved suffering and the absence of any audience waiting to judge their reactions (J. Lerner et al., 1998) allowed the participants to act upon their intuitively generated emotions rather than leading them to dispassionately search for and then report what they believed was the normatively appropriate way to act as employees, by keeping all of their pay for themselves.

Simons and Piliavin (1972) employed salient conventional norms to shape the expression of the justice imperatives when observers were unable to offer aid to an innocent victim. When the experimenter repeatedly emphasized to the participants that they were to keep in mind victims of natural disasters, they responded with compassion as they watched another participant being given painful electric shocks, supposedly as part of an experiment in human learning. The salient norms generated by the image of innocent victims of natural disasters determined that compassion was the appropriate reaction to the victim. Without that prior and continued reminder of the "appropriate" way to view the victim's suffering, however, other participants who observed the same innocent victim, rather than reacting with compassion, found ways to derogate her character, presumably as an automatic preconsciously generated reaction to minimize the injustice implicit in the victim's suffering (see Hafer, 2000a, b; Lerner, 1971).

THE NEED FOR REALISM IN RESEARCH

Documenting the ways in which norms can influence people's expression of preconsciously generated imperatives at Time 2 provides an important theoretical contribution; in addition, however, it offers a way of understanding how investigators can mistakenly attribute their participants' behavior to self-interested motives. The probability of discovering self-interest in people's thoughtfully generated reactions, that is, reactions that have been constructed under the guidance of norms, is enhanced by the prevalence of norms of justified and enlightened self-interest in most Western societies. Following thoughtful deliberations, people's subsequent reactions will typically reveal some form of self-interest, albeit more or less justified and enlightened. Because of the prevalence of those norms, investigators, like most people, naturally assume that their participants' actions and the outcomes experienced by the participants directly reveal their intentions and thus motives: if the person chose to compete and then keeps the lion's share of the outcomes, that must be evidence of the profit motive.

But often there are good, empirically backed reasons to recognize that other motives might have been generating the competitive behavior that was normatively appropriate in that situation. Rather than trying to maximize their profits, for example, the competing participants may simply have wanted to get their fair share. Evidence for this hypothesis appeared in an experiment with young children, described earlier (Lerner, 1974): referring to participants as team members or partners elicited voluntary equal sharing of jointly earned outcomes, but designating them as co-workers elicited what could be described as appropriate efforts to maximize one's individual outcomes. The label of either co-worker or team member was sufficient, even with young children, to elicit well-recognized sets of context-specific norms that designated either competitive or cooperative behavior as the appropriate way for the children to act. In either case, rather than trying to maximize their profits, the children were following the rules that defined what was fair and appropriate in each context.

Possibly the most compelling demonstration of inferring profit motivation from participants' normatively appropriate behavior resulted from the coming together of a series of unanticipated events in what had started out as a highly planned set of experiments. The important findings eventually emerged out of the need to adapt to a series of unanticipated events, and then make sense out of initially unanticipated and puzzling results with a second experiment. Fortunately, after seeing the results of the second experiment it all seemed to fall into place and generate a meaningful picture composed of the interactions among gender, norms, profit maximization, cooperation, and fairness.

Before describing the two experiments and their findings in considerable detail, it is worth considering why an investigator would go through the enormous costs and efforts of constructing and conducting field experiments in the first place. The research was designed to examine what influences people's reactions when the most rational legitimate way to maximize their own outcomes requires that they incur the risk of exploiting their co-workers. Why not design a study that presents participants with various vignettes and then ask them which they prefer, or to imagine how they would respond? Or rather than imagining how they would react, conduct experiments in which participants role-play their parts in a simulation of a real event with minimal, essentially symbolic outcomes? Those kinds of research can be designed and conducted with relatively little cost in time and effort.

The commitment to conduct the experiments reported here happened after a concerted but ultimately demoralizing preparatory immersion in the research literature that was available in our most prestigious journals. That depressing effort revealed that virtually all of the prior research reported in these prestigious journals depended upon participants recalling, pretending, imagining, and then more or less self-consciously constructing a response to an explicit simulation of an encounter or a minimal experiment involving trivial outcomes. Those were and continue to be the familiar accepted ways to discover social psychological "truths."

As a consequence, however, the published findings are extremely vulnerable to systematic errors. This is especially the case when the investigators persuade themselves and their reviewers that their participants' memories and recall required to generate a response are completely valid and relevant, and their participants' verbal reports and role-playing in simulations exactly mimics the motives that would appear when they spontaneously, or at least unselfconsciously, react to "real" events. The investigators employed familiar, manageable procedures, diligently carried out, with the participants' responses carefully analyzed with most sophisticated statistical methods available, and presented the results using the forms approved by the American Psychological Association, but with little hope of producing meaningful valid inferences.

That intense search of the literature eventually brought to mind the familiar anecdote of the inebriated man on his hands and knees apparently searching around for something on the ground. When asked about what he is looking for so late at night he says that he was trying to find a valuable watch he had dropped. When asked where he lost it, however, he points to a far distant area. In response to the obvious next question of why he is looking here rather than there, he points out the equally obvious fact that the lamppost is here and there is no light over there.

Imagine hordes of investigators groping around under the lamppost. Confounding the inevitable failure to find any watches, however, whatever they turned up employing the familiar available methods was offered and accepted as discoveries worthy of publication in the major journals. In all probability, this is a grossly distorted, cynical view of the state of the research literature, but it captures the thoughts that led to the belief in the absolute necessity to do research that did not rely upon explicit role-playing, simulations, or self-reports to generate the data that would inform the theoretically relevant inferences.

The needed research would attempt to avoid confusing the influence of psychological motives with participants' reactions based upon their conscious representations of the salient normative expectations. To do that, it might employ experiments in which the participants would be actively engaged in dealing with problems and possibilities associated with normally appearing events in their lives, both the critical and the mundane. Presumably, if the participants were unaware that they were in an experiment they would have no awareness of or need to please the experimenters hovering over them in order to examine and evaluate their behavior. Nor would they be answerable to any other person or audience that was not a natural part of the encounter. Under those conditions, absent the incentives for impression management and unnatural reflective examination and normative shaping of their reactions, hopefully, the participants' behaviors would more clearly reveal their motives and concerns, or what they intended to do and why.

If successfully constructed and carried out, confidence in the validity of important inferences would not require misplaced faith that participants invariably can and will describe their true motives and intentions, but rather, emerge out of the theoretically pertinent behavioral differences that appear among the various experimental conditions. If done correctly those observed differences should "speak for themselves," although, as will be seen in the following text, on occasion they may be misheard and require additional observations to be correctly understood, but at least they offer the opportunity and possibility of arriving at valid inferences.

Is it possible to create that kind of experimental situation and collect revealing data? With that introduction, the situations and procedures will need to be described in sufficient detail to allow readers to arrive at their own judgments.

AN ATTEMPT AT EXPERIMENTAL REALISM

The first experiment examined some preliminary hypotheses concerning when employees in a real work setting would elect to devote their productive efforts to maximizing their own pay if, in doing so, they would also unfairly profit from the productivity of other employees, that is, engage in "free-riding," and when, conversely, they would choose to contribute their efforts for an equal share of the pay generated by a common pool and risk that those efforts would be exploited by the other employees who, instead of contributing to the common pool, were working solely on their own behalf.

University students were recruited by using posters and announcements for part-time employment in a survey research agency. Initially they were given a screening interview, and if accepted they were paid a reasonable wage while they received several hours of training in how to do telephone interviews and related tasks such as making telephone contacts, coding of interviews, and so forth. Once trained, they were then notified of the place and time of their first work session.

When they arrived at the survey research center, they were greeted individually by one of their trainers and taken to a room with all the trappings and accoutrements appropriate for part-time employees doing telephone interviews and coding completed interviews for a survey research center. Along with indicating that three other employees were already in their rooms working that evening, their supervisor instructed the employee-participants concerning the jobs to be done, work procedures, and pay schedules.

To create the conflict between profit maximizing and cooperating, the supervisor explained that during the first part of the work session, they were to do three interviews or contact ten prospective respondents, for which they would be paid a flat rate of $6.00. Then, pointing to the two stacks of material on the desk (as well as telephone, telephone books, pads, pencils, etc.), the supervisor further explained that for the balance of the time, there were two jobs of equal importance and urgency that needed to be done that evening. One involved coding previously completed interviews for Company A, and the other required them to contact prospective respondents for interviews to be done later for Company Z. (The actual names of the fictitious companies were employed as well as the appropriately designated stationery.) She also described the pay schedules for each of the jobs. For making appointments for interviews, client Z paid twenty-five cents for each potential respondent successfully contacted. For the coding of interviews, client A paid thirty cents for coding each interview. After answering questions, the supervisor concluded the instructions by emphasizing that the two projects were of equal priority so the employees could devote their efforts to either or both of the jobs and divide their time as they wished.

In order to prevent the employees from attempting to resolve their conflicts by talking with each other, they were informed that because there would be telephone call-backs they could not leave their work room unattended. If they wished to go to the bathroom, for example, they should first call the supervisor to temporarily fill in for them. To convince the employees that no one, not even their supervisor, would know how they had devoted their productive efforts they were told that once the work period was over they were to put their completed work in the large envelope that was preaddressed to each of the companies, along with a self-addressed envelope with which each company could then mail their pay to them for that evening's work. No one would know what they did with their time.

The employees knew that after the initial interviews they could divide their time as they wished between the two jobs available to them, and they would be paid for all the work they did on one of them (Individual Pay company). Regardless of how they divided their work efforts, they would receive a check from the Group Share Pay company for one-fourth of the total pay earned by the combined productivity of all four of the workers that evening.

In this manner, it was clear that the rational strategy to insure the most pay for themselves and to avoid being taken advantage of by the others would be for the employees to devote the bulk of their time to the Individual Pay job. An obvious disadvantage of adhering to that strategy would come from the realization that if they devoted less time to the Group Share Pay job than the three other employees, they would be getting paid for the additional work done by the others.

For control purposes, the pay schedules were alternated between the jobs of coding and telephone interviewing. For approximately half the participants the coding job was the Individual Pay task and interviewing the Group Share Pay task; for the other half this was reversed.

Under these circumstances, would they be willing to risk profiting from the efforts of the other workers in order to maximize their own pay? Greater relative productivity at the job for which they were being paid for their individual productivity, while still receiving a share of the group productivity at the other job, indicates a greater willingness to exploit their co-workers' efforts as they pursued their own individual profit. The greater the relative efforts at the job for which they were to be paid an equal share of the group's productivity, the stronger the evidence for a greater desire to be cooperative while accepting the risk of being exploited by any of the others who pursued the maximal individual profit strategy.

The first experiment examined the effects of accountability on the employees' responses. Would they be more willing to voluntarily risk the potential costs of the cooperative strategy and less likely to pursue the rational profit-maximizing strategy with the potential of exploiting their co-workers if they were aware that they and their co-workers would each know how they had behaved after the fact, than if they were convinced no one, neither their supervisor nor the other employees, would know how they reacted? Absent the possibility of social sanctions either upon themselves or the others would they elect to pursue the more profitable, potentially exploitative, strategy rather than the more cooperative strategy?

To assess the effects of accountability, half of the employees were led to believe that at the end of the work period, all the employees would get together with the supervisor to turn in their completed work and fill out their pay forms. Participants thus had reason to believe that their task choices and level of productivity would be known to their supervisor and co-workers. For the other half, as described in the preceding text, the employees' work was mailed directly to the company, and their pay was sent directly to them in the self-addressed envelope. Their decisions as to how to allocate their efforts remained unknown to the others.

A second issue focused on gender differences in the resolution of this conflict: would women employees act differently than men? The experiment-based literature suggests that women might be more inclined to be cooperative rather than competitive (e.g., Major, Blysma, and Cozzarelli, 1989), although it is not clear that this has been documented in real employment settings. Tangentially, recent evidence based upon incidence of actual behaviors in real-world settings contradicted the generalization of gender differences derived from the experiment-based literature. For example, observational studies of what actually occurred in the real world revealed that women in many important contexts were much more inclined to engage in heroic personally risky behaviors than were men (Becker and Eagly, 2004).

Although there were no specific hypotheses concerning their interaction, both gender and group compositions were built into the experimental design. When the employees arrived for their first night's work, they were led to believe that the other three employees that evening were either the same gender as they or represented an equal mix of men and women (2 men and 2 women). What then were the results?

After considerable time, effort, and funds were devoted to pretesting, the procedure worked very nicely, in the sense of generating a compelling experience with literally no suspicion that they were participating in an experiment. Nevertheless, there were important surprises.

Surprise 1: Avoiding Interviewing

Pretesting led to the selection of pay schedules that had a roughly equivalent promise of pay earnings for the group and individual tasks. However, the pretesting had not anticipated that many of the employees would view the interviewing task as distinctly onerous, especially in comparison with the coding task.

Regardless of whether the pay was based on individual productivity or Group Share basis, 64 percent of the men and 62 percent of the women in the interviews/Group Share condition, and 60 percent of the women and 66 percent of the men in interviews/Individual Pay did no interviewing or telephone calls.

An assessment of the number of complete "freeloaders," that is, employees who did no work on the task for which they would receive a share of the total productivity (Group Share Pay), confirmed the participants' relative avoidance of interviewing and preference for doing coding. When coding was the Group Share task only 9.6 percent coded no interviews. When interviewing was the Group Share task 62 percent did no interviews, a statistically significant difference.

The participants' avoidance of telephone interviewing, even when there was no obvious pay advantage for doing the coding, created problems with using the number of interviews or telephone calls in the data analyses. As a consequence, all the analyses are based upon a comparison of the participants' performance on the preferred task: the number of interviews coded.

An analysis of variance on the amount of coding completed in the gender-homogeneous groups revealed two significant main effects (see Figure 7.3). The employees did more coding when they were paid for the number of interviews they each coded (Individual Pay $M = 18.05$) than when they were to be paid an equal share earned by the number of interviews coded by all four of them (Group Share Pay $M = 13.58$).

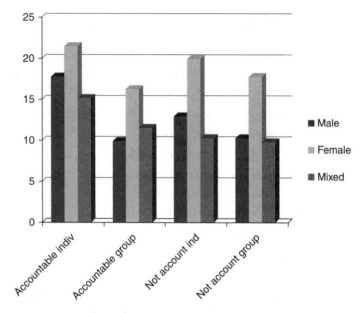

FIGURE 7.3. Number of Interviews Coded by Gender, Accountability, and Pay Condition

Contrary to expectations, the anticipation of being accountable to the other employees for their work had no appreciable effect on the employees' coding behavior: accountable $M = 16.37$, nonaccountable $M = 15.22$. None of the interactions approached significance; that is, the effect of payment mode was the same regardless of gender or level of accountability.

Surprises 2 and 3: Unexpected Gender Effects

Overall, the female employees were more productive, that is, they coded more interviews than their male counterparts: women $M = 18.88$, men $M = 12.73$. Even more intriguing was the finding that the women in the gender-mixed conditions were less productive ($M = 11.81$) than those in the all-women conditions ($M = 18.77$). The productivity of the men did not vary significantly as a function of gender composition of their work groups (gender mixed $M = 11.05$, all men $M = 12.72$). Again there were no significant interactions between gender and mode of payment (Group Share or Individual Pay).

Overall, the employees coded significantly fewer interviews when they were being paid an equal share of the pay generated by all the interviews coded by them and their co-workers than when they were paid for each interview they coded. It appears that the participants in this experiment, men and women, were not significantly deterred from trying to maximize their own pay by the possibility that in so doing they would be receiving money for work that the other employees had done. That is, they appeared to be more willing to "free ride" and exploit than to cooperate with their co-workers and risk being exploited. That is entirely consistent with the common understanding that people work in order to earn money, and they will primarily try to get the best financial deal for themselves.

The fact that the employees' behavior was not appreciably affected by their awareness that the other employees would know what they did is entirely consistent with the normative acceptability of this self-interested strategy (Bazerman et al., 1995; Miller, 1999). Apparently, these employees were not particularly ashamed of their rationally self-interested behavior or afraid of the possible sanctions from the other employees for being uncooperative or overly selfish.

The behavior of the women employees provided surprising and irresistibly intriguing results. No clear explanation came readily to mind for why women, with other women as co-workers, were more productive than men with male co-workers.

The fact that when the women believed their co-workers consisted of one other woman and two men, their productivity was significantly less than when they were working in groups of only women, and much closer to the men's level of productivity, was just as surprising as the women's greater overall productivity. What could that mean about the dynamics generated in this situation?

There is every reason to believe the women did not anticipate meeting their co-workers in the nonaccountable conditions, and so there was no way their co-workers could detect how they devoted their efforts. Nevertheless, their behavior in the gender-heterogeneous conditions, in which they expected to meet their co-workers, was virtually the same as in those conditions when they believed they would not meet the others: the average number of interviews coded in the accountable condition was 11.50, and in the nonaccountable condition it was 12.12. Apparently, whatever incentives led the women to be more productive than the men in the gender-homogeneous conditions were no longer effective when they were in gender-heterogeneous groups. The men's behavior did not seem to be affected by the presence of women among their co-workers. Obviously, additional research was needed to shed light on these issues.

The more theoretically relevant questions concern why the vast majority of these employees, men and women, were apparently willing to free ride on their co-workers' efforts, and why that free riding was not reduced by the anticipation of meeting those whose efforts they were possibly exploiting? One possible answer is that it was normatively appropriate for them, as employees, to try to maximize their own outcomes, even if that meant exploiting co-workers (Miller, 1999).

A second possible, not entirely unrelated, answer may stem from the dynamics created by presenting the participant-employees with two jobs given that one, coding, was clearly preferable to the other, interviewing. If it was readily obvious to the participants that doing the telephone interviews was a rather onerous and clearly less desirable task than doing the coding, this may have allowed them to be reasonably certain their co-workers would also much prefer coding. As a result, when coding was the Individual Pay job and interviewing would be paid on a share of the total group productivity, they could, with relatively clear conscience, avoid the Group Share task – interviewing – and concentrate their efforts on the coding job. As the evidence indicated, they would have been right in anticipating that their co-workers would be doing essentially the same thing: thus, avoiding doing interviews could be an attempt to avoid exploitation, rather than representing free riding. By coding, when it was the job that paid them each for their own productivity, the employees could avoid being exploited themselves with little expectation that they might be exploiting co-workers who were spending their time doing the Group Share paid interviews. When the clearly preferred coding was the Group Share Pay task, then it was somewhat less attractive because they were assured of only one-fourth of the pay based upon their own productivity. Although they were reasonably confident that their co-workers would also be working at the coding job, there was no assurance of how productive they would be, in comparison to themselves. As a consequence, the incentive to produce may have been somewhat (measurably but not remarkably) reduced.

If this analysis is correct then the participants in this experiment were not confronted with the intended conflict between pursuing the most rationally self-interested strategy and the possibility of their exploiting some of their co-workers. It is quite possible that being reasonably confident that their co-workers would greatly prefer to do coding, whether it was the individual or Group Share task, virtually precluded their concerns about free riding. Another experiment (or more) was needed.

In order to assess the extent to which employees will risk lessening their own pay to reduce the risk of exploiting co-workers, it was necessary to modify the original situation so that the employees would be less confident of how their co-workers were going to behave. One way of doing that would be to have the two jobs, the Group Share Pay and the Individual Pay, be more equal in attractiveness. Hopefully, that would increase the participants' belief that the more profitable strategy of devoting their efforts to the Individual Pay task could lead to exploiting the other workers' efforts at the Group Share task.

After additional pretesting, the alternative selected reduced the unpleasant features of the interviewing job by paying for each telephone call and appointment and by increasing the pay for completed interviews. If successful, the participants would believe they and the other workers were confronted with having to divide their time between two equally attractive jobs. As a result, they would be less certain of how the other workers would react. Would that lead the employees to be less willing to free ride and, in the process, expose themselves to being exploited by working on the Group Share payment task? Or would it not matter at all?

As in the previous experiment, the employees believed that they would be working with three others either of the same gender, so that groups were all male or all female, or mixed, so that groups were comprised of two men and two women.

Even without a clear explanation for the gender differences that appeared in the first experiment, the most intriguing question focuses on whether or not gender differences will appear when the employees are deciding between two relatively equally attractive jobs.

Absent any cogent theory, the safest prediction based upon generalizing from the previous findings was that there would be differences between the way men and women behave when working with others of the same gender and, when working in gender-mixed groups, the male pattern will prevail. Even with no communication before, during, or after anticipated, would the women knowing that there are male co-workers in other rooms, once again, behave more like the men than when their co-workers are all women?

Forty-four employees, approximately equal numbers of men and women, were recruited, hired, and trained in the same manner as in the previous experiment. When they appeared for their initial session of survey research they were given the same instructions, so that each believed there were three other workers that evening, whom they would not meet. For half of them the coding job was the Individual Pay task, and interviewing was paid on the basis of each worker receiving an equal share of the group's total productivity. This pay schedule was reversed for the other employee-participants.

In this experiment the pay for the interviewing job was modified to ten cents for each telephone number called and fifty cents for each appointment made. The payment for coding an interview, thirty cents, remained the same as in the previous experiment. To assess the effects of the gender composition of the work groups, approximately two-thirds of the employees believed that their co-workers were the same gender as they, while fifteen believed that they were working in a group composed of equal numbers of men and women (2 men, 2 women).

All of the participants believed they would send their completed work directly to the companies and would not meet with their co-workers at the end of the session. In this manner they all believed they were unaccountable to the other employees and their supervisors (experimenters) for their actions.

Confirming the increased attraction of interviewing as a result of the increased and altered pay schedule, 38 percent of the participant-employees in this experiment did no interviewing and made no telephone calls, compared to the 63 percent who made no calls in the previous experiment.

A statistical analysis was performed on the number of interviews coded during the work period in the gender-homogeneous conditions. Although the women tended to do more coding than the men, there was no significant difference overall. Unlike the previous experiment there was a significant interaction between gender and pay schedule. See Figure 7.4.

The male employees coded more interviews when they were each paid for what they had completed ($M = 14.4$) than when their pay would be a one-fourth share of what was earned by the number of interviews coded by them and their three co-workers ($M = 6.7$). The female employees did more coding when coding was the Group Share Pay job ($M = 16.7$) than when it was the Individual Pay job ($M = 11.1$).

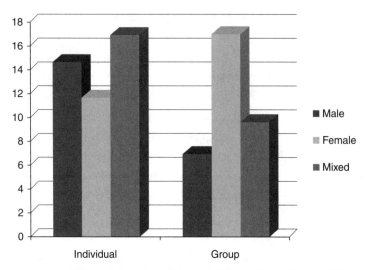

FIGURE 7.4. Effect of Pay Schedule and Work Group Composition on Number of Coded Interviews

This gender difference appears in the comparison of the number of male and female free riders, that is, those who did no work at the Group Share job. According to this definition, slightly more than half the men, 53.8 percent, and 12.5 percent of the women appeared willing to accept the benefits of free riding on the efforts of their co-workers.

As in the previous experiment, the pattern of productivity in the mixed-gender conditions resembled what occurred in the all-male conditions: more coding was done when it was the Individual Pay task ($M = 16.6$) than when it was the Group Share Pay job ($M = 9.4$). An interesting result appears if one compares the behavior of the women in the mixed-gender conditions with those in the all-women conditions. Although the women in the all-women conditions did more coding when it was the Group Share Pay ($M = 16.70$) rather than when they were paid for their individual productivity ($M = 11.10$), the opposite pattern appeared among the women in the gender-heterogeneous conditions. They did considerably more coding when it was the Individual Pay ($M = 26.23$) than when it was the Group Share Pay job ($M = 11.25$). The men's behavior did not reliably differ between the gender-homogeneous and -heterogeneous conditions.

An examination of the actual amount of pay earned by these employees provides an interesting addition to the meaning of these gender differences. Overall, the women and men did not greatly differ in the average amount earned for their evening's work. In addition to their $6.00 base pay, the women's additional earnings, on average, were $8.78, while the men earned an additional average of $6.66. They differed greatly, however, in the proportion of their pay earned from the Group Share Pay job, and the Individual Pay job. The women earned 87.5 percent of their pay from their equal share of what they and their co-workers had produced at the Group Share job. The men's share of their group's productivity provided only 15.4 percent of their total pay. Apparently, increasing the pay for interviewing and making telephone calls had the intended effect of equalizing the attractiveness of the two jobs available to the employees. There were considerably fewer men and women who avoided doing the interviews, than in the previous experiment. As a result, it is reasonable to assume that the employees were considerably less confident that the other employees in their group would avoid doing interviews and concentrate their efforts on coding. Once the employees were less certain of the other employees' task preferences then clear gender differences appeared in their responses to the conflict between maximizing their own pay and free riding on the other employees' efforts.

The women who had only other women as co-workers were remarkably less willing to maximize their profits by focusing their efforts on the Individual Pay job and exploiting their co-workers. They devoted relatively more effort to the Group Share task than to the job that paid them individually for their own productivity. The men put more effort into coding when it was the Individual Pay job than when it was the Group Share alternative. In general, considering both jobs available to them, the men were much more likely to avoid the Group Share Pay job, whether it was doing interviewing or coding.

Absent any other information, that was the most rational way to maximize their pay.

The intriguing question is what motivated the women, without any prior discussions with the other women workers, to decide to devote more time to the Group Share task? That decision appeared to be relatively consensual among the women in the gender-homogeneous groups, because the cooperating women still ended up earning, on average, slightly more pay than the men in all-male groups who appeared to take the most profitable path of working entirely for themselves and free riding on the efforts of the other men. The women collectively gave up the safest, most rational, profit-making strategy and instead allowed themselves to be vulnerable to exploitation by the other women in their group. They did that absent any opportunity to communicate, before, during, or after, with the other women. What could have motivated them?

A related question is why the women in the mixed-gender groups acted differently than those in the all-women groups. Rather than cooperating by working on the Group Share Pay job as the participants did in the all-women groups, these women devoted most of their efforts to working for themselves on the Individual Pay job. Again, there were no discussions among the group members either prior to or during the work period and none anticipated for the end. Again the men did not modify their behavior as a function of the gender composition of their group. They consistently chose to pursue the most personally profitable strategy, and, conceivably, they expected the others in their group to do the same. For the most part, they did.

At this point, it is important to recognize that if the employees in this experiment did not expect to meet their co-workers, and they made no efforts to communicate with them while working, whatever influenced their working behavior was self-generated: it went on in their own heads. If that is the case, then what led the women, in the second experiment, to systematically vary their behavior as a function of the gender composition of their co-workers?

It is possible that the women, knowing and generalizing from their own preferences and commonly recognized gender norms correctly anticipated how the other women would react. But even having that knowledge is not sufficient to explain why they, under the cloak of anonymity, would devote most of their own efforts to working at the Group Share task. They could have taken advantage of the opportunity to maximize their own pay by only working at the Individual Pay job. The women's behavior in the first experiment clearly indicated that they certainly wanted to earn money as much or more than the men. But, apparently, the women preferred to risk cooperating with rather than exploiting one another and they "knew" the other women had the same preference. Because the greatest majority acted in this way, rather than being exploited they all earned as much or more than the men who resisted working at the Group Share task. That outcome clearly revealed two things going on in the hearts and minds of the women: the recognition of how other women would react in this situation and the desire to cooperate and not exploit one another for personal profit.

To achieve a similar income, and prevent being exploited by their co-workers, the men had to avoid working at the Group Share task. Somehow, they must have known and/or did not care how the other employees would act. The hypothesis that they knew that the other employees would work primarily for themselves and free ride if possible seems plausible. For example, in the initial experiment, the men's behavior was unaffected when they were informed that all the others would know how they had spent their time and efforts at the end of the work period. Meanwhile, the women in mixed-gender groups also wisely adopted the self-interested strategy when working with men and avoided the Group Share Pay task. Conceivably, the women's behavior was a realistic defense against the valid expectation that the two men in their group would have free ridden on the women's efforts at cooperative profit sharing. The women must have known at some level of consciousness how the men as well as the women would react in this situation.

The conjecture that the women had such information available to them about men's and women's probable behavior is supported by research describing the culturally available stereotypes and normative expectations concerning men and women (Broverman et al., 1972; Eagly, 1987; Eisenberg and Lennon, 1983; Kidder, Belletrie, and Cohn, 1977): In this society, everyone "knows" that men are expected to be self-assertive and competitive, while women are considered to be more friendly and unselfish than men. Not surprisingly, these normative expectations influence people's decisions and shape their behavior.

But what do these findings have to do with the major issues addressed here? Although not expected, the gender differences in norms relevant to work and interpersonal relations provided an excellent opportunity to assess the importance of normative expectations in how people resolve the conflict between adopting a self-maximizing strategy with the risk of exploiting others and accepting the risk of being exploited in order to cooperate with them.

The findings provided a rather clear image: men did not adopt a cooperative strategy, whether or not they were accountable to others for their self-maximizing behavior. Men were not ashamed of their self-interested strategy, probably because they correctly assumed that the other men would be doing the same thing. Consistent with our theory of the justice motive, the men intuitively accepted being in a Nonunit relation with the other workers in which it seemed "right" to try to maximize one's own profits (See Lerner, 1975; Lerner et al., 1976). In addition, adopting the self-protecting and pay-maximizing strategy is the normatively acceptable way for men to act in the workplace. The women who happened to be included with men in a work group seemed to adapt their behavior to those male norms. Perhaps these women recognized that any cooperative efforts when working with men would have led to their being exploited by the men in their group.

This hypothesis was supported by how they behaved when working in all-women groups. When they believed they were working with only other women they tended to adopt a cooperative rather than a self-maximizing strategy, suggesting their clear preference for a "unit relation" with the other women (Lerner et al., 1976). The influence of a recognized normative expectation is attested to by the fact that the women employees successfully adopted a cooperative strategy without prior discussion, and reverted to a self-maximizing strategy when they were with men and women, again without any discussion. The fact that these distinct behavior patterns appeared in a context in which there was no opportunity for the employees to communicate with each other made it vividly apparent that they were all responding to both their intuitive references and awareness of relevant normative expectations for men and women.

To be sure, some postexperimental interviews or participant ratings might have helped to clarify what was going on in the participant's heads during the work session, but that would have entailed some additional risks. One is the risk of believing that the participants would be able to give valid accounts of what occurred, or accurately recalling their thoughts and feelings; were aware of what motivated their behavior; and would be willing to report their motives. A second is that after the first session there would be an entirely unacceptable risk of contaminating the behavior of subsequent "informed" participants, in spite of their well-meaning promises not to discuss what they had learned with others.

Although the difficulty of discerning the participants' motives is continually present, it is not insurmountable. For example, the behavior of the employees in the first experiment could easily have been mistakenly interpreted as *prima facie* clear evidence of self-interest: free riding. In light of the findings of the second experiment, which highlighted the presence and influence of normative expectations, it is much more plausible to infer that the male and the female employees in these experiments were acting in ways that felt like the "right," justified way to act and that they believed were normatively appropriate in that context. Absent the risk of exploiting the other employees, the participants in the first experiment simply went about their job with the completely legitimate intention of earning as much as possible without exploiting the other workers because they would be doing the same. At the same time we were able to discover that the women were more ambitious than the men, and, along with not allowing themselves to be exploited by men acting on their agendas, they were very willing to follow their justice imperatives and cooperate with other women whom they believed would not exploit their good intentions.

Mainly, the behavior of the young men and women in this "natural" work environment revealed little evidence of egoistic or self-serving motivation; although, it would have been remarkably easy, or "normative" (Miller, 1999), to have interpreted the findings of the first study as evidence that employees were willing to exploit others for their own benefit. The pattern of results from both experiments indicated that although not entirely absent from the employees' motives, their self-interest was shaped and modified by the employees' commitment to deservingness and justice for themselves as well as the other employees.

SOME CONCLUDING THOUGHTS: JUSTICE, SELF-INTEREST, NORMS, AND RESEARCH METHODS

We began with the proposition that most people in the normal course of development become strongly committed to deserving their outcomes and to the required belief that they live in a world in which people get what they deserve. As a result of these commitments the first and primary task in each encounter is to determine "who deserves what from whom." The operative rules of deservingness, along with originating in the personal contract, are internalized from the culture. Some are institutionalized obligations and entitlements associated with status roles that people occupy in the course of their

daily lives; others are greater or lesser valued social categories meriting lesser or greater fates – bad (good) people deserve bad (good)
outcomes, and bad (good) outcomes are caused by bad (good) people.
Finally, additional important rules of deservingness develop out of
regularities that occurred in the person's earliest experiences with
others: cooperating with similar others with similar outcomes, competing with different others and different outcomes. As a result of
those ingrained expectancies, the familiar cues of similarity, difference, and so forth automatically elicit the rule of deservingness people
apply in that context. But what of the dynamics involved in the
appearance of deservingness and justice in each encounter?

During the normal course of events most of the time people
naturally react "thoughtlessly" and directly express their intuitive
thoughts and feelings without consciously reflecting upon their
response to what is occurring (Haidt, 2001). As they go about their
daily lives, people automatically share equally with partners, allocate
needed resources to those dependent upon them, and distribute
earned resources on the basis of contributions with little, if any,
evidence of greed or favoritism. They are most content when they
and others get what they each deserve rather than having maximized
their own profits (see Lerner, 1977).

In critical situations, when people recognize that a serious injustice has occurred, they automatically become emotionally aroused
(Mikula, Scherer, and Athenstaedt, 1998). Investigators have dis-
cerned and measured this arousal and the various expressions of the
participants' concern with deservingness and justice in various contexts: witnessing electric shocks being administered to an innocent
victim (Lerner and Simmons, 1966), a young boy who lost arms
through electric shock (Correia et al., 2007), someone vividly describing what it is like to live with the horrible effects of being inflicted
with an HIV infection (Hafer, 2000b), someone being beaten and
publicly humiliated by a bully (J. Lerner et al., 1998; Goldberg et al.,
1999, Callan et al., 2010), or having one's partner being gratuitously

insulted and degraded by a member of an antagonistic group, or one of "them" (Meindl and Lerner, 1983). The participants' emotionally directed reactions to restore justice in some form are often neither normatively appropriate nor self-interested. Typically, they are irrational by any conventional standards and often quite costly. It is very important to recognize that the evidence consistently shows that these justice-restoring reactions are typically blended with or replaced by more conventional norm-appropriate behavior if either the participants are not emotionally aroused by the injustice and or they are given the time and incentive to consciously shape their reactions.

To understand the motives and processes that are driving participants' reactions it is essential to consider whether they are directly reacting to the events as presented or they are generating their reactions after thoughtful reflection. The available evidence points to two basic, simple, propositions:

1. The initial and thus primary influence of the justice motive in people's lives appears in their automatic reactions to familiar cues in ongoing events and their emotion-directed reactions to injustices. These intuitive reactions often appear as counter-normative thoughts, evaluations, and behaviors, directed toward reestablishing justice in the laboratory setting, everyday events, or critical situations.

2. When people have sufficient time, incentive, and cognitive resources, their thoughtful reactions will be primarily influenced by the salient normative expectations and the participants' lay psychology. In Western societies a form of rational self-interest is considered the "normal" appropriate way to respond.

Armed with these two simple ideas, it should be possible to constructively reinterpret the findings of the research literature that purports to assess the influence of self-interest and justice in people's lives and then design research that can increase our understanding of these two sources of motivation.

8

Maintaining the Commitment to Justice
in a Complex World

A common fact of living in a complex society is the prevalence of instances in which people perceive themselves as well as others to be denied what they deserve, or to suffer unjustly. These implicit, and often explicit, threats to their commitment to justice require people to defuse and manage the incessant input of new instances in ways that enable them to continue functioning. How do they do this? Typically, additional processes come into play suggesting the appearance of a third stage: Time 3.

Given the human cognitive equipment it is no surprise that most people, certainly by adulthood, acquire a repertoire of prepared responses to familiar forms of injustice. Although they may have other functions as well, these responses appear to be designed to denature threats to people's confidence that they live in a world in which people get what they deserve. Justice prevails. Even among those who have a well-rehearsed full repertoire of available prepared responses, there will almost inevitably be events and circumstances that automatically elicit the emotional reactions to the preconscious recognition of an injustice (see, e.g., Montada, Schmidt, and Dalbert, 1986, on "existential guilt"). The vast majority do adapt, more or less successfully – at least for most of the time, but probably not for all the time and all the occasions when an unanticipated compelling emotional reaction emerges.

The general culture, as well as various subcultures, provides ample material for several prepared solutions. They can be found in fully elaborated ideologies, including recognized religions, cultural myths and truisms, stereotypes, and social categories of relative merit and value. During the process of development they are communicated by various socializing agents, for example, family, peer groups, schools, religious leaders, and other authority figures, as well as the popular culture and are transmitted through the usual modes of observational and direct learning, for example, reinforcement. Not all solutions are equally salient or habitual, nor preferred for various purposes, including their effectiveness in managing the threats emanating from instances of injustice to oneself and others. Once adopted, or inculcated in the individual, their operative solution consists of one form or another of denial or suppression: there is no injustice, after all, or none that is relevant to you and your dependents' welfare.

It is worthwhile to review a sample of what is known about these prepared solutions. The review and sampling of studies will be guided by several questions: What are these solutions, substantively? Where do they originate? Do they appear to be responsive to injustices? Do they function to denature the subsequent threats to individuals' commitments to deservingness and justice? What evidence is there that these prepared solutions are employed, or at least appear in response to the recognition of injustices? The subsequent discussion will focus on some prototypical examples. A more exhaustive review of the various prepared solutions and their functioning is available from the recent work of John Jost and Aaron Kay (e.g., Kay and Jost, 2003; Kay, Jost, and Young, 2005) and the excellent theory-driven review of the literature by Hafer and Begue (2005).

PREPARED SOLUTIONS BASED ON EXCLUSION

Opotow (1990) and Deutsch (2000) proposed that individuals are indifferent to the fates of other people unless they are considered to be members of their own "moral community." They state that "dehumanizing" others leads to excluding them from considerations of justice and fairness. That seems plausible; certainly, history is full of incidents in which people apply different standards of treatment and entitlement to members of some groups as compared to members of others, and Opotow provides an important examination of the factors that might lead to the application of different standards. However, closer examination suggests that the behaviors these investigators had characterized as indifference were the derogation and rejection of particular categories of dehumanized people according to the moral community's own rules of deservingness and justice (Hafer and Olson, 2003). What Opotow describes as moral exclusion appears to conflate the psychological consequences of exclusion from a moral community with devaluation and inferior status. In actuality, some of the examples of dehumanization described, such as the Nazi dehumanization of Jews during the Holocaust, did not arise from passive exclusion and indifference but rather reflected an active form of demonization involving derogation and rejection.

The differential treatment of some groups has a long and sordid history that shows no signs of ending. In the United States, it began with the appropriation of territory that was already inhabited, included the enslavement of Africans and laws that were biased against women, and persists today in such forms as racial and gender discrimination, and in rulings that exempt foreigners or immigrants from legal protections. Such distinctions are supported by culturally supported stereotypes that suggest that the disadvantaged groups are somehow less deserving because they are less moral or less intelligent or because of their previous misconduct. But these attitudes are far from indifferent. Rather, they include an element of hostility whose explication is beyond the scope of the current work. An example closer to the moral exclusion Opotow describes may be found in the indifference of many people to the suffering of animals. Although most people like animals, they are fairly unconcerned about whether or not factory farms or euthanasia are "fair." Even in this case, however, vivid and salient instances of animal abuse, or a sense that animals share a similar identity with humans (Clayton, 2009), can awaken a sense of injustice concerning animal treatment.

The defensive exclusion of others from one's responsibility that is proposed here is quite different from what Opotow and Deutsch described as derogating and excluding others from one's moral community. It is, actually, a rather simple, almost affect-neutral establishment of responsibility for the welfare only of certain others. Because the sheer number of obviously innocent victims capable of eliciting empathy-based imperatives (Batson, 1991) is so great, most people persuade themselves, more or less convincingly, that they can only be responsible for the welfare of a limited number of certain specific victims. The recognition of the automatically experienced imperatives, however, is often more difficult to fully extinguish (e.g., Batson, 1991; Holmes et al., 2002).

Possibly the most commonly employed form of this defense is based on automatically assuming that in the absence of more compelling cues to the contrary, virtually everyone is "different" from us and they are someone else's responsibility, not mine: "I have enough responsibility looking out for my own kind." Investigators have provided good evidence that for most people this preconsciously achieved defense is only partially effective and remains vulnerable to vivid cues of "identity" relation elicited by their compelling feelings of empathy for, or similarity with, a victim (Meindl and Lerner, 1983).

The extensive program of research devoted to Batson's empathy-altruism theory has inadvertently produced considerable evidence of the prevalence of this prepared defense. He conducted several experiments to demonstrate that empathy, as the researchers defined it, elicits altruistic behavior: behavior intended to benefit someone in obvious need, often at some cost to the benefactor (Batson, 1998). Empathizing with a victim elicits consciously recognized feelings of compassion, sympathy, and caring: the empathic emotions. It is these emotions that naturally lead to acts intended to enhance the welfare of the needy victim.

Although Batson recognizes the probable origins of the empathy-altruism process in the parent-child relationship and early diffuse identities of early childhood, he wants to portray it as psychologically distinct from issues of deservingness and justice that are described in the "identity-relation" of the theory of the justice motive (Lerner, 1975, 1977, 1981; Lerner, Miller, and Holmes, 1976). A strong counter-argument, however, can be found in the most common and reliable predictor of whether or not one of Batson's research participants will experience the empathic emotions and feel responsible for the welfare of a victim. Batson, although at times manipulating perceived similarity (Batson et al., 1995), has typically employed specific instructions to elicit and/or hinder the participants' empathic emotions (e.g., Batson et al., 2007). Prior to being confronted with a victim in need, the experimenter instructed the participant either to:

> Try to imagine how ... the victim ... facing this difficulty feels and how it is affecting his or her life .... Just concentrate on trying to imagine how the victim feels.

Or to

> Try to take an objective perspective .... Try not to get caught up in how the victim ... feels ... just remain objective and detached.

Obviously, the instructions to remain objective and detached support the participants' familiar self-protective beliefs, that she or he is not responsible for the victim who is one of "them," while the empathy-inducing instructions effectively compel the cooperative participant to get caught up in the emotional world of the victim and thus naturally experience an emotional connection to the victim. Entirely consistent with justice motive theory (Lerner, 1975, 1977, 1981; Lerner et al., 1976) the elicited identity relation includes sympathetic compassionate emotions along with a sense of responsibility to promote the victim's welfare.

Evidence, previously described here, also supports the proposition that most people walk around with a constructed psychological defense against their vulnerability to empathy-induced imperatives in order to protect their commitment to their own personal contracts. Miller (1975) demonstrated that young men, contrary to the predictions of dispassionate, but otherwise similar, observers (Miller, 1977), were more motivated to work on behalf of innocently deprived victims than to increase their own profits if, and only if, in so doing they would still keep what they deserved: thus, their commitments to justice and deservingness were not violated.

Additional support for the assumed presence of defenses against justice imperatives appeared when people were given the opportunity to couch their donations to benefit children in desperate need not as donations to an obviously worthy cause, but rather as economic transactions by purchasing a commercial item (Holmes et al., 2002). The psychology of this necessary charade is apparent in the fact that similar respondents were not responsive to either the opportunity to purchase the same commercial item or a solicitation to directly donate money to the needy children. Given these findings, it is easy to believe that people automatically feel the imperative to help needy victims, but they also were aware of the need to suppress their responsiveness to victims.

As predicted, enabling them to participate in the charade that they were simply making a purchase, an economic exchange, for their own benefit was successful because it allowed them to keep their main defense of their commitment to justice intact. When confronted with the imperative to help the next needy victims, they were still able to continue to tell themselves, "Sorry, I am not responsible for your welfare: You are someone else's responsibility."

Obviously, in the light of these experimental demonstrations, when Batson's participants prior to confronting the needy victim are explicitly instructed: "try not to get caught up in how the victim . . . feels: just remain objective and detached," they are very comfortable in resorting to this familiar defense. However, when the experimenter encouraged their having an empathic reaction that would elicit an identity relation: "try to imagine how . . . the victim . . . facing this difficulty feels and how it is affecting his or her life . . . Just concentrate on trying to imagine how the victim feels," they could not maintain their separateness from the victim, and the emotions of compassion, caring, and sympathy elicited their identity-relations scripts that included the feeling of being responsible for the victim's welfare.

PREPARED SOLUTIONS BASED ON REDEFINITION

One of the most studied solutions is embodied in many religions that explicitly deny that injustice is possible: everyone's fate, good and bad, minor and severe, is a direct expression of, and thus justified by, past deeds done in this or a previous life. The expression "there are no atheists in foxholes" is an obvious example of a threat-motivated adoption of a religious perspective.

Shweder and Miller (1985) offer an example of particular interest because it is so removed, culturally and geographically, from Western societies. Following extensive fieldwork in India, they described the beliefs of the Brahmin villagers and other Hindus as manifesting the firm conviction that whatever fate someone is experiencing is the direct result of the Karma generated by past deeds in this or a previous life. This constitutes a form of immanent justice, similar in form to what Piaget (1932) observed in very young Swiss children. By contrast, some religions, as well as other ideologies, do not attempt to deny that injustices occur, but rather provide reassurance that justice will prevail in the future: ultimate justice. In either form, immanent or ultimate justice, they provide reassurance that no matter how much suffering or deprivation one experiences or sees others experience, everyone will get what they deserve, or have deserved, in the next life if not this one; and that includes the eventual deprivation or punishment of those who are clearly overbenefitted: "The last shall come first."

It is worth noting that for many members of this society and several contemporary as well as earlier ones, these solutions remain vulnerable to the intrusion of the early scripted responses to cues of suffering and deprivation leading to a "loss of faith," including among such devoted figures as Mother Teresa. An elaborate body of inquiry and dialectics has developed out of efforts to reconcile the consequences of the emotion-driven recognitions of undeniable, often quite horrible, injustices and the portrayal of the religious ideology as omniscient and omnipotent, as well as just. The automatic and often-uncontrollable emotional reactions to compelling cues of human suffering may elicit the loss of faith: if "god" is omniscient and omnipotent, why would "god" allow undeniable suffering and death and "evil" behavior to occur, even if only temporarily? Apparently faith, in spite of what one sees and feels, is then offered as the prepared solution.

The general culture as well as several subcultures provide less elaborate and organized, but no less effective, types of prepared solutions in the form of easily available myths, stereotypes, and social categories. For those who do not employ an ideological prepared solution, the recognition of an injustice, apparently undeserved deprivation or suffering, can be neutralized by retrieving familiar truisms and myths. When faced with apparent deprivation and undeserved suffering, the justice-maintaining solution is: "They are happy living like that," "That is what those people deserve," "They are just no good, lazy, shiftless," and, when confronted with apparently undeserved wealth, "It all evens out in the end" or "I wouldn't want his money with all the worries he has."

What Is the Evidence Linking These Reactions to the Justice Motive?

Sorrentino and Hardy (1974) conducted one of the earlier experiments examining the link between religious beliefs and manifestations of the justice motive. They had participants observe a woman trying to remember a series of paired nonsense syllables as part of a learning experiment. The observers subsequently described the personality of the "learner" on a series of bipolar adjectives that were highly evaluative; that is, they ascribed desirable or undesirable personal characteristics to the learner. To create an injustice, approximately half of the observers believed the learner was receiving painful shocks for each of the inevitable errors involved in remembering the list of paired nonsense syllables. For the remaining half, the learner was not punished but merely given neutral feedback.

In effect, the observers rated the characteristics of the same person after she either had been inflicted with undeserved suffering or had not. As expected, their subsequent ratings were significantly influenced by the victim's fate in a way that appeared to reveal their attempts to believe the suffering was inflected on a relatively undesirable (bad) person, although they all had viewed the same person.

Previous research that had found observers' ratings in a very similar situation became more negative as a function of the extent of the undeserved suffering provided support for this inference (Lerner and Simmons, 1966; Simons and Piliavin, 1972). Of most importance for present purposes, however, Sorrentino and Hardy (1974) had previously obtained information that enabled them to divide their participants into those for whom religion was an important part of their lives and those for whom that was not true. As it turned out, that factor had a significant association with their views of the "learner" in their experiment. The more self-described religious observers had a slightly more negative view of the learner when she or he was not suffering, or merely going through the rather simple task, in comparison with the nonreligious. The reverse was true when reacting to the same person who was being shocked while performing the same task. The nonreligious observers derogated the suffering victim, while the religiously oriented observers' views of the same victim were unaffected by her unavoidable suffering. Clearly, what had motivated the nonreligious observers' derogation of the victim did not have the same influence on the religiously oriented observers. That is consistent with the notion that the suffering victim did not threaten the religious participants' commitments to justice, or the threat was easily denatured by their faith in ultimate justice. The nonbelievers resorted, however, to another familiar method of denaturing such threats by persuading themselves that the victim was a relatively undesirable (bad) person.

But does attributing negative characteristics to a victim, someone who is unjustly deprived or harmed, actually reveal a defensively motivated reaction intended to reduce an injustice-induced threat? Several experiments, some of which have been described here, speak, albeit somewhat indirectly, to that question. They have demonstrated that the extent of the negative attributions is responsive to the severity of the injustice (Lerner, 1971b; Lerner and Simmons, 1966; Simons and Piliavin, 1972). Yet others have shown that the recognition of an injustice typically leads to preconscious focusing on issues of deservingness and justice and the extent of that preoccupation is related to the derogation of the victim (Aguiar et al., 2008; Hafer, 2000a).

Arguably, the most persuasive evidence was generated by Kay and Jost (2003, see also Kay et al., 2005) as part of their program of research devoted to "system justification theory." People are motivated to believe that they live in a society that is good and just. They conducted several studies that focused on two ways of eliminating a threat to the belief in the justness of one's world: believing that bad things happen to bad, or at least inferior, people, and believing that bad things happen to people who also have compensating good things. For example, people living in poverty are lazy and no good, or people living in poverty are leading a relatively unburdened, care-free life. These alternative paths to eliminating injustice appeared in the earlier findings in which a suffering innocent victim (receiving unavoidable electric shocks in a learning experiment) elicited observers' derogation, but not if the observers also believed the victim would be amply compensated for her suffering (Lerner, 1971b).

Among their various findings, Kay and Jost (2003) demonstrated that making their participants aware of someone inflicted with an undesirable fate that was not associated with compensating outcomes led participants to respond with measurably quicker reaction times to justice and deservingness words, suggesting an increase in their attention to issues of deservingness and justice. It also led to a subsequent decrease of their confidence that they lived in a just and good society. The fact that such reliable and rather remarkable effects were elicited by a brief written description of a relatively innocuous event – that is, one unlikely to elicit a great emotional reaction – clearly points to the participants' responses being prepared and relatively practiced reactions to such instances of apparent injustice.

Barbara Reichle and her colleagues (Reichle, Schneider, and Montada, 1998) reported results of a rather large survey in a community in West Germany, of particular relevance to the functions of prepared solutions to injustices. The researchers examined their respondents' reactions to three relatively unjustly deprived, or at least underprivileged, groups of people living in Germany at that time: migrant workers, immigrants from Third World countries, and the unemployed. The researchers assessed the extent to which respondents blamed the victims for their fates, minimized their deprivation, and justified their own relatively privileged outcomes at two time periods that were five months apart. They also assessed their respondents' belief and confidence in the justness of the world in which they lived.

At each time period, they found a large correlation between their respondents' belief they lived in a just world and their blaming and derogating the victims in their midst. But were their reactions to the victims functioning as defenses to their belief that they lived in a world in which people get what they deserve and justice prevails? Fortunately, the panel methodology allowed them to examine the cross-lag relations between these two variables, with appropriate statistical controls, and their findings were quite clear. Apparently, derogating and blaming the victims at Time 1 enabled those respondents to maintain, if not increase, their confidence that justice prevails in their world; whereas, controlling for initial beliefs, those who at Time 1 did not derogate and blame the victims, five months later revealed a significant lessening in their confidence that they lived in a just world. That is exactly what one would expect if victim derogation and blaming was a prepared solution employed by some people in some circumstances to manage threats to their commitment to justice.

Along with prepared solutions involving cognitive framing and manipulation of one's experiences to minimize or deny injustices, people develop other measures to protect and express their commitments to justice and deservingness.

It seems quite plausible that the initial justice templates and scripts as well as self-conceit and self-interested motives interact with available societal norms to generate rather enduring and habitual responses. Among the most familiar is previously described division of one's world into multiple "worlds": the relatively just one in which I live and the others in which I am not involved. The evidence confirms various aspects of that enduring reaction. One is the simple recognition that certain kinds of other people live in a relatively deprived world with no ability to change or leave it. These different worlds often have geographic markers and locations, for example, impoverished Third World countries or poverty-stricken slums in a North American city or rural area. They are also often populated with people who have distinct and relatively different identifiable features. A common response is to adopt a rationally self-interested perspective that can be paraphrased as "I didn't cause their problems, and if I try to help them, I will be unable to care for myself and those for whom I am responsible." When events elicit an automatic justice-motivated emotional reaction, for example, the sight of a suffering innocent child accompanied by helpless parents, people often resort to some form of response controlled by the rationally self-interested guide, "but, I will only do my share," that is, what others in the same position believe is an appropriate response with mainly symbolic consequences for the victims.

A more pervasive variant of this generated reaction may have its roots in the "nonunit" template script, in which people seem to be aware of an important "difference" between themselves and others, even at times intimate others, which also implies being in a competitive relationship. As a result, norms of justified and rational self-interest enable the person to continually assess "what's in it for me?" and "what do I get out of it?" in a way that allows them to limit and design how they allocate their resources to anyone at any time. In this manner, the refusal to benefit others, or victims in need, can be justified as sensible and reasonable. To do otherwise would be foolish, naive, or stupid!

The research of Holmes and colleagues (2002) nicely documents the person's control of automatic, intuitive justice imperatives elicited by the awareness of a suffering child, which can be overcome by allowing the person to act to benefit the child without relinquishing the important defense of "only doing my share." Miller's research, described in the preceding text, also provides a compelling demonstration of people not allowing themselves to believe they would be willing to share some of their earnings with suffering innocent victims (Miller, 1975). Actually, however, similar participants were highly responsive when voluntarily sharing those earnings did not threaten their receiving the pay they deserve (Miller, 1977).

It is worth noting that although the responses of the people in these experiments were eminently predictable, in all probability they would not be able to articulate the reasons for their helpful actions. They were acting in a way that was counternormative, and they would not want to be construed as fools, or as trying to be pretentious. As Miller demonstrated in more recent research, people are very reluctant to appear to be acting in any way that is counter to their own self-interest (Miller, 1999; Ratner and Miller, 2001). Because promoting one's self-interest is such a normal response, it has acquired the power to define someone acting otherwise as a *prima facie* "deviant."

The social compact, in the form of a commitment to act in a particular manner toward or on behalf of designated others, that is, an obligation to do X or provide Y for person A, is probably the most ubiquitous and generally recognized "prepared solution." It is remarkably functional for the individual as well as the social order. The individual's ability to maintain the commitment to his or her personal contract requires that he or she perform appropriate actions to eventuate in certain outcomes for themselves and others. It is commonly understood, however, that the individual, during the course of performing those actions, will almost inevitably be confronted with competing demands, some of which may come from additional justice imperatives. Other things being equal, the individual is nevertheless expected to fulfill the prior obligation. At the least the prior obligations are given priority. The normative sanctions associated with this form of contract enable the individual to solve the problem of intruding and competing demands and provide the recipients as well as relevant audiences with confidence in the order and stability of interpersonal relations.

The contract and its associated obligations appear in various forms throughout the social fabric. In its most formalized manifestation, in a complex contemporary society it plays a part in various social institutions, for example, contract law, marriage, and family relations, and provides the structural underpinnings of economic institutions, for example, employer-employee and merchant-consumer exchanges. But, similarly, and often acting in parallel, informal contracts pervade and provide the normative framework for virtually all encounters. It has been noted, for example, that even in the highest level of corporate relations, informal contractual agreements may carry special weight, because of the implied personal trust and trustworthiness, the value of which can be undermined by the introduction of the formal legal contract (Macaulay, 1963).

At the other end of the spectrum of social relations, various investigators have demonstrated that the most intimate of enduring relationships is not only built on trust between the partners but the form of that trust also involves the expectation that the other party will repay or reciprocate the benefits they received (Holmes and Rempel, 1989). Although Holmes (1981) has argued that the explicit focus on the partner's respective costs and benefits has destructive effects on the relationship, Lipkus (Lipkus and Bissonnette, 1996) reported that among long-term married couples their accommodation to one another was successful only if their "trust" included the explicit belief that they and their partners would get what they deserved, as assessed by their belief in the justness of their world.

Probably the most common and recognizable use of the "prepared solution" of contracted prior obligations appears in the individuals' control of their reactions to the obvious and pervasive signs of injustice with which they are regularly confronted. Although the signs of deprivation and suffering typically and automatically elicit the identity relation with the imperative to help the victim, most people set and maintain limits on their expression of those imperatives. Those limits are supported by the insistence that they must meet their prior obligations to themselves and those for whom they are responsible: "I cannot be responsible for every victim in this world. I can only take care of myself and those who depend upon me" – that is, meet the obligations of my prior contracts.

SUMMARY

Given the numerous occasions in which people's outcomes and experiences do not seem to match up to their entitlements, maintaining a belief in and commitment to justice takes some effort. A common strategy is to try to convince oneself that that the experiences of unrelated others is of no concern. Certainly this works for many of us most of the time, who manage to go about our lives without thinking

9

Bringing It Closer to Home: Justice in Another "American Tragedy"

In this chapter, we develop one of the scenarios introduced in Chapter 1 – the decision to institutionalize an elderly relative – in order to illustrate the main themes we have introduced, and in particular to stress the subtle but pervasive ways in which the drive for justice can affect our lived experiences in profound and, at times, tragic ways. This is very much an American story; relevant cultural mores and institutional structures would lead to different outcomes in many other societies. However, the way in which rational actions lead to unanticipated justice-based reactions can be experienced in any country.

The beginning of a common scenario occurs when elderly parents can no longer deny the inevitable fact that they are unable to meet all their needs for independent living. The increasing physical frailties and/or problems of mental functioning, together with the deterioration of their support networks will, in time, require the elderly to seek help in their daily self-sustaining activities. It is not commonly recognized in this country that the vast majority of the elderly, though they would greatly prefer to maintain their independence, turn to members of their families for this assistance, and in most cases a female member of the family becomes a primary caregiver or care manager with varying amounts of assistance from other family members (Brody, 1985).

The tragic aspects of this common event appear when the elderly parent's need for help occurs at a time when the potential caregivers are at a critical stage in their own lives: namely, their obligations as parents and even grandparents have subsided sufficiently so that they are finally able to consider how to design and enjoy their own remaining years before they become elderly. Certainly, the valued plans and expectations of the targeted family members typically did not include large investments of time and resources as filial care managers and caregivers. Nevertheless, the evidence suggests they do take on those roles and try to cope with the resulting personal deprivation and stress, typically, with only minimal success (Brody, 1985). As the parents' needs become increasingly demanding, the resultant stress often leads to deterioration in family relationships. Probably the saddest part of this scenario occurs in the "third act." As described at the outset of this volume, when the parent's increasing and undeniable needs require institutional care, finally releasing the caregivers from their obligations, the caregivers's levels of depression and stress are often undiminished or even increased by irrational self-blame and guilt (Brody et al., 1990). Presumably, with sufficient time and a caring support network, this subsides.

Much of what has been discussed here concerning the justice motive and self-interest should be evident in the scenario that evolves as the family members attempt to meet their own and their parents' needs, with particular reference to the often observed deterioration in sibling relationships.

THE PERSONAL CONTRACT

Self-Interest vs. Justice

The scenario begins with initial awareness of the parents' needs. In some sense, satisfying those needs will involve a sacrifice by some or all of the children. That leads to the more or less explicit recognition that the siblings are caught in a social dilemma concerning how to allocate their pool of resources in order to provide for their parents' need for assistance. They recognize, at least tacitly, that they are in a zero-sum relationship to each other, in the sense that the more the others contribute the less their own costs. For each of them, it is to their own benefit to have someone else, such as their siblings, contribute the required assistance. Pernicious consequences often follow if it appears that one of the potential caregivers is not willing to make the "appropriate" (fair) contribution to the common pool of required resources. Although there is sufficient evidence that the involved family members often participate in destructive defensive reactions, these reactions do not dominate what actually happens at any given time. Hopefully, the theory and evidence described here can provide insight into the psychological and interpersonal dynamics involved in how the maladaptive, as well as more constructive, reactions appear as the family members attempt to adapt to the social dilemma created by this common problem.

What Counts as Justice?

The resources that are required by the parents, and required from the children, may well include concrete resources such as money, as well as more abstract but still finite resources such as time and physical care. Beyond this, elderly parents need symbolic resources of affection, attention, and respectful treatment. Although these resources are typically associated with procedural justice rather than distributive justice, the impact is the same in that the children experience a justice-based imperative to provide these resources. When they fail to do so, perhaps by making a "rational" decision to leave these responsibilities in the hands of professional caregivers, a lingering sense of guilt may indicate the strength of the initial imperative.

Prepared Solutions

There are typically no prepared solutions easily available to allow children to detach themselves from this situation. Family bonds are too strong for the children to claim that their parents' or siblings' outcomes are of no concern, and the sense of identification is too complete to allow the use of stereotypes that encourage derogation of the others involved. Religious ideologies are likely to encourage care for one's parents rather than justify ignoring them. Children may, however, try to convince themselves that their parents are too old to enjoy their usual quality of life or too cognitively impaired to notice a decline in living standards, and thus the children justify the institutional care to themselves. They may also argue that another sibling is the preferred one and thus better able to take care of the parents, thus letting themselves off the hook. Most effectively, adult children may decide that their obligations to their own children (under the commonly accepted social contract) take priority over their obligations to their parents. As is often the case, these prepared solutions are minimally and temporarily effective, if at all.

The Importance of Relationships in the Assessment of Justice

Typically, the relevance to relationships begins when the family members' common problem becomes evident. Once informed of the parents' critical need for care and assistance in their daily lives, the initial response among siblings in a reasonably well-functioning family is shaped by the recognition of their common "identity" relationships: they each care about one another's welfare. As a result, their commonly expressed emotions of concern and compassion lead to focusing on one another's needs and a consensual agreement that the provision of the required aid should be guided by the least disruptive cost to each of them. It seems natural for them each to try to minimize not only their own but also all of their siblings' costs. So if one sibling lives closer to the parent or has lesser competing demands for their time and effort – no husband or children living at home for whom they have to be responsible, no demanding occupation – it becomes natural for them to contribute more. That would also be the case if one sibling has greater economic resources or if, as is sometimes the case, he or she would gain greater gratification from coming to the parents' aid. As in all identity relations, no one attempts to do careful calculations, but a voluntary consensus seems to emerge and is easily modified in response to the extent of self-evident and -reported needs that are being met or deprived. The emotion-based directives elicited in the identity relation appear to follow the maxim "everyone gets according to his or her needs, and gives according to their ability."

This often leads to the emergence of distinct roles, involving a primary care manager, with co- or adjunctive assistance of varying kinds from each of the others, again, depending upon what they each can give at what personal cost. This can remain relatively stable, until the effects of systematically biased information processing requires a reexamination and subsequent redefinition of their relationships with one another.

The initial identity relationship includes an implicit trust that there is a common and equally strong concern with one another's welfare (see Holmes, 1981; Holmes and Rempel, 1989). Unfortunately, this trust is too easily threatened by the typically casual, ongoing processing of the available information concerning the extent of one another's pressing needs, costs, and contributions. They each have more direct and greater access to what it is costing them, emotionally, to make their contributions. As a result, typically, people are much more aware of their own emotional costs and needs as well as their own contributions than they are of the costs and contributions of the others involved (e.g., Ross and Sicoly, 1979). That biased availability of information leads to a biased assessment of how much the other siblings are concerned with my welfare: "If they really cared about me and my needs they would do more and expect me to do less." If or when that assessment becomes consciously available, then the natural response of articulating that important observation to the others involved sets in motion the dynamics for a change in the relationship.

The expectations associated with confronting the siblings with this observation and request for a readjustment on relative contributions are often additionally biased by the self-conceited preconscious belief that "I am less unfair than others" (Messick and Sentis, 1983). So the biased assessment of one's relatively excessive contribution together with the preconscious belief that "I am not an unfair person" generates confidence that "when I inform my siblings they will agree with my accurate assessment of the situation and reasonable request." Unfortunately, there is a reasonable probability that the other participants, having gone through a similarly biased assessment of their own contributions and needs not only do not immediately agree but also offer their own diametrically opposed views: they should be contributing less not more.

If that occurs, then the apparent absence of compassion and sympathy for one another will reveal the fading if not the erosion of the trust required to maintain the initial "identity" relation. When that occurs, what remains is the glaringly obvious fact that though they may no longer agree about the extent of one another's needs and relative contribution they still have a common problem: they are similar in the sense of being children of that parent.

With the passing of the initial identity, their recognition of this important similarity would lead to a natural transition based upon the scripts associated with a "unit relation." As described in the preceding text, the unit relation–scripted elements include cooperation with equal contributions and equal costs and benefits. This transition from identity to unit relation is legendary in marital relations. Presumably, when the initial honeymoon phase (identity relation) wears off, then the couple often seeks to maintain equality in what they contribute and gain from the marital relationship (see, e.g., Steil, 1997). This cooperative implementation of equality often becomes translated into the more sophisticated form of "equivalence" or "equity" in contribution and outcomes rather than strict similarity.

As nicely reasonable, as well as democratic, as this appears, it is probably the least stable cooperative arrangement (Holmes, 1981). Unfortunately, it is highly vulnerable to the same sort of unconsciously biased assessments described as leading to the deterioration of the identity relationship. Much of the gains and costs in a close relationship are "internal," in the sense of feelings and emotions that are most directly accessible to oneself and can only be observed and indirectly inferred by and about one's partner.

Additional problems are introduced by any mutual discussions and accounting designed to resolve differences because they are not at all romantic and they actually imply a business-like distrust and distance from the other (Holmes, 1981). Further even more serious deterioration occurs when, following a resolving of differences and an agreement on how to proceed, the inevitable subsequent assessments elicit the mirror-image biased assessments of the other overconsuming or failing to contribute, that is, a betrayal. What happens next in terms of maintaining requisite degrees of trust and affection is problematic for most couples, but at that point a nonunit relationship often appears as they deal with the evidence that their spouse is actually "that kind of person," or one of "them."

This can and does occur, among siblings of dependent elderly parents, especially when the parents' needs, as they typically do, increase with time with no happy end in sight. After having tried to arrange a fair, equivalent, and equitable sharing of duties, it often appears that the other(s) are not keeping up with their mutually agreed upon share of the bargain. That judgment and disappointment may recall earlier times in the relationship with the sibling when they did something that convinced you that they were really not responsible or reliable and were actually rather selfish, or one of "them." The nonunit scripts in a situation of interdependence elicit efforts to protect oneself and, though still having to cooperate to meet the parental needs, one needs to assume that they and the others are trying to make the best deal for themselves and minimize their own costs, so you must do the same (Lerner et al., 1989, 1991).

EMPIRICAL RESEARCH

This description of the processes and dynamics involved in filial caregivers' reactions to their social dilemma is amenable to empirical examination. A full test of the predicted progressive changes in relationships would require a longitudinal panel study of assessments at several stages over time. Considerable valuable preliminary information, however, can be obtained before embarking on that time- and resource-consuming effort (Lerner et al., 1989, 1991). A first question that could be addressed in a cross-sectional study is whether or not filial caregivers do exhibit the predicted, systematically biased assessments of one another's contributions and costs. A second investigation could look for evidence of the predicted associations between the extent of their biased assessments and their relationship and regard for one another: The greater the biases the less regard for the others, and particularly those with whom they are in a nonunit relationship. Without the required longitudinal panel data it would not be possible to confirm what causes which: does the nonunit relationship predict the biased assessment of efforts, or does an assessment of insufficient effort lower the quality of the relationship? Initial results confirming the expected associations would motivate follow-up research to address the causal question, whereas a failure to confirm the predicted associations would discourage going any further.

A generous research grant from the Social Sciences and Humanities Research Council of Canada enabled a team of investigators to gain the required information from a sample of filial caregivers (Lerner et al., 1989; 1991). After an unsuccessful, very costly attempt to obtain a systematic sample of the appropriate kinds of participants, the research employed an opportunistic sample that met the general criteria required by the hypotheses.

Extensive interviews were conducted with 140 pairs of siblings. Seventy-three pairs were sisters, eleven were brothers, and fifty-six were pairs of brothers and sisters. Each sibling had to be sufficiently involved in caregiving so that it was at least "somewhat stressful" and their parents had to be able to live independently with the help given by their children. Although that reduced the probability of including caregivers for seriously demented or physically deteriorated parents, there is no reason to believe that impaired the usefulness of the sample for examining the hypotheses. The interviews covered a wide range of material, most of which were fairly explicit questions about contributions, costs, and relations to which they responded by selecting a numerical point on a dimensional scale. In addition there were items that allowed the respondent to describe themselves and the other caregiver on several bipolar evaluative adjectives, as well as items that assessed their relationship to their siblings, in terms of amount of contact, closeness, and whether the relationship was perceived as identity, unit, or nonunit, for example, "Although we are both members of the same family, and thus share things in common, we are essentially different kinds of people. We differ in important ways."

A direct comparison of the respondents' ratings with those of their siblings provided the basis for assessing the nature and extent of systematic biases in how the filial caregivers construed one another's contributions to their dependent elderly parents. If there were no systematic biases then a direct comparison of the respondents' and their siblings' ratings would yield no significant differences. The results would either be highly similar because they reflected their agreement about the same objective reality or consist of relatively random discrepancies with no particular pattern. The latter was the case with several items directly pertaining to important issues.

Contrary to what one might expect, the respondents' overall reports of the fairness of their arrangements for helping their parents to themselves and their siblings revealed no systematic differences. If taken at face value, it appeared that these arrangements were typically considered very fair to themselves and their siblings. Consistent with that benign report, their responses to items directly assessing their views of how stressful helping their parents has been, the extent to which it interfered with their personal lives, and the reasonableness of each of their contributions all confirmed essential agreement, or at least no systematic differences in their relatively rosy pictures of their status quo. Certainly the responses to these direct assessments of the most evaluatively obvious items comparing costs and contributions conveyed none of the expected biasing effects of their each having greater access to the information about their own costs and contributions than to that of their siblings.

Other responses, however, presented a different picture. The expected pattern of systematically biased responses was found in items that seemed to deal with the same issues described in the preceding text but in more specific and concrete terms that seemed less obviously evaluative, at least by implication. For example, rather than the relatively rosy picture portrayed by the respondents' general evaluation of the present arrangement, when asked about how to make the present arrangement more fair they were significantly more likely to indicate that they should be giving and doing less, and their siblings should be doing and giving more. They recognized that their siblings would not agree with that assessment. That view of a less-than-fair present arrangement was clearly supported by their biased responses to more specific questions about the frequency with which they each "do or directly arrange for someone else to do" a series of tasks for which their parents need help. They each reported doing much more than their siblings.

More complete descriptions of the findings can be found in two sources (Lerner et al., 1989, 1991), but for the present it is important to recognize the familiar pattern in which societal norms assume a dominant role in consciously constructed responses (Time 2 responses). In this context, a public portrayal of the caregivers' evaluative judgments of their siblings, it should be no surprise that they would be motivated to avoid reporting anything that might portray themselves or their siblings in a negative light: "Everything is fine and we are both doing our fair share." However, when the norm-based evaluations were less salient, or at least evident, the respondents' more candid responses revealed the expected biased views of their own and their siblings' relative costs and contributions. The direct questions elicited specific responses indicating that the respondents contributed more than their siblings, and therefore it would be more fair if they did less and the siblings did more. These are exactly the kinds of systematically biased cognitions that, often reciprocated by their siblings, generate the conflict and distrust that have pernicious effects on the participants' relationships with their siblings: "It was bad enough that I was doing more than my fair share, but when I approached him/her about doing more s/he insisted I was actually doing less than my share and s/he was the one contributing more," and "How can you trust someone like that?"

Additional evidence supported the initial conjectures concerning the underlying dynamics whereby close, compassionate feelings for one another are replaced by an emphasis on equality and independence, only to be replaced in turn by guarded distrust and the pursuit of self-interest while viewing the other as one of "them," or "that kind of person." For example, the extent of systemically biased relevant cognitions among the caregivers in this study was associated with their portrayals of themselves and their caregiving siblings on a series of bipolar adjectives (e.g., kind, warm, generous, cooperative, and responsible). The caregivers who revealed greater biases in their cognitions also characterized their siblings as less warm, generous, cooperative, and so forth. Consistent with that, a less directly evaluative measure of "distance" also yielded significant relationships with biased assessments of relative costs and contributions. Psychological distance was assessed by ignoring the evaluative direction and simply summing the self/other discrepancies of the ratings on these descriptive attributes. That measure significantly predicted systematically biased views of how much they and their sibling caregivers contributed to the overall care of their parents. The more difference between the self-descriptions and sibling descriptions, the lower the respondents rated their siblings' contributions, relative to their own.

The clearest confirmation of the expected dynamics appeared in the comparison of the extent of their systematically biased cognitions and their report of their relation to their siblings. It was mainly those participants who agreed with statements designed to assess nonunit relations who revealed significantly measurable degrees of systematically biased assessments.

Conceptually similar findings appeared in Mikula's extensive program of research, which first discovered extensive evidence of the biased views of the causes and consequences of interpersonal conflicts among partners in close relationships. When reporting about the "same" conflict, each of the partners tended to report self-benefitting mirror images as both perpetrator and victim of the extent of harm done and received as well as personal culpability when describing the same conflict. Eventually, however, Mikula (1998) discovered that those apparently defensive self-portrayals appeared only among partners who had become relatively distant and were evaluatively reversed among partners who reported having high regard for one another, that is, an identity relation. To be sure, at this point, neither set of studies can speak with confidence about the direction(s) of causality between perceived relationships and cognitively biased assessments. But the findings are nicely consistent with the proposed underlying processes.

To be of immediate social value, the description of the natural history, or rather deterioration, of sibling relationships in a social dilemma needs to include some discussion of how the process can be prevented or even reversed, at least temporarily. Some indications can be found in the nature of the preconscious templates and their eliciting cues. For example, family rituals, in which the siblings get together and share some celebratory occasion, should be able to reinforce and emphasize their commonality, enhancing a sense of unit relation and willingness to cooperate for their common good.

Sudden crises that evoke empathic concern for a family member may serve to reinstate the identity relation among siblings and thus give rise to sincere efforts to meet their needs. Finally, marriage and family therapists may have discovered techniques for preventing the most pernicious biasing processes – self-conceit, availability, or "I am more fair" – from engendering conflict-inducing assessments of one another.

CONCLUSION

An elderly parent's need for care presents a striking instance in which the children's self-interest may come into conflict with justice imperatives. The commitment to justice suggests that, because parents invested so much effort in caregiving when their children were small, the children would feel obligated to reciprocate by meeting their parents' needs. This includes providing concrete resources such as money, more abstract though still finite resources of time, and symbolic resources pertaining to interpersonal treatment. When there are multiple siblings or other potential caregivers, the concern for justice is particularly evident in the struggle to allocate responsibility to provide these resources. The family members' actions reflect their perceptions of their siblings as participants in an identity, unit, or nonunit relationship. Although the initial response to the parent's needs typically elicits an identity relationship among the siblings, over time systematic biases may distort the assessment of inputs and relative contributions and lead to a perception of injustice, with potentially destructive effects on sibling relationships. Thoughtful interventions may be able to avoid some of these negative effects. In our last chapter, we say more about the negative consequences of justice imperatives and some ways to avoid them.

10

Emotional Aftereffects: Some Negative Consequences and Thoughts on How to Avoid Them

In Chapter 7, we laid out a model that begins to describe how multiple motives are integrated. The justice motive theory is probably unique among dual-process theories in proposing that people in every encounter initially engage in preconscious processing of cues that define who deserves what from whom. If those encoded cues indicate that a person's deservingness is violated or in jeopardy they will automatically elicit justice imperatives: emotion-directed efforts to correct the injustice. Subsequent to this initial response, the person may engage in thoughtful, norm-dominated processing of motivationally relevant salient cues. In order for this secondary controlled processing to occur, there must be sufficient cognitive resources remaining after the person's initial automatic responses for him or her to attend to, and process, salient incentives and alternative courses of action: the greater the salient incentives and subsequent thoughtful deliberations, the greater the probability that some form of normatively appropriate self-interest rather than a justice imperative will shape the person's decisions and behavior.

It is obvious and important that people are often able to exert self-control and arrive at "wise" decisions concerning the most enlightened rational courses of action even while they are experiencing the presence of emotion-laden imperatives. The weaker the initial arousal and the more serious the perceived outcomes at stake, the greater the time and efforts employed to arrive at a wise or at least reasonable response. That more "rational" response typically includes the sanctions of being both the most – even the only – profitable and/or justifiable response to relevant audiences by applicable social standards (Messick and Sentis, 1983). Typically, the impact of those norm-based anticipated sanctions will be less to the extent that the initial or subsequent emotion-directed imperatives remain compelling. Familiar attempts to prevent or manage the effects of these imperatives can be paraphrased as: "Don't let your emotions cloud your mind. Take your time, consider the alternatives, think it through, don't do anything rash, or that you will regret later."

Although justice is a primary motive, there are predictable circumstances in which it can be overruled – or at least postponed or modified – by deliberate conscious processing that incorporates other concerns. Overruling the justice motive, however, is not the same as eliminating the resulting emotions. Unresolved justice concerns may have a lingering effect on the best-intentioned actors. When it comes to interpersonal treatment, people naturally rely upon conventionally accepted societal norms to define what is most appropriate and ethically acceptable when deciding among alternative courses of action that affect other people's well-being. Unfortunately the resultant, normatively legitimized, actions do not take into account the emotional responses that are automatically elicited by cues of human suffering and deprivation. As a result, the most carefully considered, rational, morally acceptable courses of action may yield unanticipated effects for all those affected, including – and especially – the decision maker.

AVOIDING THE GUILT RESPONSE

In Chapter 1, we discussed the postdecision consequences experienced by two remarkably different decision makers: corporate managers (Lerner and Becker, 1996; Levinson, 1994; Smith, 1994) and caregivers of elderly parents (Brody, 1985; Brody et al., 1990). In

these cases, decisions that were rational and justifiable according
to social norms nevertheless have been known to leave the decision
makers troubled by negative emotional consequences. These individuals, who have gone through great pains to act ethically and respon-
sibly, may subsequently experience entirely unanticipated feelings of
guilt, shame, and anger. Logically and ethically, by society's standards
they have done nothing "wrong," and yet they are reacting as if they
suddenly discovered they are responsible for someone's undeserved
suffering. Because their counternormative preconscious script "bad
things are caused by bad people" is eliciting their guilt and shame, it
is relatively futile for them to call upon the rational ethical rules to
relieve them of their "irrational" emotional anguish. An anthropologist
with training in psychoanalysis, a friend of one of the authors, drew this
conclusion in response to this scenario: it is as if our subconscious
processes do not recognize the "lesser of two evils" as a justification.
Evil is still evil. To that one should add that the preconscious processes
may define anyone who "causes" suffering, even "rationally justified"
suffering, as evil.

Are there ways to prevent or at least minimize the emotional
suffering of the managers and the daughters who are compelled to
make rational decisions that inevitably lead to signs of someone's
deprivation or unhappiness? Of course, but discovering and implementing them first require understanding the relevant cognitive-
affective processes, especially those that occur preconsciously as
described here. Relying solely on conscious, rational thought processes employing conventional norms for arriving at wise, ethically
justifiable decisions will be insufficient if not destructive. Prior recognition of the possibility of experiencing guilt at having "caused"
others to suffer or be deprived may allow the person to establish
informational defenses designed to avoid or minimize the perception
of him- or herself as the actual cause: "The rules of the game (contest)
left me no choice and the loser chose to play the game (enter the
contest)," and "I was left with no choice, it was either him or me." The

managers can remind themselves of the rules of the marketplace and their obligations to their corporate stakeholders, while family members can focus on the cost to themselves and their families and even to the long-term welfare of their parents that keeping elderly relatives at home would entail. But typically this is insufficient.

There are several structural procedures that can be introduced to prevent or preclude the unnecessary suffering of the well-intentioned decision makers. One preventive element would be to separate the decision maker from the victim, and therefore from the cues that elicit the irrational self-punitive reactions: an innocent person is suffering because of their actions. This would be easier in an organizational setting than a family one. Although there are moral counterarguments for not allowing the "victim" of the decision to become invisible, the military has institutionalized several procedures for encouraging that outcome. It is possible to make the moral hazard case that these procedures work too well at inuring those who give orders to the combatants from the human consequences of their actions.

A second procedure allows the decision maker – the manager or caregiver – to be removed as the immediate cause of the suffering by allowing others, including the "victim," to have a major role in making and even implementing the final decisions. Some European firms have successfully employed procedures wherein the employees, after being apprised of the economic realities confronting the company, were given the opportunity to decide how the downsizing would occur and who would be most affected, with management serving as a consulting resource (Lerner and Becker, 1996). There are various ways that caregivers could be relatively distanced from the final decisions concerning if and when to institutionalize their parents. If the initial preconscious automatic reactions to the justice imperatives, the guilt feelings among daughters of the elderly, are elicited by the cues of having "caused" the parents to suffer, then a possible preventive measure would involve psychologically distancing the caregiver from the actual decisions. Other family members, for example, could be called upon as natural candidates for the proxy decision makers in consultation with the relevant professionals. Following professional advice, they, rather than the care-providing daughter, would make the actual decisions of when and where to place the parent in a nursing facility.

Ironically, the recent efforts to reduce costs by various governmental agencies by offering support for family members to become caregivers in their homes may increase the caregivers' irrational guilt. Those programs provide objective evidence that the daughter has taken full responsibility for the total care and welfare of her parents. Such programs do not preclude the eventual institutionalization of the deteriorating parent but merely rather postpone the inevitable. At the same time, taking the parent into one's home and administering to their needs may enhance the daughters' feelings of intimacy and recognition of personal responsibility for their parents' care and well-being, perhaps by strengthening the sense that this is a unit (we are kin) or even an identity (we are one family) relationship. That might also increase their subsequent feelings of failure and self-blame when the inevitable actually occurs. There must be better alternatives for all concerned, ones that maximize the ability of the decision makers to meet their own needs as well as do what is best for their parents without leaving them feeling as if they have acted unjustly.

AVOIDING VICTIM DEROGATION

The failure to recognize the effects of preconsciously generated justice imperatives can generate other potentially insidious effects. An important one appears in the rather frequent tendency, described in earlier chapters, for people to engage in what some have described as secondary or even tertiary victimization of innocent victims. One rather dramatic example, amply demonstrated in several experiments, revealed observers derogating the character of an innocent victim: the greater the undeserved suffering, the more negatively they portrayed the victims' character. There is at least one set of experiments, however, that inadvertently demonstrated the consequences of this derogation in the way people treated the victim in the next situation.

Carolyn Simmons (Simmons and Lerner, 1968) initially intended to provide a compelling test of the hypothesis that people who believed that they had been treated unjustly would be most responsive to an opportunity to help other innocent victims. To that end, she employed an experimental situation that had been previously used to confirm the prediction, based on the norm of social responsibility, that people who had been previously rewarded would be more willing to comply with the norm and act in a socially responsible manner, by helping a victim, than would those who had just suffered an unhappy fate.

The findings of that previous study were sufficiently intriguing to invite a replication and extension employing the same procedures. In a simulation of a supervisor-worker employment situation, participants assigned the role of employees, after receiving written instructions from their supervisor, constructed simple paper products for which their designated supervisor would then receive payment. The more products completed by the participants during the work period, the greater their supervisor's pay. In addition to the previous research history, that situation had the appeal of having a discrete, countable dependent variable easily amenable to interpretation as an index of the participants' motivation to benefit their supervisor.

The experiment varied the immediately prior fate of the participant designated to be the employee as well as beliefs about the prior fate of their current supervisor. The initial random-assignment procedure had the participants functioning as supervisors or as control participants, working on their own task. The initial "supervisors" were led to believe that they had either been exceptionally benefitted by their workers' extreme efforts or that their workers had done remarkably little work for them, and they would receive very little pay.

These successful and failed participants, as well as participants who were given a task to work on alone in a control condition, were then assigned to be workers for supervisors whose previous pay indicated that they had been highly rewarded, received very little pay, or were in a control condition. They all received instructions from their supervisor on how to construct another paper product and, following a brief practice session, were left alone to perform the task for which their supervisors would be paid. Finally they responded to some questions involving their impressions of their supervisor. The final design included three conditions of participants' prior fate, highly paid by their workers, underpaid by their workers, and control, and three conditions of their supervisors' prior fate, highly paid, underpaid, and control. The main prediction was that the previously underpaid, essentially betrayed participants would be most productive, especially for a supervisor who had suffered a similar fate.

That did not occur. The previously overbenefitted participants produced much more for their supervisors who had been under-benefitted or were in a control condition , and did less for a supervisor who had also been previously highly paid. The participants who had been betrayed by their own workers or were in a control condition did the most for a previously highly paid supervisor and the least for one who had received little previous pay. Why were the predictions so wrong?

The participants' subsequent ratings of their supervisors suggested an explanation for these rather surprising findings. Their responses to the question "Would you want your partner from this task as a roommate?" yielded a simple main effect. The participants rated their partners who had previously received little pay, the ones who had been betrayed by their previous workers, as significantly less desirable as a potential roommate than either a supervisor who had previously worked alone or one who had been highly paid.

Apparently, the information about the desirability of their supervisors' prior fate had elicited the automatic, preconscious processing "bad things happen to bad people." As a result, the participants, who had no previous contact with their supervisors, might be inclined to put out less effort for a rather undesirable person; unless the participants were experiencing the warm glow of believing they had been an exceptionally good (i.e., highly rewarded) supervisor. That feeling of elation might have allowed them to express compassion for their less than adequate present supervisor, that "poor thing." Thus the extra effort expended on behalf of the "loser."

These possible explanations suggested a second experiment in which the automatic preconscious "blaming" of a supervisor whose worker-generated pay was considerably less than average was prevented by initially providing objective feedback that their supervisors' instructions to their workers were more than adequate. By rational (i.e., Time 2) standards, the workers' poor performances could not be blamed on their supervisors. Obviously, the underpaid supervisors were innocent victims and the participants had the opportunity to compensate those victims by their productive efforts. In addition, it meant that they might infer that the initially highly rewarded supervisors probably had not deserved all of their pay.

The findings in the second experiment nicely confirmed these predictions. Consistent with the initial hypotheses, the participants, overall, produced most for their previously victimized supervisors, and by far the greatest productivity for their victimized supervisor appeared among the participants who had been similarly victimized. The previously underpaid, that is, worker-betrayed, supervisor became much more acceptable as a potential roommate.

This pattern of justice-driven behavior did not appear in the participants' productive efforts for their supervisors in the first experiment. The procedure in that experiment, however, had not taken into account the possibility, even probability, that the participants' initial reactions to their own fates and those of their supervisors would be shaped by preconsciously elicited justice imperatives. Those automatically elicited interpretations, that bad outcomes happen to bad people, and good outcomes happen to good people, would lead them to believe their supervisors' fates revealed their merit. As long as subsequent, more controlled processes, as in the second experiment, did not interfere with the participants acting upon those initial imperatives, the participants' behavior would perpetuate the consequences of their assumption that people get what they deserve. They would not be motivated to benefit their inadequate supervisors; they even disliked them, somewhat.

It is relatively relieving to find that if people have sufficient cognitive resources available early in the processing of information and incentives to engage in controlled processing, the preconsciously elicited derogation of innocent victims may not appear. This derogation may even be replaced with more constructive behavior designed to bring about justice: compensating the victims, and if possible punishing their harm doers, rather than adding to their victimization. For example, research has shown that the influence of the initial preconscious, automatic justice imperatives will be relatively neutralized or precluded from occurring when people have prior information to the effect that the innocent victim will ultimately be sufficiently compensated for the suffering they are witnessing (Lerner, 1971; Lerner and Simmons, 1966) or that the harm doer who brought about the suffering has been punished. That is, the person's experienced injustice associated with the victimization has been reduced or eliminated (Goldberg et al., 1999).

There is also evidence that if the person is given sufficient compelling information prior to experiencing the automatic justice imperative, they may be able to replace the initial imperative with an alternative response. In some cases, as when the person is convinced in advance that the victim is a desirable person, for example, highly similar or intimately connected to the person, that person tends to engage in psychological denial by avoiding the awareness of what has occurred rather than derogate the victim (Lerner and Agar, 1972; Novak and Lerner, 1968). One set of experiments repeatedly made the cultural image of the unfortunate truly innocent victim of an "accident" vividly salient prior to their participants observing the suffering victim. Those participants did not derogate the victim – who, however, was derogated by other similar observers who had not been previously primed with that cultural image (Simons and Piliavin, 1972). That procedure was conceptually similar to the one employed in Simmons and Lerner's (1968) second experiment, in which the experimenter in advance emphasized the conventional rules for assigning blame and responsibility. Primed with those rules, the participants' subsequent reactions did not reveal the automatic preconscious imperative that "bad things happen to bad people."

There is good reason to believe that people who (at Time 3) have adopted a prepared solution, a belief system that promises ultimate, if not immediate, justice, will be prepared to redefine the victim's fate and therefore not view them as having been truly victimized: therefore, no derogation. Sorrentino and Hardy (1974) conducted an experiment that indirectly confirmed this prediction. Students who held strong religious beliefs were measurably less likely than their relatively nonreligious peers to derogate an innocent victim. Jurgen Maes (1998) generated additional evidence consistent with this finding from survey and questionnaire data that examined the reactions to victims among those people who subscribed to the belief in "ultimate" justice. Apparently, the operative factor is the belief that the fates people experience now are relatively unimportant because through the power of "god," the revolution, natural forces, or whatever, everyone ultimately gets what she or he deserves, in the next life, if not this one. Justice prevails.

The research by Shweder and Miller (1985), described in Chapter 8, provides another example of a belief system that allows people to believe they live in a just world, a world in which obvious suffering or deprivation never constitute an injustice. The deeply held religious faith of members of a community of Brahmins in India leads them to the conviction that all good and bad things that happen to people now are the inevitable results of their good or bad deeds in a past life. In this manner, there is no injustice. In their world everyone always gets what they deserve.

More recently available evidence, however, confirms the unanticipated effects found in Simmons and Lerner (1968), experiment 1: Controlled, more rational thought processes, and encompassing belief systems do not invariably override the pervasive and potentially insidious tendency for people to form of impressions of others by automatically generalizing from their outcomes to their personal attributes: "bad things happen to, are caused by, bad people" and similarly good things happen to, are caused by good.

In several studies, children, including those who are very young, as well as adults of various ages revealed compelling evidence of what these investigators termed "affective tagging" or "generalization of affect" (Olson et al., 2006, 2008). Their participants' revealed the tendency to evaluate people more negatively if they were informed that something bad happened to that person than if something desirable occurred. More importantly, those measurable relative preferences appeared even when the outcomes were explicitly described as the outcomes of events over which the person had no control. Even more surprising, however, were the findings that these evaluative preferences persisted over time, even when the participants were unable to recall the initial instigating events.

In some studies (Olson et al., 2006), the participants also generalized the outcome-generated preferences to others on the basis of their association with the initial accidental victim or fortunate beneficiary. All of these evaluations appeared to be generated merely by the desirability of the outcome associated with the person being evaluated. A recent article by economists argued that this tendency operates on a group level when adult citizens of a society see members of a particular social group being victimized at a greater rate than average (as in the case of hate crimes): in the absence of explanatory circumstances, the assumption is made that the members of this group somehow deserve the negative treatment they receive (Dharmapala, Garoupa, and McAdams, 2009).

These outcome-based evaluative reactions are consistent with what one would expect from the desire to believe that people get what they deserve and deserve what they get; however, they appear to be rather automatic preconscious reactions rather than defensively constructed responses to protect a belief system. These reactions appear to be a virtually automatic manifestation of the person's belief in a just world: the assumption that people deserve what they get, rather than a defensive effort to maintain that belief. Whether they are a result of an assumed belief or a defensive effort to maintain that belief, it is clear that these evaluations, as shown in the previously described research, can have important consequences for how people behave toward one another and react to themselves. Whom do they help, whom do they condemn, and when do they feel guilty or ashamed?

Actually, as seen in the Simmons and Lerner (1968) research, the preconscious evaluative reactions often interact with conventional norms to shape the person's ultimate behavior. At other times, as in the guilt responses of the supervisors (Levinson, 1994) and the care-managing daughters of institutionalized elderly parents (Brody, 1985; Brody et al., 1990), they can occur in spite of conventionally accepted norm-based rules for assigning blame and culpability. The main determinant of how they are expressed appears to be the magnitude of the original affective concomitant of the automatic preconscious reactions.

CONTROLLING PUNITIVE REACTIONS

The desire to punish is a strong emotional reaction to a perceived violation of justice. Multiple arguments can be advanced for the function of punishment, such as the idea that it will deter that offender or other offenders from future offenses, or that it affirms the values of the society. However, work by Carlsmith (Carlsmith, Darley, and Robinson, 2002) suggests that the desire to inflict "just deserts" on an offender is a stronger motive than future deterrence. Thus, the desire for retribution persists. Even though punishment can lead to negative emotional consequences for the punisher (Carlsmith, Wilson, and Gilbert, 2008) and can entail the sacrifice of self-interest in an phenomenon known as "altruistic punishment" (e.g., Fehr and Gachter, 2002), recent neurological evidence suggests that effective punishment is experienced as rewarding while it is occurring (De Quervain et al., 2004). Because it may entail a cost to the self, the automatic desire for retribution may be overridden when circumstances allow for a more thoughtful reaction. However, if the emotion-directed imperatives are intense and persist, the conventional controlled processes will be less influential, if they have any influence at all.

Intense emotion-driven imperatives may not leave the person with sufficient cognitive resources to engage in rational processing of additional information. In addition, weaker, but still substantial, emotion-driven imperatives may persist and influence subsequent consciously controlled responses. A clear example of that was demonstrated in Jennifer Lerner and colleagues (1998) and Goldberg and colleagues (1999). Their participants, previously angered by witnessing a vividly portrayed injustice, expressed that anger in their exaggerated punitive reactions to an entirely different harm doer in the next situation. When their participants were prompted to think more rationally about their subsequent responses, they continued to express their anger in enhanced punishment, but they also justified their reactions by employing conventional norms for assigning blame. Absent the extra inducement to be "rational," the participants directly expressed their anger in their punitive responses without the rational application of conventional norms. In either case, the effects of the previously induced anger influenced their subsequent reactions to a harm doer, directly or through rational justifications. The only cognition that effectively eliminated the subsequent anger-based punitive response involved prior information that the initial "bully" harm doer had been caught and punished: justice, at least partially, had been done.

Interestingly, although there is ample evidence that a "cooling-off" period may prevent people from engaging in irrational, self-harmful punishments, many societal practices seem to privilege the punitive response. Thus, victim provocation can be a legal defense for battery and even (in some cases) homicide; sentencing guidelines sometimes encourage the consideration of victim input and allow victims to witness executions; movies celebrate vigilantes who "take justice into their own hands"; and politicians gain points by showing they can be "tough" on crime and/or terrorists. In these cases, the emotion-based imperative to restore justice is valued more than the more rational desire to protect oneself and to preserve due process.

These findings concerning punitive reactions to observed injustice raise the question of what happens when people are directly involved in an encounter involving prior arousal of emotions and competitive relations between groups. Jim Meindl (Meindl and Lerner, 1984) conducted a series of experiments that produced a number of important findings some of which, though anticipated and remarkably familiar, nevertheless remain difficult to fully comprehend and explain.

One compelling experimental situation he constructed led male university students to believe that they were hired by a private firm to test new parlor games. They were assigned a female "partner" and a team designation and led to believe that they would play a game in competition with a second, designated two-person team. Actually, the participants did not meet nor were they aware of the identities of any of the other participants (who were fictitious).

The critical events occurred during the practice session prior to the competitive encounter. In all conditions, the participant, his partner, and a member of the other team took turns describing their recommended strategy for playing the practice game while they were in separate cubicles communicating through intercoms (the comments from the fictitious participants were audiotapes). The second member of the other team, speaking last, then launched into a vicious verbal assault on the intelligence, maturity, and decency of one of the previous speakers: the participant, the participant's partner, or the member of the other team. The victim of the assault had no opportunity to defend him- or herself before engaging in the game for which they were to be paid.

The participants were then given the opportunity to either play a game in which they and the other person would earn considerably more money, or they could play a game of less profit and potential cost to themselves as well as another – the insulter. Additional measures confirmed that the procedure successfully created the intended effects: the participants recognized that they were given an opportunity either to avoid the insulter at greater profit to themselves, or give up that profit in order to cause the insulter to have less. They could choose to punish the harm doer but at a considerable cost to themselves.

The theoretical explanations offered thus far would clearly predict that the participants who had been insulted would be most motivated to punish their harm doer; then somewhat, but less so, to punish a harm doer who had insulted their partner who, by virtue of being on the same team, was someone "similar" to them; and finally least willing to give up the more profitable alternative when the harm doer had insulted his own partner.

In two very similar experiments (the second involving only males on a team from the participants' university competing against two students from the "other" university), the participants' choices revealed the same surprising findings. These young men were considerably, dramatically more motivated to punish the harm doer who had insulted their partner than the one who had directed the same nasty diatribe against them. They were virtually not at all motivated to punish the harm doer who victimized his own partner.

Two important questions emerge out of these findings: What was the source of the participants' greater motivation to punish someone who had insulted their partner in comparison to having directly insulted them? Why were the participants apparently indifferent when the harm doer similarly degraded his partner?

The assumption that people are motivated to retaliate and punish someone who harms them out of self-interest, maintaining a positive, if not necessarily superior, self- and social impression (Hogan and Emler, 1981), would not provide a sufficient explanation. The situation was intentionally constructed so that the participants would believe that the only audience for their actions would be the harm doer and themselves. They all were led to believe that their partner, whom they had never met, and whose identity they did not know, would not know of their attempt to punish the harm doer, and the experimenter was absent during the practice session when the harm doing occurred. There was no one else to impress or ingratiate with a "noble" economic self-sacrifice. They certainly could not have felt their vanity or social reputation was more harmed by the harm doer insulting their partner than themselves. Because there is no direct self-interested benefit for the participants to be gained by their punishing the harm doer, as in the previous experiments, it is necessary to consider the symbolic meaning of what had occurred: what it represented to the participants.

Conceivably, the participants felt less compelled to respond to the injustice to themselves because selecting the legitimate opportunity to earn more money could at least partially justify their not electing to punish the harm doer. After all, that is why they were all there: they had agreed to participate in the experiment to earn some money. They had no such alternative opportunity to legitimize their not attempting to punish the harm doer who had so terribly degraded their partner. The participants had no reason to believe that their partners would be benefitted by their decision to earn more money and not punish the harm doer. Symbolically, by electing the opportunistic alternative to enhance their economic profit instead of punishing the person who harmed their partners, the participants would have compounded the relative injustice to their partner: I will get more money and the person who degraded my partner will get off scot-free. So they could choose to avoid retribution and the opportunity to restore justice on their own behalf because self-interest was a legitimate competing principle. However, choosing not to restore justice for another person in order to enhance their own self-interest was a less legitimate choice.

Some additional evidence consistent with these conjectures appeared in a third experiment employing essentially the same procedure. In that experiment the participants were not given the opportunity to confront and punish the harm doer. They were told the experiment had to be terminated. Immediately after leaving the room, they were approached by someone who presented them with the request to volunteer their time to help other investigators who, for lack of volunteers, were at risk of not completing their research in time for graduation. The participants who had witnessed their partners being harmed volunteered measurably more time to help these investigators in desperate need than those in any of the other experimental conditions, including their having been the target of the insult. Whatever was driving the participants who had witnessed the unprovoked and undeserved assault on their partners, it obviously had little if anything to do with protecting their egoistic vanity. They were primarily disturbed by the injustice of what they had witnessed and felt impelled to correct it, in some way, including punishing the harm doer or, failing that, preventing other innocent victims from undeserved suffering.

But then why the apparent indifference to the verbal assault on the member of the other team? It is possible that people somehow have adopted norms that instruct them, or at least allow them, to "mind their own business" and thus override or preclude the justice imperative. Further, without any explicit connection to people who have been defined as "them," or the competitors, the participants may feel no sense of responsibility for how they treat one another: that is their business and up to them to work out, "We just have to look out for ourselves, and our own welfare." This is true moral exclusion: a lack of concern for the extent to which others receive deserved or undeserved outcomes. These may reflect familiar cultural themes that have their historic origins in the initial "individualistic" frontier ethic and that still have currency in contemporary mores and norms. It is well recognized that people who intervene in the lives of others with whom they have no specific relationship or obligations do so at their own risk: "Who do you think you are! Mind your own goddam business!" may be just as likely a response as "Thank you for being so kind and generous .... I count on the kindness of strangers" (Miller, 1999). It is only fairly recently that "good Samaritan" laws have been passed in some jurisdictions in order to reduce the possibility that voluntary attempts to help victims will be rewarded with legal liabilities and penalties. These norms of unconcern can prevent the individual, in a typical situation, from incurring great personal cost in order to restore justice for unrelated others.

Group Memberships and Vicarious Retribution

An additional set of experiments (Meindl and Lerner, 1984) examined the effects of being a representative of one's group when confronted with the responsibility of responding to a verbal attack on the group by one of "them," or an outgroup member. In these experiments, the "attack" consisted of a vigorous, rather strident expression of a not unfamiliar complaint: the participants' social category, or group (English-speaking Canada), had unfairly employed its greater economic and political power to subjugate, exploit, and unfairly deprive the members of the accuser's group (French-speaking Canadians

from Quebec). Given the history of these two areas, the complaining
attack does have a familiar but arguably hollow ring. The relative
political power and general economic well-being of these two groups
provides some, but rather weak, credibility to these claims of discrimination and relative deprivation, but it is probably not true that
these rather marginal differences in relative well-being are the result
of the English-speaking majority exploiting or discriminating against
the Quebecois. As a consequence, the recipient of the assault has
available a range of options in terms of how to respond. It could
easily be construed as an insulting unfair assault based on groundless
accusations or, alternatively, as an impassioned appeal with some
legitimacy.

In a pretest, university students who listened to the tape ostensibly
from a student attending a university in Quebec were asked to
evaluate the appropriateness of several possible responses. The ones
receiving the greatest approval involved an appeal to engage in a
mutually respectful dialogue in the attempt to resolve the problem.
Alternatives that expressed anger and threatened to punish the
Quebecois or, at the other extreme, insultingly generous offers to
nurture the obviously immature, underdeveloped Quebecois were
rated as considerably less appropriate.

How would similar students who believed it was a genuine communication from a Quebec student react when given the responsibility to fashion a response to the attacker? There was reason to
believe that the students' reactions would differ if they believed they
were responding as a representative of their group ("a member of the
English-speaking majority in Canada"), or as themselves ("an individual"). Simply extrapolating from the research cited in the preceding text one might expect that being a representative of their group
might lead the participants to feel a greater sense of injustice and
the imperative to punish the person who verbally attacked not just
them but also everyone in their group, and that the other victims had
no opportunity to respond for themselves. But as in many such

encounters, these students had the opportunity to adopt either perspective: I as an individual am responding to the Quebec student, or I am representing my group in responding to the Quebec student who represents the outgroup. What will determine which one prevails?

Identity is flexible, and whether one feels most conscious of oneself as an individual or as a group member depends on external factors – what is made salient by the situation – and internal motivations, such as the desire for a positive self-image. Jim Meindl (1984) reasoned that in this culture most people typically behave as "I," myself, an individual. In this manner the person experiences the benefits of successes and the challenges to overcome or compensate for failures. Typically, an extra event must occur for people to view themselves and react as a member of a social category. One eliciting event that, historically, may have some social consequences associated with it, is the experience of lowered self-esteem resulting from economic failure, or social disgrace. The inner dialogue and, at times, public declaration that has been observed to follow from such painful experiences is "I may be poor, but at least (as a white man, a Christian) I am better than them." Apparently those ascribed identities, though somewhat ego bolstering, may also elicit and accompany extreme acts to demonstrate that "we" are better than "they." Typically, these acts are much more extreme than the person would have felt impelled to do as "I," an individual.

Meindl's (Meindl and Lerner, 1984) carefully constructed situation was designed to provide a clear experimental test of these hypotheses. Half of his participants were led to believe they had accidentally caused harm to someone. At the outset of the experiment the participants were instructed to take a seat at a table and complete some forms. It was arranged so that by pulling out their chair they "accidentally" caused serious disarray of someone's research material, which would jeopardize the completion of a required project. Pretesting confirmed that this event, though clearly accidental and unforeseeable, led the participants to become measurably depressed and lowered their self-esteem. The remaining half of the participants had an affectively neutral prior experience. Regardless of their prior experience, half of the participants who heard the audiotape described in the preceding text were asked, either as an individual or as a representative of his group that had been attacked, to rate the desirability of various ways of responding to the Quebec students.

The results of three experiments clearly confirmed the main hypothesis: those participants who had experienced a lowering of their self-esteem and then were asked, as a member of the group that had been verbally attacked, to respond to the Quebec attacker, rated the most extreme responses as considerably more desirable than those students who were either reacting as individuals and/or who had not had their self-esteem threatened. The preferred extreme reactions included threats of punitive hostility and degradingly solicitous offers, that is, as one would treat a child or an inferior. These messages expressed either contempt or anger. By contrast, those participants who were either reacting as individuals or had not had their self-esteem lowered clearly preferred sending a more cooperative, less strident message. These findings were replicated in a third experiment in which the participants' reacted by agreeing to sign a petition reflecting the content of the various messages.

Additional insight into the meaning of those findings may be found in the results of the participants' predictions as to what proportion of their peers would approve of each of the alternatives. Those predictions were not reliably influenced by either their own preferences or the experimental inductions and were remarkably similar to the responses of their peers when responding dispassionately in the pretest: they predicted that the balanced reasonable response would be the most endorsed by others. But, apparently, that did not dissuade them from their own extreme reactions.

There is now evidence that experiencing the self-esteem–lowering effects of perceiving oneself as having accidentally causing someone else harm, "I am a harm doer," can persist into the next situation and cause the person to adopt a group identity, when offered, and stridently attempt to maintain the superiority and integrity of that identity when confronted by an undeserved attack. "How dare you assault us English-speaking Canadians! We can and will teach you a lesson!" Apparently, bad things are more likely to happen when people's individual identities are spoiled, and they are offered the opportunity to identify themselves with and defend the integrity of their "group." They are willing to do things to "them" in the defense of "us" that they would not have considered acceptable as individuals with a normal amount of self-respect.

It is important to note that the participants' self-esteem was lowered when they automatically and irrationally perceived themselves as harm doers. Clearly, they were the proximal cause of harm when they followed instructions and pulled out the chair, but every conventional rule of assigning culpability and blame would have labeled them as completely innocent. Instead, the preconscious justice imperative they applied to themselves elicited feelings of guilt and shame. How much more intense and compelling these emotional reactions must be for employees who have just been dismissed and are now the proximal cause of their families' deprivation and suffering! As the evidence shows, explaining to themselves and their families that they are not to blame, and they could do nothing to stop or prevent it, will probably do little to reduce the self-blame, anguish, and guilt when confronted with the effects of their job loss on their families.

Group memberships can highlight injustices and exaggerate the emotional responses, making it more likely that the justice imperatives will lead people to take action in opposition to their own rational self-interest. Such actions can include vicarious retribution, in which people are held accountable for actions that they did not commit but that were committed by other members of their own group. Although such responses are occasionally useful, when injustices are directed at others purely on the basis of their group membership, they can also lead to a vicious cycle of continued conflict, in a Hatfield versus McCoy situation. The likelihood of such responses may be reduced if individuals are not given the cues to interpret injustices on the basis of group identifications. Individual and situational factors can promote such interpretations (Clayton, 2009). Certainly situational as well as political factors can highlight group identities, which makes interpretation of events on the basis of those identities more likely. Interventions can encourage individual-level processing, for example, by individuating members of outgroups and ingroups, or by encouraging superordinate identities that incorporate the victim and the offender.

IN SUMMARY

The bottom line is that people's commitments to justice often influence their reactions to important encounters involving good and bad outcomes. There are publicly recognized norms that define the rules of deservingness and justice. However, there are other equal if not more powerful preconscious processes inherent in the justice motive. These influences are the result of imperatives that are automatically elicited, often without the person's conscious awareness or ability to anticipate. Though the effects of these imperatives are not always pernicious they can be, especially when the outcomes are very important and those involved are not forewarned or prepared for the power and persistent influence of these imperatives to compel people to find or reestablish justice.

The consequences can be particularly serious when events are interpreted as threatening justice relations between groups rather than simply between individuals. The involvement of group identities means that attempts to restore justice by punishing or derogating an individual can expand to others who were not involved in the original situation: blaming the victim can lead to blaming an entire social category (Dharmapala et al., 2009), and punishing an aggressor can lead to vicarious retribution against other members of the aggressor's group. Those justice-seeking reactions can appear as heroic personal sacrifices, take forms that are counterproductive for all concerned, or be self-sacrificing and destructive. However, if we recognize the power of the justice motive to override self-interested, rational, and normative reactions, we can try to construct situations that provide the time and the support for reconsidering the preconscious, automatic reaction. Emotions of guilt, blame, or outrage following apparent violations of justice should serve as cues that alert us to the importance of a situation but should not be allowed to dictate a response without the guidance of more thoughtful information processing. Ironically, the motivation to maintain justice can sometimes result in more negative consequences than the drive for self-interest.

POSITIVE EFFECTS

We have presented considerable evidence documenting some of the personally costly and interpersonally destructive consequences that can be attributed to people's automatic expression and defense of their commitment to justice. But to leave it at that would be to minimize by implication the positive roles the commitments to justice and deservingness appear to play in the lives of most people. Some of the more important functions may occur virtually unnoticed except in the breach. These include providing the psychological bases for people's collective willingness to engage in mutually beneficial "fair" exchanges of goods and services and to tailor their activities so as not to interfere with and, at times, to promote one another's ability to avoid harm as they go about their daily activities.

Arguably, a collective agreement to live by rules of deservingness and justice promotes the comfort and enabling security of a civilized society in which people, by and large, can get what they deserve and be relatively free from harm. But clearly establishing the relationships between the individual's commitments to justice and specific

constructive psychological and interpersonal outcomes requires additional evidence. The vast majority of the available relevant research
was enabled by the development of relatively simple procedures for
assessing individual differences in the extent to which people report
holding beliefs and opinions that they live in a "just world" (BJW).
Essentially, their agreement or disagreement with a series of statements describing various ways that people get what they deserve and
deserve what they get is correlated with other measures and events
(Rubin and Peplau, 1973, 1975).

A large and growing research literature explores the correlates
of people's BJW (Furnham, 2003; Furnham and Procter, 1989). Much,
if not all, of the most relevant research can be found in Claudia
Dalbert's thorough and thoughtful portrayal of the constructive contributions of the BJW (Dalbert, 2001) followed by a coedited volume
on a similar theme, devoted expressly to research with adolescents
and young adults and the development of the BJW (Dalbert and
Sallay, 2004). A rather consistent picture emerges from this literature
revealing many of the expected associations between the extent of
individuals' BJW and measures of their life satisfaction, dispositional
optimism, internal locus of control, and sense of well-being, leading
to the conclusion that "Taken collectively, we can thus assume that
the more individuals believe in a just world, the more satisfied they are
with their life" (Dalbert, 2001, p. 258). This is in addition to promoting
trust, particularly in institutions; providing meaning in their lives;
and encouraging people to behave fairly.

There is much more, but often the empirical relations are under-
standably more complex, for example, the relation of BJW to self-
esteem, reactions to life crises, seeking employment, and so forth. It is
not appropriate within the scope of this volume to delve much further
into these complexities and provide a more complete review of the
published literatures. Fortunately, those are both eminently available
in the previously mentioned reviews of the literature (Furnham, 2003;
Furnham and Procter, 1989) and especially in the excellent volumes

published by Claudia Dalbert and her colleagues (Dalbert, 2001; Dalbert and Sallay, 2004). Before leaving this literature, however, it is important to note that the near-complete absence of experimental or longitudinal panel studies seriously limits the ability to confidently arrive at inferences about what causes what. Although many of the investigators employed the most sophisticated statistical methods, the most that can be inferred is that there are associations, for example, between BJW and reports of a sense of well-being, that are consistent with the assertion that BJW fosters satisfaction with one's life. But could that just as easily be reversed, or could a correlated third variable elicit both? Obviously, much remains for the future generations of investigators to do, and hopefully, the presently available rather remarkable accomplishments will provide the incentive and encouragement to take it on.

GENERAL CONCLUSION

The desire for justice is a motive so fundamental and powerful that it permeates our lives, affecting the way we respond to others, creating behavioral imperatives, and influencing even our self-assessments. Although self-centered and self-interested motives can affect our reactions, the justice motive can also trump self-interest and sometimes leads us to negative personal consequences, both emotional and material. In this book, we have reviewed some major threads of justice research to evaluate which claims about justice have merit and which might be overstated, and to provide a preliminary model that integrates the two motives. Our conclusion based on all of this is clear and fundamental: though people are often portrayed as essentially selfish, only recognition of the way in which their central commitments to justice interact with these more self-centered motives can provide a complete understanding of how humans exist in a social world.

REFERENCES

Adams, J. S. (1963). Toward an understanding of inequity. *Journal of Abnormal and Social Psychology*, 67, 422–36.

Aguiar, P., Vala, J., Correia, I., and Pereira, C. (2008). Justice in our world and in that of others: Belief in a just world and reactions to victims. *Social Justice Research*, 21, 50–68.

Alicke, M. D. (2000). Culpable control and the psychology of blame. *Psychological Bulletin*, 126, 556–74.

Apsler, R., and Friedman, H. (1975). Chance outcomes and the just world: A comparison of observers and recipients. *Journal of Personality and Social Psychology*, 31, 887–94.

Arkin, R. M., and Duval, S. (1975). Focus of attention and causal attributions of actors and observers. *Journal of Experimental Social Psychology*, 11 (5), 427–38.

Armstrong-Stassen, M., and Latack, J. C. (1992). Coping with work-force reduction: The effects of layoff exposure on survivors' reactions. Best paper proceedings. *Academy of Management*, 207–11.

Aronson, E., Ellsworth, P. C., Carlsmith, J. M., and Gonzales, M. H. (1990). *Methods of research in social psychology* (2nd ed.). New York: McGraw-Hill.

Austin, W. (1980). Friendship and fairness: Effects of type of relationship and task performance on choice of distribution rule. *Personality and Social Psychology Bulletin*, 6, 402–8.

Babcock, L., Loewenstein, G., Issacharoff, S., and Camerer, C. (1995). Biased judgments for fairness in bargaining. *American Economic Review*, 85 (5), 1337–43.

Batson, C. D. (1991). *The altruism question: Toward a social-psychological answer*. Hillsdale, NJ: Erlbaum.

Batson, C. D. (1998). Altruism and prosocial behavior. In D. Gilbert, S. Fiske and G. Lindzey (Eds.), *Handbook of social psychology* (pp. 282–316). New York: McGraw-Hill.

Batson, C. D., Early, S., and Salvarani, G. (1997). Perspective taking: Imagining how another feels versus imagining how you would feel. *Personality and Social Psychology Bulletin*, 23 (7), 751–8.

Batson, C. D., Kennedy, C. L., Nord, L., Stocksy, E. L., Fleming, D. A., Marzette, C. M., Lishner, D. A., Hayes, R. E., Kochinsky, L. M., and Zerger, T. (2007). Anger at unfairness, is it moral outrage? *European Journal of Social Psychology*, 37, 1272–85.

Batson, C. D., Kobrynowicz, D., Dinnerstein, J. L., Kampf, H. C., and Wilson, A. D. (1997). In a very different voice: Unmasking moral hypocrisy. *Journal of Personality and Social Psychology*, 72, 1335–48.

Batson, C. D., Thompson, E. R., and Chen, H. (2002). Moral hypocrisy: Addressing some alternatives. *Journal of Personality and Social Psychology*, 83, 330–9.

Batson, C. D., Thompson, E. R., Seuferling, G., Whitney, H., and Strongman, J. A. (1999). Moral hypocrisy: Appearing moral to oneself without being so. *Journal of Personality and Social Psychology*, 77, 525–37.

Batson, C. D., Turk, C. L., Shaw, L. L., and Klein, T. R. (1995). Information function of empathic emotion. *Journal of Personality and Social Psychology*, 68 (2), 300–13.

Baumeister, R. (1998). The self. In D. Gilbert, S. Fiske and G. Lindzey (Eds.), *Handbook of Social Psychology* (pp. 680–740). Boston: McGraw-Hill.

Baumeister, R., and Vohs, K., eds. (2004). *Handbook of self-regulation: Research, theory, and applications.* New York: Guilford.

Bazerman, M. H., White, S. B., and Loewenstein, G. F. (1995). Perceptions of fairness in interpersonal and individual choice situations. *Current Directions in Psychological Science*, 4, 39–42.

Becker, S. W., and Eagly, A. (2004). Heroism in men and women. *American Psychologist*, 59, 150–62.

Bekoff, M., and Pierce, J. (2009). *Wild justice: The moral lives of animals.* Chicago: University of Chicago Press.

Benedict, R. F. (1934). *Patterns of culture.* Boston: Houghton Mifflin.

Benton, A. A. (1971). Productivity, distributive justice, and bargaining among children. *Journal of Personality and Social Psychology*, 18, 68–78.

Blader, S. L., and Tyler, T. R. (2003). A four-component model of procedural justice: Defining the meaning of a "fair" process. *Personality and Social Psychology Bulletin*, 29, 747–58.

Braband, J., and Lerner, M. J. (1975). "A little time and effort" . . . Who deserves what from whom? *Personality and Social Psychology Bulletin*, 1, 177–80.

Brockner, J. (1990). Scope of justice in the workplace: How survivors react to co-worker layoffs. *Journal of Social Issues*, 46, 95–106.

Brockner, J., Heuer, L., Siegel, P., Wiesenfeld, B., Martin, C., Grover, S., Reed, T., and Bjorgvinsson, S. (1998). The moderating effect of self-esteem: Converging evidence from four studies. *Journal of Personality and Social Psychology*, 75, 394–407.

Brockner, J., and Wiesenfeld, B. M. (1996). An integrative framework for explaining reactions to decisions: Interactive effects of outcomes and procedures. *Psychological Bulletin*, 120, 189–208.

Brody, E. M. (1985). Parent care as normative family stress. *Gerontologist*, 25, 19–29.

Brody, E. M., Dempsey, N., and Pruchno, R. (1990). Mental health of sons and daughters of the institutionalized aged. *Gerontologist*, 30, 212–19.

Brosnan, S., and De Waal, F. (2003). Monkeys reject unequal pay. *Nature*, 425 (6955), 297–9.

Broverman, I. K., Vogel, S. R., Broverman, D. M., Clarkson, F. E., and Rosenkrantz, P. S. (1972). Sex-role stereotypes: A current appraisal. *Journal of Social Issues*, 28, 59–78.

Buunk, B. P., Doosje, B. J. Jans, L. G. J. M., and Hopstaken, L. E. M. (1993). Perceived reciprocity, social support, and stress at work: The role of exchange and communal orientation. *Journal of Personality and Social Psychology*, 65, 801–11.

Callan, M. J. (2010). Justice motive effects in memory reconstruction. Unpublished manuscript.

Callan, M. J., Ellard, J. H., and Nicol, J. E. (2006). Belief in a just world and immanent justice reasoning. *Personality and Social Psychology Bulletin*, 32, 1–13.

Callan, M. J., Kay, A. C., Davidenko, N., and Ellard, J. H. (2009). The effects of justice motivation on memory for self- and other-relevant events. *Journal of Experimental Social Psychology*, 45, 614–23.

Callan, M. J., Powell, N. G., and Ellard, J. H. (2007). The consequences of victim's physical attractiveness on reactions to injustice: The role of observer's belief in a just world. *Social Justice Research*, 20, 433–56.

Callan, M. J., Shead, N. W., and Olson, J. M. (2009). Foregoing the labor for the fruits: The effect of just world threat on the desire for immediate monetary rewards, *Journal of Experimental Social Psychology*, 45, 246–9.

Callan, M. J., Sutton, R. M., and Dovale, C. (2010). When deserving = causing: The effect of cognitive load on immanent justice reasoning. *Journal of Experimental Social Psychology*, 46, 1097–100.

Carlsmith, K. M., Darley, J. M., and Robinson, P. H. (2002). Why do we punish? Deterrence and just deserts as motives for punishment. *Journal of Personality and Social Psychology*, 83 (2), 284–99.

Carlsmith, K. M., Wilson, T. D., and Gilbert, D. T. (2008). The paradoxical consequences of revenge. *Journal of Personality and Social Psychology*, 95 (6), 1316–24.

Clark, M. S., and Mills, J. (1979). Interpersonal attraction in exchange and communal relationships. *Journal of Personality and Social Psychology*, 37, 12–24.

Clayton, S. (2009). Attending to identity: Ideology, group membership, and perceptions of justice. In K. Hegtvedt and J. Clay-Warner (Eds.), *Advances in group processes: Justice* (pp. 241–66). Bingley, UK: Emerald.

Clayton, S., and Opotow, S. (2003). Justice and identity: Changing perspectives on what is fair. *Personality and Social Psychology Review*, 7, 298–310.

Correia, I., Vala, J., and Aguiar, P. (2007). Victim's innocence, social categorization, and the threat to the belief in a just world. *Journal of Experimental Social Psychology*, 43, 31–8.

Crosby, F. (1976). A model of egoistical relative deprivation. *Psychological Review*, 83, 85–113.

Dalbert, C. (2001). *The justice motive as a personal resource.* New York: Springer.

Dalbert, C., and Sallay, H. (Eds.). (2004). *The justice motive in adolescence and young adulthood.* London: Routledge.

Damon, W. (1975). Early conceptions of positive justice as related to the development of logical operations. *Child Development*, 46, 301–12.

Darley, J. S., and Pittman, T. S. (2003). The psychology of compensatory and retributive justice. *Personality and Social Psychology Review*, 7 (4), 324–36.

De Quervain, D. J., Fischbacher, U., Treyer, V., Schellhammer, M., Schnyder, U., Buck, A., and Fehr, E. (2004). The neural basis of altruistic punishment. *Science*, 305 (5688), 1254–8.

Deutsch, M. (1975). Equity, equality, and need: What determines which value will be used as the basis of distributive justice? *Journal of Social Issues*, 31, 137–50.

Deutsch, M. (2000). *Distributive justice.* New Haven, CT: Yale University Press.

Dharmapala, D., Garoupa, N., and McAdams, R. (2009). Belief in a just world, blaming the victim, and hate crimes statutes. *Review of Law and Economics*, 5, 311–45.

Dion, K. L., and Dion, K. K. (1987). Belief in a just world and physical attractiveness stereotyping. *Journal of Personality and Social Psychology*, 52, 775–80.

Dols, J. F., Aguilar, P., Campo, S., Vallacher, R., Janowsky, A., Rabbia, H., Brussino, S., and Lerner, M. J. (2010). Moral hypocrisy or legitimate self interest? Normative conflict and decision-making in zero-sum situations. *Journal of Experimental Social Psychology*, 46, 525–30.

Eagly, A. H. (1987). *Sex differences in social behavior: A social role interpretation*. Hilllsdale, NJ: Erlbaum.

Eisenberg, N., and Lennon, R. (1983). Sex differences in empathy and related capacities. *Psychological Bulletin*, 94, 100–31.

Ellard, J. H., Meindl, J. R., and Lerner, M. J. (2000). How do self-interest and justice appear in people's lives? The interplay of social norms and individual processes. Unpublished manuscript. University of Waterloo.

Epley, N., and Caruso, E. M. (2004). Egocentric ethics. *Social Justice Research*, 17, 171–88.

Epley, N., and Dunning, D. (2000). Feeling "holier than thou": Are self-serving assessments produced by errors in self- or social prediction? *Journal of Personality and Social Psychology*, 79, 861–75.

Feather, N. T. (2003). Distinguishing between deservingness and entitlement: Earned outcomes versus lawful outcomes. *European Journal of Social Psychology*, 33, 367–85.

Feather, N. T. (2006). Deservingness and emotions: Applying the structural model of deservingness to the analysis of affective reactions to outcomes. *European Review of Social Psychology*, 17, 38–73.

Feather, N. T. (2008). Perceived legitimacy of a promotion decision in relation to deservingness, entitlement and resentment in the context of affirmative action and performance. *Journal of Applied Social Psychology*, 38, 1230–54.

Feather, N. T., and Johnstone, C. (2001). Social norms, entitlement, and deservingness: Differential reactions to aggressive behavior of schizophrenic and personality disorder patients. *Personality and Social Psychology Bulletin*, 27, 755–67.

Feather, N. T., and Nairn, K. (2005). Resentment, envy, schadenfreude, and sympathy: Effects of own and other's deserved or undeserved status. *Australian Journal of Psychology*, 57, 87–102.

Fehr, E., and Gachter, S. (2002). Altruistic punishment in humans. *Nature*, 415 (6868), 137–40.

Fischer, R., and Smith, P. (2003). Reward allocation and culture: A meta-analysis. *Journal of Cross-Cultural Psychology*, 34, 251–68.

Foa, U. G., and Foa, E. B. (1976). Resource theory of social exchange. In J. W. Thibaut, J. T. Spence and R. C. Carson (Eds.), *Contemporary topics in social psychology* (pp. 99–131). Morristown, NJ: General Learning Press.

Freedman, J. L., Wallington, S. A., and Bless, E. (1967). Compliance without pressure: The effects of guilt. *Journal of Personality and Social Psychology*, 7, 117–24.

Freud, Sigmund (1953). *The standard edition of the complete psychological works of Sigmund Freud* (James Strachey, Trans.). London: Hogarth.

Frohlich, N., Oppenheimer, J., and Moore, B. (2001). Some doubts about measuring self-interest using dictator experiments: The costs of anonymity. *Journal of Economic Behavior and Organizations*, 46, 271–90.

Furnham, A. (2003). "Belief in a just world": Research progress over the past decade. *Personality and Individual Differences*, 34, 795–817.

Furnham, A., and Procter, E. (1989). Belief in a just world: Review and critique of the individual difference literature. *British Journal of Social Psychology*, 28, 365–84.

Gaucher, D. Hafer, C., Kay, A., and Davidenko, N. (2010). Compensatory rationalizations and the resolution of everyday undeserved outcomes. *Personality and Social Psychology Bulletin*, 36, 109–18.

Gilbert, D. T., Pinel, E. C., Wilson, T. D., Blumberg, S. J., and Wheatley, T. P. (1998). Immune neglect: A source of durability bias in affective forecasting. *Journal of Personality and Social Psychology*, 75, 617–38.

Goldberg, J., Lerner, J., and Tetlock, P. (1999). Rage and reason: The psychology of the intuitive prosecutor. *The European Journal of Social Psychology*, 29, 781–95.

Gouldner, A. (1960). The norm of reciprocity: A preliminary statement. *American Sociological Review*, 25, 161–78.

Greenberg, J. (1990). Looking fair vs. being fair: Managing impressions of organizational justice. In B. M. Staw and L. L. Cummings (Eds.), *Research in organizational behavior* (Vol. 12) (pp. 111–57). Greenwich, CT: JAI Press.

Greenberg, J., and Cohen, R. L. (1982). *Equity and justice in social behavior*. New York: Academic Press.

Gross, J. J., and Levenson, R. W. (1995). Emotion elicitation using films. *Cognition and Emotion*, 9, 87–108.

Hafer, C. L. (2000a). Do innocent victims threaten the belief in a just world? Evidence from a modified Stroop task. *Journal of Personality and Social Psychology*, 79, 165–73.

Hafer, C. L. (2000b). Investment in long term goals and commitment to just means drive the need to believe in a just world. *Personality and Social Psychology Bulletin*, 26, 1059–73.

Hafer, C. L., and Begue, L. (2005). Experimental research on just world theory: Problems, developments and future challenges. *Psychological Bulletin*, 131, 128–67.

Hafer, C. L., and Olson, J. M (2003). An analysis of empirical research on the scope of justice. *Personality and Social Psychology Review*, 7, 311–23.

Haidt, J. (2001). The emotional dog and its rational tail: A social intuitionist approach to moral judgment. *Psychological Review*, 108, 814–34.

Hastorf, A. H., and Cantril, H. (1954). They saw a game: A case study. *Journal of Abnormal and Social Psychology*, 49, 129–34.

Heider, F. (1958). *The psychology of interpersonal relations*. New York: Wiley.

Hessing, D. J., Elfers, H., and Weigel, R. H. (1988). Exploring the limits of self-reports and reasoned action: An investigation of the psychology of tax evasion behavior. *Journal of Personality and Social Psychology*, 54, 405–13.

Heuer, L., Blumenthal, E., Douglas, A., and Weinblatt, T. (1999). A deservingness approach to respect as a relationally based fairness judgment. *Personality and Social Psychology Bulletin*, 25 (10), 1279–92.

Hoffman, M. (1970). Moral development. In P. Mussen (Ed.), *Carmichael's manual of child psychology* (pp. 261–359). New York: Wiley.

Hogan, R., and Emler N. P. (1981). Retributive justice. In M. J. Lerner and S. C. Lerner (Eds.), *The justice motive in social behavior: Adapting to times of scarcity and change* (pp. 126–44). New York: Plenum.

Holmes, J. (1981). The exchange process in close relationships: Microbehavior and macromotives. In M. J. Lerner and S. C. Lerner (Eds.), *The justice motive in social behavior: Adapting to times of scarcity and change* (pp. 261–84). New York: Plenum.

Holmes, J. G., and Rempel, J. (1989) Trust in close relationships. In C. Hendrick, (Ed.), *Review of personality and social psychology, close relationships* (Vol. 10). London: Sage.

Holmes, J. G., Miller, D. T., and Lerner, M. J. (2002). Committing altruism under the cloak of self-interest: The exchange fiction. *Journal of Experimental Social Psychology*, 38, 144–51.

Homans, G. C. (1958). Social behavior as exchange. *American Journal of Sociology*, 62, 597–606.

Homans, G. C. (1961). *Social behavior: Its elementary forms*. New York: Harcourt, Brace, and World.

Huo, Y. (2002). Justice and the regulation of social relations: When and why do group members deny claims to social goods? *British Journal of Social Psychology*, 41, 535–62.

Janoff-Bulman, R. (1979) Characterological versus behavioral self-blame: Inquiries into depression and rape. *Journal of Personality and Social Psychology*, 37, 1798–1809.

Joreskog, K. G., and Sorbom, D. (1986). *LISREL* (version 7). Mooresville, IN: Scientific Software.

Kahneman, D., Knetsch, J. L., and Thaler, R. H. (1986). Fairness and the assumptions of economics. *Journal of Business*, 59, S285–S300.

Kay, A. C., and Jost, J. T. (2003). Complementary justice: Effects of "poor but happy" and "poor but honest" stereotype exemplars on system justification and implicit activation of the justice motive. *Journal of Personality and Social Psychology*, 85, 823–37.

Kay, A. C., Jost, J. T., and Young, S. (2005). Victim derogation and victim enhancement as alternate routes to system justification. *Psychological Science*, 16, 240–6.

Keltner, D., Ellsworth, P. C., and Edwards, K. (1993). Beyond simple pessimism: Effects of sadness and anger on social perception. *Journal of Personality and Social Psychology* 64, 740–52.

Kidder, L. H., Belletrie, G., and Cohn, E. S. (1977). Secret ambitions and public performances: The effect of anonymity on reward allocations made by men and women. *Journal of Experimental Social Psychology*, 13, 70–80.

Klein, O., and Azzi, A. (2001). Procedural justice in majority-minority relations: Studies involving Belgian linguistic groups. *Social Justice Research*, 14 (1), 25–44.

Konow, J. (2005). Blind spots: The effects of information and stakes on fairness bias and dispersion. *Social Justice Research*, 18, 349–90.

Kozlowski, S. W. J., Chao, G. T., Smith, E. M., and Hedlund, J. (1993). Organizational downsizing: Strategies, interventions, and research implications. *International Review of Industrial and Organizational Psychology*. New York: John Wiley.

Kurtines, W. M., and Gewirtz, J. L. (Eds.). (1991). *Handbook of moral behavior and development* (Vol. 1–3). Hillsdale, NJ: Erlbaum.

Lerner, J., Goldberg, J., and Tetlock, P. (1998). Sober second thoughts: The effects of accountability, anger, and authoritarianism on attributions of responsibility. *Personality and Social Psychology Bulletin*, 24, 563–74.

Lerner, M. J. (1971a). Justified self-interest: A replication and extension. *Journal of Human Relations*, 19, 550–9.

Lerner, M. J. (1971b). Observer's evaluation of a victim: Justice, guilt, and veridical perception. *Journal of Personality and Social Psychology*, 20, 127–35.

Lerner, M. J. (1974). The justice motive: "Equity" and "parity" among children. *Journal of Personality and Social Psychology*, 29, 539–50.

Lerner, M. J. (1975). The justice motive in social behavior: Introduction. *Journal of Social Issues*, 31, 1–20.

Lerner, M. J. (1977). The justice motive: Some hypotheses as to its origins and forms. *Journal of Personality*, 45, 1–52.

Lerner, M. J. (1980). *The belief in a just world: A fundamental delusion.* New York: Plenum.

Lerner, M. J. (1981). The justice motive in human relations: Some thoughts on what we know and need to know about justice. In M. J. Lerner and S. C. Lerner (Eds.), *The justice motive in social behavior: Adapting to times of scarcity and change* (pp. 11–35). New York: Plenum.

Lerner, M. J., and Agar, E. (1972). The consequences of perceived similarity: Attraction and rejection, approach and avoidance. *Journal of Experimental Research in Personality*, 6, 69–75.

Lerner, M. J., and Becker, S. W. (1962). Interpersonal choice as a function of ascribed similarity and definition of the situation. *Human Relations*, 15, 27–34.

Lerner, M. J., and Becker, S. W. (1996). Managers at risk: The hidden costs of normatively justified harm doing. *Quality Management Journal*, 3, 23–35.

Lerner, M. J., and Grant, P. R. (1990). The influence of commitment to justice and ethnocentrism on children's allocations of pay. *Social Psychology Quarterly*, 53, 229–38.

Lerner, M. J., and Lerner, S. C. (Eds.). (1981). *The justice motive in social behavior: Adapting to times of scarcity and change.* New York: Plenum Press.

Lerner, M. J., and Lichtman, R. R. (1968). Effects of perceived norms on attitudes and altruistic behavior toward a dependent other. *Journal of Personality and Social Psychology*, 9, 226–32.

Lerner, M. J., and Simmons, C. H. (1966). The observer's reaction to the "innocent victim": Compassion or rejection. *Journal of Personality and Social Psychology*, 4, 203–10.

Lerner, M. J., and Torstrick, R. (Eds.). (1994). Special issue on social justice issues. *Social Justice Research*, 7 (4).

Lerner, M. J., Dillehay, R. C., and Sherer, W. C. (1967). Similarity and attraction in social contexts. *Journal of Personality and Social Psychology*, 5, 481–6.

Lerner, M. J., Miller, D. T., and Holmes, J. G. (1976). Deserving and the emergence of forms of justice. In L. Berkowitz (Ed.), *Advances in experimental social psychology* (Vol. 9) (pp. 134–62). New York: Academic Press.

Lerner, M. J., Somers, D., Reid, D., and Tierney, M. (1989). Sibling conflicts induced by dependent elderly parents: The social psychology of individual and social dilemmas. In S. Spacapan and S. Oskamp (Eds.), *The social psychology of aging: Claremont Symposium on Applied Social Psychology* (pp. 53–80). Newbury Park, CA: Sage.

Lerner, M. J., Somers, D. G., Reid, D. G., Chiriboga, D., and Tierney, M. (1991). Adult children as caregivers: Egocentric biases in judgments of sibling contributions. *The Gerontologist*, 31, 746–55.

Leventhal, G. S. (1976). Fairness in social relationships. In J. W. Thibaut, J. T. Spence and R. C. Carson (Eds.), *Contemporary topics in social psychology* (pp. 211–40). Morristown, NJ: General Learning Press.

Leventhal, G. S., and Anderson, D. (1970). Self-interest and the maintenance of equity. *Journal of Personality and Social Psychology*, 15, 312–16.

Levinson, H. (1994). Why the behemoths fell: Psychological roots of corporate failure. *American Psychologist*, 49, 428–36.

Lind, E. A., Kanfer, R., and Earley, P. C. (1990). Voice, control, and procedural justice: Instrumental and noninstrumental concerns in fairness judgments. *Journal of Personality and Social Psychology*, 59, 952–9.

Lind, E. A., and Tyler, T. R. (1988). *The social psychology of procedural justice*. New York: Plenum.

Lipkus, I. M., and Bissonnette, V. (1996) Relationships among the beliefs in a just world, willingness to accommodate, and marital well-being. *Personality and Social Psychology Bulletin*, 22, 666–77.

Lipkus, I. M., Dalbert, C., and Siegler, I. C. (1996). The importance of distinguishing the belief in a just world for self versus for others: Implications for psychological well-being. *Personality and Social Psychology Bulletin*, 22, 666–77.

Long, G. T., and Lerner, M. J. (1974). Deserving, the "Personal Contract," and altruistic behavior by children. *Journal of Personality and Social Psychology*, 29, 551–6.

Loewenstein, G., Thompson, L., and Bazerman, M. H. (1989). Social utility and decision making in interpersonal contexts. *Journal of Personality and Social Psychology*, 57, 426–41.

Macaulay, S. (1963). Non-contractual relations in business. *American Sociological Review*, 28, 55–67.

Maes, J. (1998). Immanent justice and ultimate justice: Two ways of believing in justice. In L. Montada and M. J. Lerner (Eds.), *Responses to victimizations and belief in a just world* (pp. 9–40). New York: Plenum.

Major, B., Blysma, W. H., and Cozzarelli, C. (1989). Gender differences in distributive justice preferences: The impact of domain. *Sex Roles*, 21, 487–97.

Major, B., McFarlin, D., and Gagnon, D. (1984). Overworked and underpaid: On the nature of gender differences in personal entitlement. *Journal of Personality and Social Psychology*, 47 (6) 1399–1412.

Markovsky. B. (1988). Injustice and arousal. *Social Justice Research*, 2, 223–33.

McClintock, C. G. (1978). Social values: Their definition, measurement and development. *Journal of Research and Development in Education*, 12, 121–36.

Mead, M. (1939). *From the south seas*. New York: Morrow.

Meindl, J., and Lerner, M. J. (1983). The heroic motive in interpersonal relations. *Journal of Experimental Social Psychology*, 19, 1–20.

Meindl, J. R., and Lerner, M. J. (1984). Exacerbation of extreme responses to an out-group. *Journal of Personality and Social Psychology*, 47 (1), 71–84.

Messick, D. M., and Sentis K. (1983). Fairness preference and fairness biases. In D. M. Messick, and K. S. Cook (Eds.), *Equity theory: Psychological and sociological perspectives* (pp. 61–94). New York: Praeger.

Meyer, C. B., and Taylor, S. E. (1986). Adjustment to rape. *Journal of Personality and Social Psychology*, 50, 1226–34.

Mikula, G. (1998). Does it only depend on the point of view? Perspective-related differences in justice evaluations of negative incidents in personal relationships. *European Journal of Social Psychology*, 28, 931–62.

Mikula, G., Scherer, K. R., and Athenstaedt, U. (1998). The role of injustice in the elicitation of differential emotional reactions. *Personality and Social Psychology Bulletin*, 24, 769–83.

Milgram, S. (1974). *Obedience to authority: An experimental view.* New York: Harper and Row.

Miller, D. T. (1975). *Personal deserving vs. justice for others: An exploration of the justice motive* (Doctoral dissertation). University of Waterloo.

Miller, D. T. (1977). Personal deserving and justice for others: An exploration of the justice motive. *Journal of Experimental Social Psychology*, 13, 1–13.

Miller, D. T. (1999). The norm of self-interest. *American Psychologist*, 54, 1053–60.

Miller, D. T., and Gunasegaram, S. (1990). Temporal order and the perceived mutability of events: Implications for blame assignment. *Journal of Personality and Social Psychology*, 59, 1111–18.

Mischel, W. (1961). Preference for delayed reinforcement and social responsibility. *Journal of Abnormal and Social Psychology*, 62, 1–7.

Mischel, W., Shoda, Y., and Peake, P. K. (1988). The nature of adolescent competencies predicted by preschool delay of gratification. *Journal of Personality and Social Psychology*, 54 (4), 687–96.

Montada, L., and Lerner, M. J. (Eds.). (1996). *Current societal concerns about justice.* New York: Plenum Press.

Montada, L., and Lerner, M. J. (Eds.). (1998). *Responses to victimization and belief in a just world.* New York: Plenum Press.

Montada, L., Schmidt, M., and Dalbert, C. (1986). Thinking about justice and dealing with one's own privileges: A study of existential guilt. In H. W. Bierhoff, R. L. Cohen and J. Greenberg (Eds.), *Justice in social relations* (pp. 125–44). New York: Plenum Press.

Moore, D. O., and Loewenstein, G. (2004). Self-interest, automaticity, and the psychology of conflict of interest. *Social Justice Research*, 17, 189–202.

Murphy-Berman, V., and Berman, J. J. (2002). Cross-cultural differences in perceptions of distributive justice: A comparison of Hong Kong and Indonesia. *Journal of Cross-Cultural Psychology*, 33, 157–70.

Nemeth, C. (1970). Effects of free versus constrained behavior on attraction between people. *Journal of Personality and Social Psychology*, 15, 302–11.

Nisbett, R. E., and Wilson, T. D. (1977). Telling more than we can know: Verbal reports on mental processes. *Psychological Review*, 84, 231–57.

Novak, D. W., and Lerner, M. J. (1968). Rejection as a consequence of perceived similarity. *Journal of Personality and Social Psychology*, 9, 147–52.

Olson, K. R., Banaji, M. R., Dweck, C. S., and Spelke, E. S. (2006). Children's bias against lucky vs. unlucky people and their social groups. *Psychological Science*, 17, 845–6.

Olson, K. R., Dunham, Y., Dweck, C. S., Spelke, E. S., and Banaji, M. R. (2008). Judgments of the lucky across development and culture. *Journal of Personality and Social Psychology*, 94, 757–76.

Opotow, S. (1990). Moral exclusion and injustice: An introduction. *Journal of Social Issues*, 46, 1–20.

Piaget, J. (1932). *The moral judgment of the child*. New York: Harcourt, Brace.

Ratner, R. K., and Miller, D. T. (2001). The norm of self-interest and its effects on social action. *Journal of Personality and Social Psychology*, 81, 5–16.

Rawls J. (1971). *A theory of justice*. Cambridge, MA: Harvard University Press.

Reichle, B., Schneider, A., and Montada, L. (1998). How do observers of victimization preserve their belief in a just world cognitively or actionally? Findings from a longitudinal study. In L. Montada and M. J. Lerner (Eds.), *Responses to victimization and belief in a just world* (pp. 55–64). New York: Plenum Press.

Rivera, A. N., and Tedeschi, J. T. (1976). Public versus private reactions to positive inequity. *Journal of Personality and Social Psychology*, 34, 895–900.

Ross, M. A. (1989). The relation of implicit theories to the construction of personal histories. *Psychological Review*, 96, 341–7.

Ross, M. A., and DiTecco, D. (1975). An attributional analysis of moral judgments. *Journal of Social Issues*, 31, 91–110.

Ross, M. A., and Sicoly, F. (1979) Egocentric biases in availability and attribution. *Journal of Personality and Social Psychology*, 37, 322–36.

Rubin, Z., and Peplau, L. A. (1973). Belief in a just world and reactions to another's lot: A study of participants in the national draft lottery. *Journal of Social Issues*, 29, 73–93.

Rubin, Z., and Peplau, L. A. (1975). Who believes in a just world? *Journal of Social Issues*, 31, 65–89.

Rusbult, C. E., Lowery, D., Hubbard, M. L., Maravankin, O. J., and Neises, M. (1988). Impact of employee mobility and employee performance on the allocation of rewards under conditions of constraint. *Journal of Personality and Social Psychology*, 54, 605–15.

Scher, S., and Cooper, J. (1989). Motivational basis of dissonance: The singular role of behavioral consequences. *Journal of Personality and Social Psychology*, 56, 899–906.

Shaver, K. G. (1985). *The attribution of blame: Causality, responsibility, and blameworthiness*. New York: Springer-Verlag.

Shweder, R. A., and Haidt, J. (1993). The future of moral psychology: Truth, intuition, and the pluralist way. *Psychological Science*, 4, 360–5.

Shweder, R. A., and Miller, J. G. (1985). The social construction of the person: How is it possible? In K. J. Gergen and K. E. Davis (Eds.), *The social construction of the person* (pp. 41–69). New York: Springer-Verlag.

Simmons, C. H., and Lerner, M. J. (1968). Altruism as a search for justice. *Journal of Personality and Social Psychology*, 9, 216–25.

Simons, C., and Piliavin, J. (1972). The effects of deception on reactions to a victim. *Journal of Personality and Social Psychology*, 21, 56–60.

Skitka, L. J. (2002). Do the means always justify the ends or do the ends sometimes justify the means? A value protection model of justice. *Personality and Social Psychology Bulletin*, 28, 452–61.

Skitka, L., Aramavich, M. P., Lytle, B. L., and Sargis, E. G. (2009). Knitting together an elephant: An integrative approach to understanding the psychology of justice reasoning. In D. R. Bobocel, A. C. Kay, M. P. Zanna, and J. M. Olson (Eds.), *The psychology of justice and legitimacy: The Ontario symposium* (Vol. 11) (pp. 1–26). Philadelphia: Psychology Press.

Smith, L. (1994). Burned out Bosses. *Fortune*, 25, 44–52.

Sorrentino, R. M., and Hardy, J. (1974). Religiousness and derogation of a victim. *Journal of Personality*, 42, 372–82.

Steil, J. (1997). *Marital equality: Its relationship to the well-being of husbands and wives*. Newbury Park, CA: Sage.

Stillwell, A. M., and Baumeister, R. F. (1997). The construction of victim and perpetrator memories: Accuracy and distortion in role-based accounts. *Personality and Social Psychology Bulletin*, 23, 1157–72.

Stokols, D., and Schopler, J. (1973). Reactions to victims under conditions of situational detachment: The effects of responsibility, severity, and expected future interaction. *Journal of Personality and Social Psychology*, 25, 199–209.

Sunshine, J., and Heuer, L. (2002) Deservingness and perceptions of procedural justice in citizen encounters with the police. In Ross, M., and Miller. D. T. (Eds.), *The justice motive in everyday life* (pp. 397–415). Cambridge: Cambridge University Press.

Tajfel, H., and Turner, J. C. (1986). The social identity theory of intergroup behavior. In S. Worchel and W. G. Austin (Eds.), *Psychology of intergroup relations* (pp. 7–24). Chicago: Nelson-Hall.

Tetlock, P. E., Kristel, O. V., Elson, B., Green, M., and Lerner, J. (2000). The psychology of the unthinkable: Taboo trade-offs, forbidden base rates, and heretical counterfactuals. *Journal of Personality and Social Psychology*, 78, 853–970.

Thibaut, J. W., and Walker, L. (1975). *Procedural justice: A psychological analysis.* Hillsdale, NJ: Erlbaum.

Thornton, B. (1984). Defensive attribution of responsibility: Evidence for an arousal-based motivational bias. *Journal of Personality and Social Psychology*, 46, 721–34.

Tomaka, J., and Blascovich, J. (1994). Effects of justice beliefs on cognitive appraisal of and subjective, physiological, and behavioral responses to potential stress. *Journal of Personality and Social Psychology*, 67, 732–40.

Towson, S., Lerner, M. J., and de Carufel, A. (1981). Justice rules or ingroup loyalties: The effects of competition on children's allocation behavior. *Personality and Social Psychology Bulletin*, 7, 696–74.

Tyler, T. R. (1990). *Why people obey the law.* New Haven, CT: Yale University Press.

Tyler, T. R. (1994). Psychological models of the justice motive: Antecedents of distributive and procedural justice. *Journal of Personality and Social Psychology*, 67, 850–63.

Tyler, T. R., and Blader, S. L. (2003). The group engagement model: Procedural justice, social identity, and cooperative behavior. *Personality and Social Psychology Review*, 7, 349–61.

Tyler, T. R., Boeckmann, R. J., Smith, H. J., and Huo, Y. J. (1997). *Social justice in a diverse society.* Boulder, CO: Westview.

Valdesolo, P., and DeSteno, D. (2007). Moral hypocrisy: Social groups and the flexibility of virtue. *Psychological Science*, 18, 689–90.

Van den Bos, K., Wilke, H. E. M., and Lind, E. A. (1998). When do we need procedural fairness? The role of trust in authority. *Journal of Personality and Social Psychology*, 75, 1449–58.

Van den Bos, K., Lind, E. A., Vermunt, R., and Wilke, A. M. (1997). How do I judge my outcomes when I do not know the outcome of others? The psychology of the fair process effect. *Journal of Personality and Social Psychology*, 72, 1034–46.

Van den Bos, K., Peters, S. L., Bobocel, R., and Ybema, J. F. (2006). On preferences and doing the right thing: Satisfaction with advantageous inequity when cognitive processing is limited. *Journal of Experimental Social Psychology*, 42, 273–89.

Van den Bos, K., Wilke, H. E. M., Lind, E. A., and Vermunt, R. (1998). Evaluating outcomes by means of fair process effect: Evidence for different process in fairness and satisfaction judgments. *Journal of Personality and Social Psychology*, 74, 1493–1503.

Van Yperen, N. W., and Buunk, B. P. (1994). Social comparison and social exchange in marital relationships. In M. J. Lerner and G. Mikula (Eds.), *Entitlement and the affectional bond* (pp. 98–110). New York: Plenum Press.

Vermunt, R., and Steensma, H. (Eds.). (1991). *Social justice in human relations: Societal and psychological origins of justice* (Vol. 1). New York: Plenum.

Walster, E., Walster, G. W., and Berscheid, E. (1978). *Equity theory and research*. New York: Allyn Bacon.

Weiner, B. (1993). On sin versus sickness: A theory of perceived responsibility and social motivation. *American Psychologist*, 48, 957–65.

Wicker, G., and Bushweiler, G. (1970). Perceived fairness, and pleasantness of social exchange situations. *Journal of Personality and Social Psychology*, 151, 63–75.

Williams, J. M. G., Mathews, A., and MacLeod, C. (1996). The emotional Stroop task and psychopathology. *Psychological Bulletin*, 120, 3–24.

Zanna, M., Crosby, F., and Loewenstein, G. (1987). Male reference groups and discontent among female professionals. In B. Gutek and L. Larwood (Eds.), *Women's career development* (pp. 28–41). Thousand Oaks, CA: Sage.

Zuckerman, M. (1975). Belief in a just world and altruistic behavior. *Journal of Personality and Social Psychology*, 31, 972–6.

Zuckerman, M., and Gerbasi, K. C. (1977). Belief in internal control or belief in a just world: The use and misuse of the I-E scale in prediction of attitudes and behavior. *Journal of Personality*, 45, 356–78.

AUTHOR INDEX

SUBJECT INDEX